In
they
days

In they days

Dex Cameron

clear water books

Paperback ISBN 0 9543041 2 8

Published
by

cwb

clear water books

www.clearwaterbooks.com
PO Box 81
Liskeard
Cornwall
PL14 6WZ

Printed By
Swift Print
St. Austell Cornwall
01726 70700

About the author

Dex Cameron, who moved to Cornwall with his family in 1998, has found a second career in writing. He has been active in the life assurance industry for more than forty years, and has now, with *In They Days,* completed his third book.

It continues the story of his family's life in the magic county of Cornwall which began with *Where Are You To?,* published in July 2002. He lives with wife Mel and their cats, horses and dogs, their three sons continuing to come and go.

His first work of fiction, *Embedded Values,* was published in October 2002 and he is already well advanced in the writing of its sequel, *Finite Differences* which he hopes to publish later in 2003.

He plans to continue the Cornish saga with a third book, *Rising in the West,* which he expects to start in the coming months.

For my wife, sons and animals

Dex Cameron

Acknowledgements

Thanks to all who read *Where Are You To?*, said they liked it and asked for more, thus diminishing my own responsibility for what follows!

Foreword

Akin to that of the *Minack Chronicles* written by the master of the genre - Derek Tangye - the charm of Dex Cameron's writing is his ability to bring to everyday happenings that elusive 'feel-good' factor from which we, who live in such stressful times, can derive a measure of comfort, courage and optimism.

Once again in this, the sequel to his first book *Where Are You To?*, the characters - on two legs and four - leap out from the text, inspiring the reader with their continuing enthusiasm for their new lifestyle: surrounded by the glory of the natural world and the special magic that only rural, ancient, mystical Cornwall can offer. Written in the author's easy, ambling style which perfectly captures Cornwall's quiet ambience, this book leaves the reader in no doubt that the 'good life' is still out there, waiting to be discovered and enjoyed by those with the courage and determination to seek it.

The spiritual uplift I experienced whilst reading Dex Cameron's first book made it difficult to put down, at the same time never wanting to reach the last page - something I had only previously tasted when reading Derek Tangye's *Minack Chronicles*. I have, therefore, been eagerly awaiting this sequel. Dex has not disappointed me.

Pauline Ruffles
Founder
Friends of Minack Society
Somerset
May 2003

In They Days

1 Field Sports

The warm August breeze across the top of the field was refreshing on my brow, damp after the climb up from the sultry depths of the house below. As I stopped to take in my familiar view across to the rounded green hills on the other side of the valley, I noticed, out of the corner of my eye, a small black, brown and white streak carving out an arc through the rippling green shag-pile carpet which stretched out and fell away in front of me.

Chan was in hot pursuit of nothing at all. Did Basenjis ever run in straight lines, I wondered? Was it something to do with their instinctive hunting strategy in the African bush? Behind me poor old Jake, our brindle Great Dane, ambled in, I suppose, cold pursuit of my limping shadow. Only a week or so before he had started a ghastly retching, eventually being unable to keep down any food and we had marched him in to see Simon Draper, our vet, the next day, Friday.

While Jake's heart was beating vigorously, his pulse was up, his blood pressure down and his temperature way up at 105°. Simon focused on his heart rather than his digestive system. He quickly diagnosed fluid on his lungs but, as we stood there in the consulting room, Jake was weakening and needed to lie down.

'Ideally, I'd like to x-ray him but I'm worried he might not stand the strain of the anaesthetic.'

'No, we're really not sure he's up to it,' Mel agreed.

'I'll put him on an antibiotic to deal with whatever is causing that temperature, a diuretic to reduce his fluid retention and ease his lungs, something to stop the vomiting reflex and some heart stimulant tablets to keep him going over the weekend.' Simon's downbeat comments prepared us for the possibility of losing him, just two months off his ninth birthday. But more of that in due time. And of my limp!

The three months or so since Smartie, Mel's three year-old Morgan mare, returned home from training had seen much water pass under the bridge, metaphorically and, with the particularly wet spring and early summer, literally. Anyone who has acquired a fear, as Mel had of riding in recent years, knows the constant battle involved in vaulting each new hurdle that presents itself. Mel had certainly succeeded in her self-imposed task of taking on and riding as many different horses as she could, both in Wiltshire before our move and at the Chiverton Riding Centre in Cornwall prior to the big challenge of riding several Morgans, including an entire stallion, at Monnington-on-Wye in Herefordshire where Smartie was born and trained.

She had gone on to ride Smartie immediately after she was broken to saddle at Monnington by Lionel Ferreira, a South African, and under his tutelage, expert beyond his years, had encountered few problems. As we neared the end of April in that millennium year she had to decide whether to leave Smartie to readjust her mind to life at home for a while or ride her straightaway. Her instinct, usually so sound, was to leave her for a few days, particularly in view of her protracted journey home. My own, so often less sound, was to ride her the next day, taking advantage of any residual tiredness which would take the edge off any exuberance on Smartie's part. More to the point, I thought to myself, it gave Mel less time to brood on the potential for things to go awry!

To her credit, Mel saw the wisdom in this and the next morning began to groom Smartie in preparation for her first lesson at home. Her fingers worked away twitchily on the buckles of the girth, bridle and Martingale, itself a challenge to fit correctly, as the big moment loomed. Mel used my massive mounting block to climb aboard while I steadied Smartie at her head. 'Don't let her go,' instructed Mel anxiously.

'No darling, I've got her and she's perfectly...' I was going to say 'still' when she fidgeted causing Mel to remove her left foot from the stirrup and start again.

'This time hold her!'

'Yes, dear.' I knew the turmoil in her head at that point. So much depended on the next half-hour or so going well and with all the cumulative effort of the last few weeks, months and years I shared the apprehension, though, with so much at stake, was not about to show it. 'She's fine, just a bit green that's all. Try to keep calm yourself and then calm her. You're in charge here.' I was rewarded with a disavowing look.

She was on. 'Don't just stand there, open the gate,' said the nerves. Understanding that the gate closing behind her would at least give Mel the security of knowing she was not about to be carted off down Penwithiel Lane, I hurriedly swung it open and then when they were through clanged it shut. 'Come on, I can't do this if you're not with me,' Mel complained as she walked Smartie up into the field. I drew in a deep breath and, as I exhaled, I exuded, I hoped, an air of relaxed confidence. My mind's ear began to ring with Lionel's oft-repeated assurances to Mel in moments of worry, such as Smartie's little bucking sessions.

'That's all she's going to do,' he would say emphatically, and I now found myself saying as Smartie walked rather enthusiastically and slightly erratically across the field towards the one flat area at the bottom behind the house.

'A-a-h,' panicked Mel as they descended the small but steep slope down to the 'school'. I had hoped to at least have fenced it off by now but it had not proved possible in time. I knew Mel felt she needed the comfort of a contained area but I had decided to turn the lack of one to psychological advantage.

'If you can ride her there without a fence it will make it much easier when you come to ride her out for the first time,' I had said encouragingly a few days before but not, I concluded, totally convincingly, judging by the stern look on Mel's face. Now all her concerns were being contained just beneath the surface.

'OK, there you are, no problem at all,' I said with relief as they reached the bottom safely. Sensing the need to take control of the proceedings while Mel found her, or more accurately, Smartie's feet I launched into my totally unproven role as trainer. 'Just walk her round the school for a while,' I said with as much authority as I could muster. To my amazement Mel began to respond as pupil rather than as, more usually, wife! 'Now reverse and walk the other way,' and, as soon as I felt things were going smoothly, 'terrot!' Mel shot me a slightly startled glance but obliged.

A somewhat untidy trot emerged from somewhere under the saddle then, just as quickly, evaporated. Mel tried again. This time Smartie gave a little buck of objection, trotted a few yards and stopped. 'Why is she doing that?' asked Mel with not a little frustration in her voice. My mind racked across the hours of lessons at Monnington in search of the answer. Suddenly it came.

'Hands up and forward,' I yelled in what came out in an uncannily South African-sounding accent! 'Up and forward,' I shouted again, this time with accompanying movements of my hands and arms. Mel's glance of recognition was quickly transformed into action.

'Brilliant! A perfect Morgan trot,' I shouted as Smartie pistoned her way along the boundary hedge. Her - their - confidence was beginning to build. 'Now trot her in a figure of eight,' and, mission accomplished, 'OK walk.' After a brief rest, 'take her into trot again.' Smartie kicked out with her left hind foot, half trotted and then resumed her rather messy walk. 'Trot,' I yelled knowing now was not the time to lose the initiative. 'Hands up and forward...give her the reins!' I commanded. Mel meekly responded, to be rewarded once more with a perfect Morgan action.

'Perfect' was the word I found escaping Lionel-like from my mouth. 'How do you feel about cantering?' I asked, getting the answer I expected.

'I think that's enough for today,' Mel threw over her shoulder as she trotted across the end of the school. Concluding that it was important that I should take that particular decision and not her, I shot a glance at my watch, saw that Mel had been in the saddle for fifteen minutes and ordered her to walk. She did so without demur. I was secretly smiling to myself at this new-found, uncharacteristic obedience on Mel's part.

'Now pick up your trot again.' She did so without quite knowing why. But *I* did! She was temporarily dependent on me. 'After the corner put her into canter.' Mel gave me a potentially mutinous look before going along with Smartie's anticipation of what, after all, usually came next. Smartie gave two or three small bucks when I called out, 'give her the reins, Mel. Trust her.' She did and got a few yards of uncomplicated canter in return.

'Great,' I said with relief and satisfaction. 'Now walk her in a couple of serpentines to give her some leg-yielding practice,' I said, now more as a suggestion than an instruction, as the five-minute countdown to a resumption of normal roles I had settled for continued. 'Good,' I said, 'you should be pleased with that,' as I myself was that we had ended on such a positive note.

'What was it like, honestly?' she asked as she walked Smartie towards me, gently patting the base of her neck.

'For your first ride on her at home, it could hardly be better. You saw the worst she was going to do: just a small bounce...'

'It felt more like a big buck,' she rejoined.

'No, I can tell you, it was nothing.' Mel looked unconvinced but, as the two of them walked slowly back up the slope to the gate, the hard lines of tension in her face gave way to the soft creases of relief and, did I detect, a little smile of pleasure? Back at the barn Mel asked me to hold Smartie's head as she dismounted. Another small step forward I thought with some gratification.

All our new animals over the years had wormed their way into our affections without our being conscious of it. Chan was not only no exception but, in view of his natural predilection to destroying his environment if left to his own devices for too long, in practice just a few minutes, managed it against the odds. It soon became apparent that any adjustment to this state of affairs was going to have to come from us rather than him. All the hard-learned principles of dog-training which we had acquired over the years simply did not apply to a Basenji! Better, we concluded, to treat him like a totally different species. While it was true that, as we had been told, Basenjis exhibited a number of cat-like tendencies, the immaculate washing routine, readiness to ascend the cat tower we had bought for Moss, Clover and Dandy, our Burmese kittens, and deftness at escaping through the tiniest of gaps carelessly left when closing a door were where the similarities ended. He had little concept of the need for house-training for example, considering that any old place would do, any old time. Even a Dane, to which even the most devoted of owners would ascribe no great intelligence, always got the basic message in a couple of weeks. We resigned ourselves for a long haul.

However, we were left in no doubt of the total trust this little dog was placing in us, never more so than on those frequent occasions when he sought a lap for a nap. First he coiled himself on you, head turned towards yours, then he gazed into your eyes, silently of course because Basenjis don't bark, as if to seek total reassurance that he was going to be safe. Then he would go limp and fall into a deep sleep so that you could not move for half an hour or more. There was no doubt, Mel and I agreed, that here was the most affectionate of dogs, though she would never agree with my contention that he had much to be affectionate for! For the periodic damp patches on the carpet, for the frequent shredded newspaper or for the odd chewed slipper, for example.

To our continuing amazement, his relationship with Moss, our big lilac Burmese male, continued to blossom. For some reason Moss did not object to having his tail pulled, his neck nibbled, his head grabbed or even, on one memorable occasion, to being dragged along on his back by his collar as Chan walked backwards a pace at a time across the sitting room floor! Even more surprising was the slow thawing in Chan's relations with Dandy and Cloey who had retained a female feline aloofness from the moment he had arrived unannounced in their midst but who had never quite succeeded in ignoring him altogether!

Sukie, our beloved geriatric fawn Great Dane, continued to plough through her ups and downs, quite literally as her weak quarters sometimes let her down with a bump when she clambered up the steps into the utility room she shared with Jake and Angus, our eight year-old black American Cocker. Every so often I rearranged the building blocks I had deployed to reduce the steepness of the steps in order to make it easier for her. On her down days she might need to be helped to her feet first thing in the morning, before her system got into its stride, while on her up days she would happily get up on her own and go up and down the steps without difficulty. It was, of course, on the down days that our thoughts turned to how long she would be with us. This then seemed to act as a spur to her to resume her ups, which far out-numbered the downs. Her sheer determination and courage were always enough to keep us positive and the affection and interest she showed were an ample reward for our efforts.

We had never taken particular notice of the animals' birthdays over the years but tended to become more aware of them as they aged. Sukie was certainly the oldest Dane or dog we had had but Daisy, our Burmese female, outstripped them all, reaching the grand age of seventeen as the end of April approached. To our delight she had continued to increase in sprightliness as a direct result, we believed, of the arrival of the kittens, though at just over a year old, Moss and Dandy were now quite grown up. Daisy not only stood her ground against Chan, alone among the cats, but, having seen him off, would then stride with purposeful authority across the kitchen floor and leap with adroit confidence up to her bed in pride of place next to the Rayburn where she would then enjoy a recuperative sleep of some hours!

Max, my wonderful 17-hand Westphalian gelding, continued his unruffled life, patiently awaiting, it seemed, the inevitable day when Smartie, accompanied by Mel, would join us on a ride out. This was never more in evidence than when he watched in silent attention through his stable grille as Mel took Smartie through her paces in the field. Mel had one lesson on Smartie at Chiverton, after which she had agreed with Debi that she would come to our house, Upper Penwithiel, once a week to give her tuition since Smartie would be more relaxed at home.

So relaxed was she, in fact, that Mel's next 'lesson' with me in the field was characterised by Smartie continually stopping. As I reminded Mel, Lionel had always said a small buck, or stopping altogether, was all she was ever going to do. Mel's historical experience had been with horses whose bucks were anything but small and whose 'fail-safe' was anything but stop. Rather, it was to gallop hell for leather! After a frustrating and less-than-satisfactory twenty minutes we called it a day.

We puzzled over why things were not continuing along the path started so successfully at Monnington, watched videos of Mel's lessons there but reached no clear conclusions. I encouraged Mel to try again the next morning but things were worse. Smartie seemed to resort to bucking, or rather her little kicks at fresh air, whenever Mel tried to trot her, precluding any attempt at a canter. I then put my secret plan into action. I had decided that if she repeated her antics I would sit on her myself! Mel looked horrified at my suggestion. 'You'll flatten her!' I was well aware that my 6'2" and 16 stones were not explicitly catered for in Smartie's design specification but I said, 'you never know, I might just persuade her to behave.'

I got on her in my wellies and, exceptionally, without a hat and waited for Mel to adjust the stirrups. As I walked her on I detected signs of surprise and apprehension in the way she swivelled her ears back towards me. I then pushed her into a trot, inducing a buck or two, but, because of my extra weight, they were smaller and more short-lived than when Mel was riding her. The slightly erratic responses to my reins and legs jolted me into the reality of what Mel was handling: a young, green, worried and easily distracted young horse. As I looked down at her head and neck stretched out in front of me I was struck at the difference between her head carriage and Max's. Why, yes, it was just like Finn's: the only Morgan I had ever ridden. He was at Monnington and it was Trudy Connolly, the yard manager there, who had first suggested that I should ride him.

That realisation acted as a mental trigger. Suddenly, in my mind, I was back on Finn and started to ride Smartie in the quite idiosyncratic saddle-seat style: gripping with my knees and inner thighs, I released my lower leg and ankles, holding them away from the horse, with heels down and toes parallel to her body. I raised my hands and loosened them, maintaining the very lightest of contacts with her mouth. Her head went up and her neck arched as we went into the most elegant of high-stepping trots. 'How did you do that?' asked Mel, trailing in my wake. When I explained, her face relaxed with a slight nod of realisation. 'Yes, of course. I've been trying to ride her English style...'

I hopped off and helped Mel back on. The improvement was immediate as she too slotted her mind back into saddle-seat mode and Smartie, with an almost palpable relaxation in relief, did exactly as she had been taught. To this day, however, whenever I walk up to her when she is tacked-up, I can detect a mental 'oh no' reaction from her but I do not intend to put her through the trauma of being ridden by me again unless, of course, the circumstances demanded it!

The arrival of May Day jogged our memories but, having decided that Padstow could manage without our attendance on the 'obby 'oss, we ordered our hanging baskets from the Trelawney Garden Centre instead. At a cost in excess of £200 we couldn't help wondering what else we could have done for that. Perhaps a meal for Mel, James, Justin and me at Rick Stein's Seafood Restaurant or for the whole family at Trawlers in Looe? Certainly ten of us could have had a side-bursting meal at the Blisland Inn. It would buy the two new tyres I needed for the Jag or most of the service then due. It would even cover our vet's bill for the month! Ah, wonderful things priorities: all I knew was that we had had hanging baskets for years and I wasn't about to drop the habit, despite the pain of having to water them each dry day.

A day or two later Steve Masters arrived with his JCB to do his annual clear up of our muck heap. He waited, engine idling, while I opened the gate into the field for him. I smiled and nodded at him and saw his lips move. I moved closer to his cab. 'Did you say something Steve?'

He leant over and raised his voice. 'Dog's not dead then,' he observed cheerily. He was looking at the still empty pit he had dug some months earlier for Sukie when we thought her demise was imminent.

'Oh, no,' I grinned. 'I think watching you dig it gave her a new lease of life.' He threw back his head and laughed as he wound up the engine to creep carefully between the posts before wiggling up through the second gate.

Mel's first home lesson with Debi was scheduled for a week later so I seized the opportunity to build upon my new-found and, no doubt, short-lived standing as chief riding instructor to get Mel to ride out on Smartie with Max and me. To my delight Mel took this in her stride, merely asserting that she didn't want to go too far. I assured her that a short trek up Penwithiel Lane was all I had in mind and that she could turn round and head for home whenever she wished. Being totally confident of Max's mature, sensible calmness and its likely effect on Smartie, my undisclosed objective was to go to the very top of the lane where it hit a busy road, a distance of about a mile and a half.

Once out on the lane I suggested we went straight into trot as I knew this would not only give Mel and Smartie something to think about but it would cream off Smartie's excess energy and Mel's tangible tension while allowing Max to assume a cloak of courage on his first expedition into this particular unknown, as we had only ever gone down the lane before. While he turned his head to left and right to satisfy himself all was well, he gave Smartie just the confidence we hoped he would. Why, it was just as though he came up here every day! Max it was, however, who brought us back to walk as his below-par fitness struggled to carry my bulk up the relentless hill, one-in-three in one place.

They both flinched at the ancient sheep which came to the bottom of next door's field for a closer look and Max twitched at the sight of the brightly coloured farm machinery parked in the Trevithicks' yard further on. My usual assurance that it was 'only a thing' calmed him instantly. On and up we went, all of us jumping as the Labradors at the next house leapt up at their gate and barked at us. But Max and Smartie looked askance as they were used to bigger things!

'How much further are we going?' asked Mel breathlessly but sensing the answer.

'Oh, just to the top,' I replied nonchalantly, knowing what was coming next.

'I don't want to go too near the main road,' she said. I had already decided that that was not the day to try to get Smartie used to juggernauts.

'No, we'll turn round at the farm entrance at the top,' I soothed. Just as we approached it a car came up behind us on the single-track lane. Mel immediately gave me a 'what do we do now?' sort of look.

'In here,' I said, leading the way into a small area of clear ground between the trees. I then swung Max round to face back the way we had come, placing him between Smartie and the road, and waved the car past. 'There you are. She's coped with everything today. She's brilliant - just right for you,' I purred.

'Mmm,' said Mel, pondering the truth of my statement. At the track which led down to Pencarris Farm we stopped and faced the horses in the direction of the busy road some two hundred yards ahead. The chrome barrel of a petrol tanker flashed across the narrow lane entrance emphasising the potential difficulty of ever getting across the road on horse-back: it was hard enough in a car. Mel then said what I was thinking. 'I can't see how we could ever go across there. Look at the speed they're going.'

'And the road to the left is almost blind. But I think we'll be alright going across the road at the bottom,' I ventured, half expecting to be shot down in flames.

'Yes, but not just yet,' she said smiling ruefully in my direction.

'What's down there?' I asked, nodding to my left down the farm track.

'Pencarris Farm,' she shot back, knowingly unhelpful.

'Yes, I know, but how far is it? Can you ride a horse down there?'

'Oh, I don't think so. There's just the house at the end of the track.'

'How far is the house?' I persisted.

'Half a mile or so?' she replied uncertainly.

'Let's look,' I said decisively, turning Max through 120 degrees.

'Oh we can't,' she said, with one of her forbidding looks.

'Yes we can. We'll just keep going until we can see the house. We won't intrude on their privacy.' She had little choice but to follow as she would not, I thought, want to go back down the lane on her own. The three hundred degree view was spectacular. In front and to the right of us the patchwork farmland dropped down to the valley below and beyond that lay Bodmin Moor, a resplendent brown and green in the bright sunlight. To our right the land declined to the east and disappeared in the spring haze. To our left and behind us, in the far distance, we could see the conical china clay tips around St Austell with a passing resemblance to white sand dunes in a multi-coloured desert.

The single dirt track wound down through a succession of right-angled bends, past a number of open fields, each with its own track, until we were almost upon the house. Mel was getting twitchy behind me. 'Come on, let's go back now,' she urged.

'Now we're here we might as well find someone and ask if it's OK to ride down here.' She gave me a knowing, somewhat resigned look, edged with a forgiving smile. Finding no one about, we retraced our steps back to the lane. At each field entrance we stopped to try to work out how far the track went but did not trespass beyond the gate. We were limited to a walk back down the lane because of the gradient. In fact, in places, Mel was limited to a standstill! Smartie just kept stopping, infuriating Mel.

'What's up with this horse? She just keeps stopping for no reason.'

'Perhaps she's tired,' I suggested as a somewhat unlikely explanation.

'Just being difficult, more like,' she retorted. This stop-start continued all the way home.

'But at least she's defaulting the right way - she's not carting you off!' Mel's expression told me this was of small comfort.

'I suppose you're right but it's an absolute pain.'

'But she's so young, only just coming up to three,' I reasoned. 'Give her time. She'll be fine. Each hour in the saddle is putting miles on the clock. She's perfect for you.' Max descended slowly with the usual accompanying grunts which showed his disapproval of going downhill and with the occasional slipping of a shoe which this usually entailed. I joined in with a periodical curse as I was buzzed by flies which, like holiday-makers, had started to make an appearance though, also like them, not yet in the bothersome numbers we knew we could expect in August! As we passed the Trevithicks', one of the farm cats, marmalade in colour, shot across the lane and up over the bank into the field opposite the farm. This caused but a momentary pause in the horses' plodding walk home.

'We never did see Thomas again did we?' said Mel.

'Thomas who? Oh you mean Thomas Arnold, the little black feral cat,' I said answering my own question. 'No, funny that. The last time we saw him was when he first met Chan.'

'Do you think Chan frightened him off?' asked Mel.

'Probably,' I replied idly without really meaning it. 'No,' I continued, 'he wouldn't have put him off coming for food, I wouldn't have thought. Even if he had, I can't imagine we would have gone all this time without catching a glimpse of him. He was always around.'

'Maybe someone poisoned him. Or shot him...' rambled Mel. 'He might have been considered vermin by some,' she added. 'But I liked him, he was a harmless little thing.' This caused me to reflect on our erstwhile neighbour's, Dixon Warburton's, reported sighting, just before he moved, of Moritz, our lilac Burmese male who had so mysteriously gone missing in November 1998. His daughter Julia had dismissed this as probably being a grey squirrel which he had mistaken as our cat after having a few drinks! Being so unlikely anyway, we had consequently given it no more thought.

Over the following week we alternated between lessons in the field and rides out. I managed to contact the farmer who leased the farmland through which our track meandered who, in turn, talked to the people who rented Pencarris Farm from him and they both consented to our using the farm track, and the tracks through the fields, for riding provided, of course, we did no damage to crops. I could hardly avoid noticing, however, that in the morning prior to riding Smartie, Mel was winding herself up with worry. It was not so much worry about coming off, which is what she used to think about - with good reason - but about whether it was all going to work out. Sure enough, after each ride, she would be on a high because of how well it had gone.

'Why don't you keep a written note of exactly how you feel each morning before you ride her and then again afterwards? Over a short period of time I'm sure you'll be amazed at how you're progressing,' I suggested.

'Could do,' was the less than enthusiastic response. But she did, and by the time Debi turned up for their first lesson in the field together she was saying to me, 'it's really fantastic that what was worrying me a few days ago just isn't an issue any more.'

'Good!' I replied without surprise. 'Just keep writing down your feelings before and afterwards.'

As Debi took Mel through her paces in the field I couldn't help peering out of our bedroom window once or twice to check everything was OK. On the third occasion, I saw Mel jump off Smartie and thought she had had a crisis of confidence. In the event Debi had decided to ride her to try to get to the bottom of the bucking. Later Mel explained that it was Smartie trying to balance herself on the uneven ground, something which didn't come easily to such a young, inexperienced horse. Mel had rounded off her lesson by riding Smartie round the perimeter of the field. 'Did you enjoy the view from the top?' I asked earnestly.

'You must be joking!' she retorted. 'I was concentrating on keeping her walking quietly.'

The next day saw the arrival of the hanging baskets, just a few days before our friends Jim and Tricia Carter and Carl and Barbara Wellings were due to arrive for a short weekend with us. The new double bed we had ordered cut things even finer by turning up the day after that. Mel had decided that James' room, which we did not expect him to need after leaving Bath with his Masters degree in Management and Marketing followed by the hoped-for career move, would become a potential guest room requiring us to replace his old single bed with a new double.

The day before their arrival Mel decided she would still put up with another lesson from me in the field but I suspected Debi was doing more for her confidence than I was. I therefore took a tactical decision to be there in body and spirit but to leave Mel to find her own way forward. She subconsciously took the hint and put herself through her usual schooling routine. For the first time she was no longer reliant on someone on the ground telling her what to do. That evening she seemed more relaxed than for sometime. 'How are your 'before and after' notes looking now?' I asked, sensing some improvement in her outlook.

'Oh, I haven't been keeping those recently,' she admitted sniffily. 'Don't feel the need to anymore.' Maybe yet another small corner had just been turned...

I was still hosing the winter's debris from our cobbled drive when the Carters and Wellings arrived on Saturday morning. The new hanging baskets, though their contents had still not filled out, were in sparse bloom and provided welcoming splishes of colour against the brown and grey stonework of the house and cottage. After a brief discussion among themselves, our visitors decided that Jim and Tricia would stay in the cottage while Carl and Barbara would use James' room and the boys' bathroom.

We enjoyed our usual catching up with each other's news over lunch, then went off to Constantine Bay on the north coast just west of Padstow, parked in the car park above it, and set off for a cliff-top stroll in the sunshine towards Trevose Head. Past the lighthouse we wandered over to the cliff-top and sat on the warm, if slightly damp, springy grass. The women talked excitedly behind us while we men exchanged thoughts on the tranquillity of just being able to sit and gaze across the lightly rippling water below. While it was true I no longer had the day-to-day stresses of work, I had enough of my own pressures to be able to share the benefits of relaxing and enjoying the quietness of the day. We watched and chatted as a scuba-diving training session took place on a small boat bobbing gently above the rocks underneath the cliff.

I had booked a table for 8.00pm at the Blisland Inn where we enjoyed the usual grand helpings and sampled landlord Gary's superb real ales. Carl related the sad tale of the time he and Barbara had agreed to look after their new neighbour's cat while they were away for a few days. The sadness related to the cat's tragic end, to Carl and Barbara's horror, under the wheels of a passing car a day or so later. Carl felt it was his responsibility to give the cat a decent burial at a carefully chosen spot in their neighbour's garden but on returning from their break, their neighbours' initial shock was rapidly overtaken by indignation as they dug it up and reburied it in what they considered to be a more suitable final resting place. 'If I'd known their reaction I wouldn't have bothered,' said a somewhat put out Carl to gales of laughter from the rest of us.

We hit upon Mevagissey as the place we would visit on Sunday, as the others had never been there. Mel and I had been there just once several years before and, finding it full of the worst sort of tourist shops from souvenirs to cheap clothing and greasy spoon cafés, had had little compunction to return. We therefore disowned the decision to go there but were curious to see whether there had been any change.

The drive down to the small working fishing port from the A390 was through some delightful scenery, though our recollection of our earlier visit came into focus as we parked the cars in the small back street car park. Soon, however, we were captivated by the range of entirely different shops, almost all of them open that spring Sunday morning. There were fabric shops, clothes shops, some with ethnic designs, and a large number of art studios. I was particularly taken with the work of Kevin Platt who was from Manchester, born the same year as me and who had painted in Mevagissey for some years. Indeed he was at work in his gallery as we browsed and he stopped to talk to us. Yes, he would be happy to undertake a commission at the same price as his paintings on display and paint a scene of our choice. I immediately thought of my view from the top of our field and made a mental note to come back after the season was over.

We also had a splendid lunch of fresh seafood, from succulent scallops to juicy John Dory. We learned from the proprietor that the harbour was privately owned and that little investment was made in the upkeep or refurbishment of premises which explained the somewhat scruffy appearance of many of the buildings. Even so we all agreed we had enjoyed our visit and the stroll to the mouth of the harbour past the racks of nets, lobster pots and general detritus which was the by-product of the day-to-day work of the port.

After a leisurely tea back at Upper Penwithiel, it was time for our visitors to pack up their cars and head back home to resume their normal working routines. It was only after waving them down the drive when Mel and I turned to go in the front door that we realised it had shut behind us with all our keys inside. Having returned from our day out only half-an-hour or so before, all the doors and windows in the house were closed and locked with the sole exception of the boys' bathroom window which Carl had told us he had opened before he left. Having got various expletives out of our systems and abandoned the futile idea of trying to allocate responsibility for this minor disaster, we focused on how to get back in!

'You'll have to break a window,' concluded Mel after a few seconds' thought.

'No. Not yet. Let me think about it.' Mel sighed impatiently while I pondered. I looked up at the first floor bathroom window, sitting a few inches ajar with its arm on its peg, directly above my study window next to the utility room door and almost willed myself up and through it.

Reading my thoughts Mel said, 'there's no way you can get up there without a ladder.'

'Hmmmm,' I responded thoughtfully. 'The ladders are locked in the garage...but the bathroom window is the only way in. I have to get in there somehow.' My thoughts turned to what 'equipment' I could lay my hands on for the purpose and lit upon the scaffolding planks in the barn. 'Planks!' I expostulated to Mel's astonishment.

'Planks? Are you going to lean them against the wall and climb up them or what?' she joked. I had in fact seriously contemplated that but rapidly realised I'd never manage the gradient. I started to think about resting them on the top of the stone wall between the house and the barn but could not work out what to do with the other end! My meanderings took me up to the barn to find some inspiration. First I found the planks, ranging from six feet to sixteen feet in length. The long ones would reach the window but for some reason I concentrated on the shorter ones. I dragged them out in front of the barn. Then I saw them. The carefully stacked pile of green polythene-wrapped bales of shredded paper - the horse bedding.

'Yes!' I said out loud.

'What?' asked Mel who had eventually followed me up.

'I've got it. I'll build a small tower of bales and climb up it,' I said, rather pleased with myself.

'Won't it be a bit wobbly?' Mel asked.

'Yes, but it's the only way in,' I repeated firmly. I loaded up the mucking-out barrow with three bales and wheeled them down to the house and continued until I had seven or eight. As I piled them one on top of the other, they did indeed resemble a green plastic leaning tower of Pisa.

'You can't get up on that,' Mel said, 'you'll break your neck.' I looked up once more and the open window tantalisingly beckoned.

'I'll get a few more bales,' I said, hurriedly returning to the barn. Having built a solid base two deep and two wide, I stacked them up with the top three layers of single bales rising above the study window sill. As I contemplated climbing on them to check for height, I realised I could not reach the topmost bale! 'I need to use one of the short planks,' I explained. After bringing one down from the barn I could not see how to use it without pushing over the delicately balanced pile.

'I've got that old kitchen stool in the tack-room,' offered Mel. After a second's thought I asked her to fetch it. I then laid the plank across the top of the stool which, itself, was placed on the utility room steps, and then onto the top bale. I found I could just get up on the plank and edge across to the top of the pile of bales. I stretched up to find that, while my fingers reached the bathroom window sill, there was no way I could haul myself up but I managed to unhitch the arm from the peg.

'I think I can do it with one more bale,' I said over my shoulder to Mel below. With that she shot up to the barn and half-carried, half-dragged another of the heavy tightly-packed bales down to the house. As I perched precariously atop my wobbling tower of paper she just managed to manoeuvre the new bale onto the plank where I could lift it, with her pushing it up from underneath, onto the bale I was standing on. Once I had it in place I stood on it and managed to get my elbows onto the bathroom window sill.

As I scrambled up, lifting my feet off the bales, Mel shrieked, 'watch the study window.' Too late, my heavy Timberland boots crashed against the glass, rocking the unstable and suddenly soft tower, dislodging the top bale. My luck, and, more to the point, the glass, held as I hauled myself up. I then had to twist and turn to get my bulky girth and long legs in through the narrow opening, experiencing an unwelcome and uncomfortable intimacy with the peg. But I was in and the sense of triumph was exhilarating. I leaned out to see a grinning Mel looking up at me, as much as anything, in relief that my vertical progress had been up rather than down!

'I'm not letting you in the front door though. You'll have to climb in the window,' I yelled down at her. Her reply was not one I could repeat here. I relented, went down and let her in.

Mel's next lesson with Debi was very encouraging for her as they began the process of educating Smartie in the English way of riding which she, Mel, was so used to. 'It won't take long to get her to canter on an English aid. The saddle-seat way is all very well but can be confusing in dressage,' Mel explained. This seemed to hold good on our next ride out together when Mel cantered Smartie in open country for the first time. We were getting accustomed to breaking new ground in one way or other each time we went out. That was also to be the day when Mel first insisted that Smartie went through puddles and not round them! After some delicate negotiations, the deal was finally done. Morgans, being the exceptionally smart horses they are, will do their best to arrange for everything to be done on their terms, deferring only at the very last minute to your will, and only then if they happen to care for you! There was no doubt, however, that each additional minute in the saddle was increasing their trust in each other and lowering the tension. The resulting increasingly relaxed approach improved their riding teamwork dramatically.

Over the following week Sukie became increasingly wobbly and fell once or twice but past experience told me to give her a day or two before reaching any conclusions. I felt that her various lumps and bumps could not be helping her.

A welcome break from the pressures at home came with the annual 'leaping cat run' organised by the Cornwall branch of the Jaguar Enthusiasts' Club. The drive started once again in the Lemon Quay car park in Truro but this time we arranged to join it just after the A39 roundabout above Wadebridge thus avoiding the needless journey to and from Truro. We sat in the lay-by at the appointed time with our engine running and were waved into the middle of the convoy as it approached. We made for Tintagel and parked at the King Arthur's Castle Hotel where we had coffee. From there we walked to The Cornishman pub for lunch.

Inside, we all met up with Mike Godwin, a JEC member and, intriguingly, a fellow member of the Institute of Directors, who was the proprietor of King Arthur's Great Halls which we were later shown round as his guests. While built after a mediaeval style, they were actually opened in 1933. Despite the lack of any direct historical links to King Arthur, the halls were painstakingly constructed of local granite and slate, featured internal stonework from many of Cornwall's quarries and boasted some impressive stained glass windows, making it worth a visit for these features alone. It was also interesting to hear that the original motivation of the founder was the espousal of Arthurian principles.

On returning home to reality, I found that while Sukie was more stable she was unable to support herself when spending a penny last thing that night. That was to me a key factor in determining that it was no longer right to let her continue: her dignity counted for everything in the equation I would have preferred not to have to contemplate. However we had to take Daisy to the vet because of an eye infection and also got a course of antibiotics to help Sukie one more time with her cysts.

The following day brought scant improvement but Sukie just insisted on getting to her feet, following me out and generally carrying on as usual. Browsing through a book called 'Aloe Vera in Veterinary Practice' by David Urch, himself a vet, to see whether our administration of this amazing substance was likely to be of continuing help, I was reminded of the benefits of cod liver oil for arthritic conditions and joint problems. Considering these to be likely factors in Sukie's difficulties, I bought her a supply of both. Within a few days the improvement was clear and her instabilities diminished. She enjoyed yet another new, if capped, lease of life.

❦

Our next ride out was distinguished by Smartie deciding to canter sideways. As it was, I always had to hold Max back when Mel started to canter Smartie and this always resulted in us going backwards, rearing or spinning until I was able to slowly unleash his power and catch them up. Mel's total preoccupation with handling her own horse luckily enabled me to conceal these shenanigans which I knew would have otherwise unsettled her!

Several days of rain ensued, in true Cornish, non-stop style, precluding further progress with Smartie. Sukie, however, had continued her almost miraculous recovery, progressing to such an extent that I felt she was able to resume her walks with us - Jake, Chan and me - round the field. There had been a break in the rain that late May morning, allowing us to make our way up to the field. As the horses were at the far end of the big field, I decided to take the dogs up into the small paddock which was connected to it by gates at the top and bottom. This was so that Sukie would not be worried by the attentions of the horses, notably Smartie. As usual, both gates were open to allow the horses to move around freely. Sukie seemed content to wander around in the sheltered small paddock while Jake, Chan and I strode off towards the top gate for a walk along the top of the big field.

Just as I turned to check that Sukie was OK before disappearing through the gate, the thunder of hooves behind me announced that Smartie and Max had arrived at speed from the far end to investigate. This was always a magnificent sight but on this occasion I stood in the gateway to deter them from going through and frightening the still-fragile Sukie. They then charged down to the bottom of the big field and through the bottom connecting gate. I spun round and headed back towards Sukie as fast as I could. While I knew the horses posed no direct threat or danger to her, I knew she would be worried so I determined to get to her first to reassure her and then gently lead her out of the paddock.

I rode the undulations and ruts of the small paddock, very much in the manner of a downhill skier, though in wellies rather than on skis. The grass and the clay soil beneath it, being still wet, contrived, in turn, to mimic the properties of a ski slope. This combination resulted in a crunch and crack as my left foot attempted to take the line round one particular 'flag' or tussock rather faster than the rest of me was able to. The searing pain which tore through my ankle and up towards my shin, as my foot bent under my full weight, more than justified the particular expletive with which I shocked a quivering geriatric Great Dane bitch, small inquisitive Basenji puppy, lumbering curious Great Dane dog and stock-still grazing Morgan!

There was only one casualty that morning and he stubbornly refused to go to hospital for fear of being prevented by plaster from walking, driving or riding for an indefinite period, thus interrupting the normal flow of life and, not least, the promising progress of an increasingly confident rider with her increasingly competent horse.

The pain and delayed shock were sufficient to write off the next two days but by the third I was definitely hobbling better! David Urch's book had suddenly come into its own as I added doses of aloe vera and cod liver oil to my own obligatory 'Deep Heat' and crêpe bandage treatment. It seemed that May was determined to go out with a bang: in addition to my ankle, Chan's unplanned abandonment in the utility room with the other dogs that morning resulted in his chewing through the power cable to the boiler tripping out all the power in the house.

The next day I felt able to ride and, discovering I could not mount in the normal way, left foot into left stirrup first, had to throw my right leg over Max first and then put my feet in the stirrups. As ever, Max did not bat an eyelid at this unconventional and, for both of us, uncomfortable approach. We walked and trotted up the lane with Mel continually asking how my ankle was. It was fine, in fact remarkably comfortable considering I couldn't walk on it properly! However, I found this growing confidence to be misplaced when Mel took the initiative and shot off into a smart canter along the edge of one of the Pencarris Farm fields. Ouch, ouch, ouch, throb, throb, throb in time with each downbeat of Max's front left hoof!

My mind was taken off my swollen ankle as we made our way back along the track, the ruts still full of water from the recent rain, when Mel, in front as usual, insisted yet again that Smartie go through the puddles and not round them. Smartie duly did her earnest best, accompanied by uncontrollable giggles from Mel, as she paced with legs either side of the puddles with an action not unlike that of a commando running through staggered car tyres on an obstacle course!

Thankfully my discomfort did nothing to slow Mel's and Smartie's joint progress that day. 'I've learned so much today,' Mel said on our way back down the lane. 'When I relax and trust her she responds by being, well, just brilliant.' She carried on chattering excitedly about her ride as we dismounted by the barn. What more could I have asked for, I thought, as I led Max in to be untacked, other than the ability to walk in a straight line without wincing...

2 Adam and Eve It

June had arrived and it would soon be time to meet Joan Collins. No, I was not about to audition for her romantic lead, though it would not have taken much to resurrect the old youthful fantasy of a romp with a more, um, mature woman. The less promising, though still exciting, reality was that she was going to open new offices in Shropshire for the company of which I was a director. Mel couldn't wait to meet her, being a long term admirer of her, though more because of her positive, feisty approach to life than her screen roles as such.

Yet another of life's little coincidences jumped out and grabbed my attention. I had come across a man who had recently moved to Cornwall from London but whose career had spanned both years and continents, involved as he had been in show business and films. He had worked with Barry Humphries, or rather Dame Edna Everage, and, he had confided, with Joan Collins. How strange that this should have happened just a few weeks prior to my meeting her.

When we came to planning our two day trek north we found a natural stopping place overnight: Bredwardine. It was time, we thought, to revisit Sue and Jim Whittall. Their lovely old stone farmhouse was perfectly placed, not only to break the journey but to give us the excuse to drop in on the Monnington crew to update Trudy Connolly and Lionel Ferreira on Mel's and Smartie's excellent progress.

While quite used to leaving Cornwall, we never felt completely comfortable at putting too many miles between us and the animals even though we had total confidence in middle son James who had returned home specially to look after them. By the time we reached the Severn Bridge, however, the mild apprehension was turning into keen anticipation.

We had to eat, so what better way to swap notes than to meet up with them both at the Sun Inn at Winforton? As ever, it was Wills, the Whittalls' lovely Border Collie who saw us first as we got out of the car outside Old Court Farm around 7pm. He raced over to greet us, silently and enthusiastically wagging his tail and, indeed, his whole body. 'Wills, come here,' commanded Jim from inside one of his barns.

'It's OK, Jim,' I said as I bent over to fuss the smiling dog.

'I didn't want him plastering you with mud,' Jim grinned, a little in relief, I guessed, that we really didn't mind.

'How are you?' I asked. 'Busy as usual, I suppose,' I said, knowing the answer.

'Yes, we had a good crop of lambs this year. Plenty to keep me going well into the evening,' he replied against a background of baas and bleats from within.

Wills waited as I unloaded our bags and then escorted us to the front door. But no further: as a working dog he knew his rightful place was outside. As we went in he resumed his attendance on his master.

'How are you both?' Sue sang out as she emerged from her kitchen on hearing the huge front door close behind us. After our usual exchange of news she said, 'I've put you in the granary like last time, if that's OK with you.' It was, we acknowledged, giving us, with its external steps, the freedom to get in when we wished after our meal later without disturbing anyone.

There was much banter over dinner as we imparted the story of Mel's progress with Smartie since bringing her home from her period of training. Was that quiet smile I noticed crossing Lionel's face one of relief that nothing untoward had happened? Despite his undoubted prowess as a trainer, obvious confidence and evident charm, I thought I detected the merest indication of a need for reassurance from his clients that they were happy with him. While unnecessary I concluded it was no bad thing and certainly preferable to the arrogance that some might exude.

While we had easily slipped back into the Morgan world with talk of showing, breeding, training and personalities, we couldn't help being aware that our perspective and priorities were different. The most important thing for Mel was that she had a beautifully trained horse with character, manners and temperament. The Morgan elegance and intelligence were things she had long aspired to have in a horse but were nonetheless a distinct bonus compared with the prize of owning a horse she could trust.

It was no later than around 11pm when we arrived back at Old Court Farm and as we got out of the car we were startled by Wills who emerged barking from the shadows by the front door. Once we started our ascent to our room he wagged his tail and quietly disappeared from view once more.

The next morning saw us, after a hearty Whittall breakfast, meandering through northern Herefordshire back roads before crossing into Shropshire. We were in good time to join a guided tour of the company's new offices in a small group of visitors and unattached executive wives, none of whom were involved in the business. I decided to kill two birds not only putting the staff and management at their ease but fulfilling my own need for information by asking what I hoped were relevant, intelligent and penetrating questions. This enabled our hosts to focus on someone who was not only showing interest but who might actually want to hear the answers and far from putting them off, this seemed to relax them by letting them talk about what they knew best!

'I hope you weren't bored by that,' I muttered to Mel as we returned to the gathering point for the grand opening.

'No, why, should I have been?' she answered.

'Well I was conscious that the rest of our group might not know what we were talking about but I know what it's like having to show round visitors. It's much more motivational if they're genuinely interested,' I explained.

'No, it was fine,' she said. 'In fact I could see how relieved the staff were that they could just answer your questions.'

'You don't think the others felt I was monopolising things?'

'No, of course not. If they were anything like me they were probably relieved at not having to look intelligent by asking any themselves,' she replied with a twinkle of honesty in her eyes.

We were shepherded back to reception which was filling up with guests ranging from architects to builders and planners as well as other directors and senior executives and their partners. After a few minutes Hugh Broadhurst, the Chief Executive, appeared with Joan Collins who was smiling broadly under her wide-brimmed hat. As he introduced her, staff gathered at the open windows above us in the atrium. She performed the brief opening ceremony with style and panache to a futtering of camera flashes. She took her time to give a regal wave and smile to all of us surrounding her before, professional to the tips of her flickering eyelashes, turning her attention to the staff in the gods. She truly was the next best thing to royalty, though my only brushes with the real thing were an introduction to the Duchess of York as a representative of my then company who had supported a particular charity and to the Princess Royal in Buckingham Palace. This too was charity-related as the Princess had invited in a group of business representatives to try to interest them in sponsoring Save the Children. I'm not sure which had the greatest impact on me, the total lack of apparent security (long since tightened up I'm sure), the view up the Mall from the room behind that balcony or the conversation I had with Her Royal Highness in which I mentioned to her genuine amusement that at a recent cricket match between her son's school and mine, hers had cheered on his team from the boundary in a most un-Lords like fashion!

We then got into our cars and proceeded in a protracted convoy to the magnificent Weston Park, a large 17th century house near Shifnal. Once inside we enjoyed pre-lunch drinks and then the opportunity arose. Joan had been escorted by one of the aides from her management company and had been introduced to one or two guests by Hugh. Then followed a lull and, as sometimes happens with celebrities I've noticed, she was rather left to one side with no one feeling bold enough to go up to her.

'Excuse me, my name's Dex Cameron,' I said to a protective look from her companion and one hovering between curiosity and ennui from Joan. Once they had accepted I was neither going to harm her nor bore her to death she switched on a smile from under the hat the top of which, even with her five inch heels, was still a good five or six inches below my eye level. As we shook hands I explained, 'I'm one of the directors here. The opening went well. I'm sure we'll get a lot of local publicity,' I mumbled. She smiled again.

'Where have you come from?' she asked.

'Up from Cornwall,' I replied.

'You live there?' she asked, giving a bravura performance in disguising her indifference. I realised she was still on her fee time so was giving me time she otherwise wouldn't.

'Yes,' I replied. 'We've been there a couple of years now.'

'Really?' Her eyes lit up for the first time as she went on, 'my daughter's on holiday there at the moment.'

As everyone does I instinctively asked, 'oh, where?' Her look changed the subject. 'Can I introduce Mel, my wife,' I swiftly said, feeling I had worked the ground sufficiently to do so.

'Nice to meet you,' Joan smiled sweetly.

'It's wonderful to meet you too,' replied Mel. 'I've long admired you.' Joan's smile broadened. 'I've got several of your books. I just love the positive approach you have to everything.'

'Well, that's important I think, don't you?' she asked.

'By coincidence,' I began, after a near-terminal pause in the conversation, 'I spoke to someone recently who has just moved to Cornwall and who says he knows you.' She showed renewed interest by slightly raising a finely-plucked eyebrow. 'Said he'd worked with you on one or two films.'

'What's his name?' she asked and on cocking her ear for my reply said, 'never heard of him I'm afraid, but then I have made over 50 films so I can't know everyone,' she added with a thin dismissive smile. We continued briefly before it was announced that luncheon was served.

So what did I think of her close to? There is no doubt that she looks as good in the flesh as on television or in the papers. It was amazing to think of her true age: she really did appear to be defying the passage of time. But was she attractive? Of course! There was no doubt that that adolescent fantasy of many a man of my age had been standing in front of me. How this was to be put into sharp perspective a year or so later when she married a man half my age! Lunch was in the orangery to the accompaniment of electric violins played by attractive young women from the Vanessa-Mae school of bowing.

After lunch Hugh gave a short speech of welcome and explanation of the company's need for additional accommodation before introducing Joan who, most unusually for a PR celebrity, gave a short to-the-point speech.

On returning to our car we put in a call to Ron and Freda Lewis, of Walkmyll Great Dane fame, whose house was on our way home via the M5. Yes, of course we could drop in, we were told by Freda. 'I'll have some tea ready.'

Half-an-hour or so later we turned into their familiar farm driveway near Cheslyn Hay to the wonderful sound of deep-throated barks that can only come from a large number of Great Danes. After changing from our glad rags into sad rags or, more specifically, jeans and casual shirts, we enjoyed several cups of tea, accompanied by the attentions of two indoor Danes, and caught up with all the news and gossip before going out to meet the current generation of Walkmylls. Once again I found myself waxing lyrical on the properties of aloe vera as a response to some of Freda's aches and pains.

'Is this the stuff you mean?' she asked, producing a familiar plastic container.

'Yes. Oh, you already know about it,' I laughed.

'Well I bought some because someone recommended it but it's so darned expensive I haven't got round to opening it yet,' she chuckled.

'Oh you must,' I said. 'I'm sure you'll be glad you did.'

Our return home brought us back to the reality that Sukie was in decline. The sight of Ron and Freda's younger and healthier Danes had served only to sharpen the contrast with Sukie's condition. I renewed my promise to her not to let her suffer but stepped up her aloe vera dose.

On the following Sunday Andrew arrived for a week. He continued to demonstrate a greater knowledge of our part of Cornwall than we had by telling us all the short-cuts, pubs of interest and quieter beaches. Oh to have the time to be on holiday here again! The difference was we were lucky enough to be able to grab mini-holidays of a few hours here and there whenever we liked and we never took for granted the view that appeared as we drove up this road or that.

That was the reason why the meal I booked at Trawlers in Looe for later in the week would not be the first that year for us. Our culinary tastes are nothing if not broad and so it was in the Southern States restaurant next to the multiplex cinema in Plymouth the following evening that we found ourselves enjoying a meal, while waiting to go in to see 'Gladiator'. Visiting Plymouth seemed to have become one of those things we only ever did when one or more of the boys suggested it: in other words it did not hold a natural attraction for us!

The undoubted highlight of the week, however, was our first visit to the amazing Eden Project at Bodelva near St Austell. While the project was still under construction, the PR prowess of Tim Smit, whose baby it was, had resulted in unprecedented interest and thousands of visitors who, like us, were curious to see the progress to date. Tim had some years before been responsible for 'finding' the Lost Gardens of Heligan at Pentewan. In that project he had literally been involved in unearthing the landscaping and planting done many years earlier by others. It had in those years become totally overgrown and virtually lost for good before he came to the rescue. How rewarding it must be for him to be the architect of this fabulous new project in the heart of Cornwall's less well-known south-east corner.

We had, of course, followed the progress on local TV and radio as well as in the local press. All we really knew was that these huge structures of metal and transparent plastic were to be built, on the same principles as greenhouses, in a disused china clay pit of which there are a few in the locality.

Nothing could have prepared us for the excitement we felt as we parked the car amidst a forest of fluttering vertical banners lining the car park and walkway down to the reception area. The car parks, paths and buildings were, of course, all new. As we descended into the valley the sight before us was staggering. Not only was the scale of the site beyond our imagination but the sheer level of activity on the 'biomes' below, sprouting from the earth like some giant man-made fungi, was reminiscent of a set of a James Bond movie.

There were people sitting on top, a hundred feet or more up, fixing the hexagonal 'pillows' of triple-skinned inflated transparent foil into place, others suspended inside working on the internal structure, which we now knew was of tubular steel, and yet others abseiling down to the ground to move on to the next task. Across the floor of what had until fairly recently been a white-lined man-made lake were sprinkled dozens of others driving dumper trucks, lorries, bulldozers, cranes and all the other mechanical aides such large scale works require.

After working our way to the front of the queue, we bought our tickets, donned the requisite hard hats and luminous yellow safety tops, making us wonder whether we were about to become forced labour to help speed things up a bit, and boarded a small rubber-tyred train to make the quarter mile journey to the edge of the largest of the biomes. There was, as yet, no vegetation to be seen, other than the natural flora sprouting from the huge Cornish bank behind and into which the massive earth anchors had clearly been secured.

On our way out we visited the shop with its wealth of mementoes, plants, books and foodstuffs. I looked up at one point to see disc jockey Dave Lee Travis browsing in front of me. Unlike Joan Collins, he was not on duty so I, along with everyone else who recognised him, did not invade his privacy.

While we were aware of the local feeling against the loss of amenity which the inevitable incursion of hundreds of thousands of visitors to Eden would bring each year, we could not but marvel at the transformation of what, with the best will in the world, was otherwise only ever going to be an eyesore. One thing was certain and that was that the local economy, so long supported by the old fishing, agriculture, mining and china clay industries was in need of the boost that such an imaginative scheme was surely going to bring as people flocked from across the world to see this eighth wonder.

The next day saw us taking Andrew to the Nare Hotel for the first time where, yet again, I could not resist their huge platter of fresh sea-food. After that we went on to St Mawes for the first time in a few years and were pleasantly surprised at how much it had improved: the buildings seemed better cared for and there had been a distinct improvement in the quality of shops and restaurants. We had heard about a smart new hotel that was opening but didn't manage to locate it.

That evening brought a different atmosphere altogether. The four of us went banger racing at St Columb, as spectators of course!

❧

I am pleased to say that Andrew has inherited my own, not uncritical, interest in seeking out good eating places and he was impressed with Trawlers. Andrew, and I enjoyed a plateful of the largest, juiciest scallops as a starter while I, for once, was able to eat fresh local lobster without feeling guilty about the cost.

While it was true that we had eaten out a few times that week, it was something we tended to do more when we had visitors and particularly when they were special to us.

Soon his inevitable return to his daily life meant it was time for goodbyes once more but, while sad to see him go, the raw emotion of our early days in Cornwall had faded.

As Mel and I got back to our own individual routines I could not help noticing the improvement in Sukie's whole outlook. While she was a little slower, she seemed more relaxed than for a while. I wondered, though, whether she would still be with us on Andrew's next visit.

Another continuing cause for concern had been Angus, our black American Cocker. The allergy to house dust he had had since birth was affecting his eyes. We noticed a milky film appearing which told us he was, as Simon Draper had warned he might, slowly losing his sight. Being younger than Sukie it had not affected his general brightness and ability to get around so we just resigned ourselves to making his life as tolerable as we could. On re-reading our book on the veterinary applications of aloe vera we discovered it was also potentially useful in managing allergies so decided to try it on Angus. The early signs were hopeful as he seemed markedly less irritated than he had been.

It was not only the domestic pets who, like their owners, were showing signs of wear and tear but the domestic fixtures as well.

'Come and look at this,' Mel called out urgently from the landing one morning. I left my computer screen to go and investigate the cause of her concern.

'Whatever is it?' I asked breathlessly after racing up the stairs.

'Here,' she said, leading the way into the boys' bathroom. My heart sank at the thought that the loo seat needed fixing again or a tap washer needed replacing. But no, the source of her consternation was evidently inside the airing cupboard. 'The hot water tank's leaking.'

I peered into the gloom. 'Where?' I asked from my usual optimistic perspective which told me there would be some simple explanation.

'There,' she replied, pointing to a damp patch on the floor. I brushed it lightly with the tips of my fingers.

'That's nothing,' I said dismissively. 'Probably a bit of condensation. Certainly not enough to worry about.'

'Are you sure? We don't want the ceiling to come down in your study.'

'No, there's no sign of any leak,' I said with as much reassurance as I could. Seeing this had done little to satisfy her, I made great play of getting down on my hands and knees to get a better look. I ran the tip of my forefinger round the seam at the bottom of the tank. To my surprise I disturbed a small drip.

'Well?' she asked insistently. I muttered a non-committal reply which she missed. 'Let *me* see,' she said joining me on all fours. 'It's wet,' she exclaimed. 'There *is* a leak.'

'Well the seam might be weeping slightly,' I conceded, 'but let's just keep an eye on it to see how bad it is. Have you got a small bowl to put under it?' Her look told me she was unconvinced but off she went to find one. I put it in place and closed the door deep in thought. A slight lack of watertightness was only to be expected after ten years I told myself but something was nagging away at me.

Supposing it was the cumulative effect of the slight acidity in the spring water. Maybe the joints were corroding and what I'd felt was the result of water running down a pipe and collecting at the bottom of the tank. Either way there was no great pressure in the system. But there was a considerable weight of water that I certainly did not want cascading over my computer immediately below. It was with some relief on checking the bowl the next morning that I found just a couple of millimetres of water in the bowl.

These, it turned out, were not to be our only waterworks problems. Dear old Jake's retching had subsided over the weeks then very suddenly returned but this time accompanied by his repeatedly throwing up his food together with bile. An urgent appointment with Simon Draper had him stroking his chin in thought. 'It could be one of several things,' he said as he shook down his thermometer.

A minute or two later he peered over his half-moon glasses and said, 'his temperature's up a bit. Not dramatically but it may indicate a bit of an infection somewhere.' After grilling us about other symptoms he checked Jake's heart which he said was strong before finally concluding, 'it could be a prostate problem but we'll give him some antibiotics to help sort out whatever it is. I'd like to see him again in a couple of days.'

We went off to weigh Jake on the weighing platform, standing just an inch or two above the floor, which all vets seem to have. They are usually just a little too small for the giant breeds. After persuading Jake that it was safe to put all four feet on the platform rather than using one to anchor himself firmly to the floor, we all agreed the right reading was 69 kilograms or around 11 stones in old money.

Jake seemed to perk up a little in the days that followed but we knew we had to keep a close eye on him. Just as we thought we had enough to think about, we heard from Bill, Mel's father, that Mary, her mother, had gone into hospital.

❧

I couldn't bring myself to believe the large, warm, fawn head I held in my hands might not be with us for very much longer but Sukie was having a distinctly down day and I felt the inevitable decision closing in. We had never fooled ourselves into thinking that the aloe vera she was having was going to do any more than make life more comfortable: it was not capable of keeping her going indefinitely. Now she had reached the grand old age of eleven-and-a-half, each day was a precious bonus.

In the middle of July we found ourselves in the middle of the Royal Cornwall Showground. Not, this time, for the show itself but for 'Wheels 2000', a classic car show. Other members of the Jaguar Enthusiasts' Club had convinced me that our XJS was on the very threshold of becoming a classic car. Though uncertain whether this was good news, I had decided to enter for fun. The main purpose seemed to be to allow members of the public to look over the collections of cars grouped by marque.

Later I was to agree to join a cavalcade in which each car stopped in front of the announcer's tent to allow him to read from the notes prepared by the owner on his pride and joy. I felt something of a fraud sitting there in the blazing sun with my air conditioning full on while the genuine petrolheads sweltered. By the end of the afternoon my pristine, freshly washed and buffed paintwork was the same colour as every other car: a light tan from the thin layer of showground dust that had settled on every surface except, thanks to the aircon, the interior ones!

But on that day we had an added attraction: it was Chan's first outing where there was a crowd of people. He not only took everything in his stride but also grabbed the attention of many a passing child. 'What is he? A Jack Russell?' asked one young boy, more knowledgeably than his father who had asked whether the car was an XJ40.

'A Jack Russell with attitude,' I joked. The boy's expression remained as blank as his father's had when I had told him the car was a special edition.

'What's special about it?' the father had asked.

'What's attitude?' the boy had wanted to know. I wasn't sure where or whether to start!

That evening the setting sun treated us to a lava flow of clouds coloured crimson, purple and violet. Days later the arrival home of James and Justin for the summer presented Mel with an avalanche of dirty washing.

❦

The sea was as flat and inviting as the Med as Mel and I turned the nose of the Jag down the familiar steep descent to the Nare Hotel in time for lunch at our favourite spot in Cornwall. The view itself was enough to settle us instantly into the feeling of calm we had experienced on our previous stays there. Now we lived so near, that was no longer something we could sensibly indulge in, so a few hours' lingering would have to do.

After a leisurely lunch on the terrace by the pool on what was a very hot and sunny day, we spied the owner, Bettye Gray, alas sadly widowed since we had last stayed. After a brief chat, we talked about 'Oh My Dear Life!', the book she was publishing about her and her family's involvement over many years in the Cornish tourist industry. She told us the running of the hotel had passed into the capable hands of her grandson Toby Ashworth, perpetuating the dynasty.

Later we strolled along Carne beach. The sea looked inviting though something told me it would not be as warm as the previous August when I had convinced myself the sea was as warm as in Greece. 'It's freezing,' Mel exclaimed as she slipped off her shoes and walked through the sea's gently lapping wavelets.

'Can't be,' I exclaimed with total certainty.

'You try it then,' she replied.

'No thanks,' I said, moving too slowly to avoid the spray she kicked in my direction. 'OK, I believe you,' I said, narrowly avoiding a more serious soaking. We walked hand-in-hand for a while. Instantly I was back at Rinsey on our first holiday together thirty years earlier. It is true that sights, sounds, smells, tastes and touch can all have the effect of transporting you back to where you had a vivid experience of them, whether good or bad. On that occasion it was the shimmering heat haze, the soft rippling of the water, the warm scent of seaweed, the salt tang of the breeze and the warm, gentle grip of Mel's fingers that briefly wafted me back to my mid-twenties. 'Let's run up to those rocks,' I said more enthusiastically than was sensible.

After a few breathless yards, 'let's not,' Mel said with a grin as she pulled me down to sit on them next to her.

Soon we were sufficiently refreshed to begin thinking about our return home. 'Jake's not so good again,' Mel said as we pulled ourselves up the slipway onto the road back to the Nare's car park.

'No,' I replied. 'I'm not very happy about him, not least because we don't really know what's wrong with him.' Mel nodded silently in agreement.

When we arrived home Justin seemed quite pleased with himself. 'I've got a holiday job at Tesco's,' he announced with a grin. While we all knew this would be a limited challenge for him, we also all knew he was going to have a much better summer with some money in his pocket. 'It's good I contacted them at Easter. All the jobs had gone by the end of June,' he told us.

James' reaction was less ebullient as he had not planned so far ahead. 'All I know is that whatever I do it won't be in a supermarket,' he grunted, the memories of Asda not yet distant enough for him to appreciate the value of that particular experience.

'Do you mean all your food hygiene expertise is going to go to waste?' I asked. His withering look gave me his answer.

'For one thing I've got to finish my dissertation and so I want something where the time commitment is flexible and for another I want something I might actually enjoy,' he explained more in hope than expectation.

'Good luck,' was all I could think to say.

That evening Mel and I walked the dogs round the field together. As we turned to look at the view from the top of the field, Mel said, 'look! The sky's on fire.' And it was; the clouds were shot with an orange-crimson glow through 360 degrees. We could clearly see in the clouds in the east the familiar shape of Queen Victoria's head and, in the west a Christ-like man with a flowing white beard. We had had a good day!

I had to pay for our 'day in Cornwall' as Mel and I described any break from our routine when we were able to get away for a few hours. My ankle flared up the following morning requiring an increase in multi-vitamin and mineral pills and cod-liver oil capsules. They seemed to help.

Somehow I managed to hobble round the Jag with a bucket of car shampoo and a sponge before finishing it off with a vigorous polishing ready for the Jaguar Enthusiasts' Club's annual rally at the Shire Park near Wadebridge. On our return from that we were greeted by good news and bad.

'I've found it,' said James as he told us about his day.

'What?' Mel and I asked in unison, being unsure what he had lost.

'My holiday job,' he replied.

'Go on then, what is it?' asked Mel.

'Bike hire,' he said with a smirk of satisfaction. Before we could ask where, what hours or how well paid he went on, 'it's only two miles away and I can get there when I like within reason, can work on my dissertation when it's quiet and rent out bikes whenever anyone turns up.'

'Sounds ideal,' Mel said with her usual enthusiasm.

'Do they pay you for this?' I asked tentatively.

'Of course. It's not much but then I don't need much,' he explained as a mental flurry of the pound notes it would continue to require from me to cover such things as his food and car insurance passed behind my eyes. 'I have to repair any bikes that go wrong,' he added, 'but that's not difficult'.

I decided to settle for the fact that whatever he earned was money I would not have to provide and the completion of his dissertation would surely take him a step nearer to full financial independence. These thoughts were just settling contentedly in my mind when he switched subjects. 'Jake's not too good, I don't think. He keeps trying to be sick.'

'Right, I'll take a look at him,' I said turning to go into the utility room. While the small pool of clear fluid on the floor told me James had been absolutely right, dear old Jake got up as quickly as ever to greet me with his old exuberance.

'It's a complete puzzle,' I said to Mel over my shoulder as I heard her footsteps follow me in. 'Something's clearly not right but he seems so normal in other respects.'

'Hmm,' she said non-committally. 'When is he due to go back to the vet's?'

'Simon Draper said to wait and see what the antibiotics did,' I said, 'and they ran out a couple of days ago.'

'Maybe he should go back,' she suggested.

'Let's see how he is in the morning,' I replied. 'I'll take him for a walk later to see how he is.'

The next morning, after eating quite normally, Jake just sicked up a little undigested terrier meal but nothing else so I resolved to soak it from then on. He enjoyed a walk and seemed generally brighter.

Mel and I decided we would take the horses out. Max and I led Smartie and her down to the lane. I stopped briefly at the bottom of the drive, turning to say as calmly as I could, 'I think we'll go left today.' I knew this would have a double impact on Mel. First it would mean passing new hedges, gateways and 'things' and secondly it would mean going towards the busy main road at the bottom. Could it also mean, I knew she would be wondering, that I was about to spring on her a ride along the Barnweathers' (our neighbours') track and, worse, the dreaded crossing of the road to go on 'my' ride. Tempted and impatient though I was to introduce them both to my favourite track - the 'Rim of the World' - I was not that insensitive. That was something I knew would have to be worked up to gradually.

'Why, where are we going?' she asked nervously.

'Just down to the main road to get you used to the traffic,' I explained.

'Me? What about Smartie?' she asked jumpily.

'Oh, she's used to it already, remember?' I asked, referring to the fact that a year earlier we had tentatively taken her down on a lead rope only to discover she didn't bat an eyelid, even at petrol tankers.

Max and I led the way down the hill, he looking loftily over the hedges that were just too high for Smartie to be able to do the same. He started as we passed the corner of the Littles' property with its duck pond surrounded by ducks. This jumpiness was immediately transmitted to Smartie and of course Mel. 'Good girl, steady,' she murmured. As we approached the busy main road I edged Max in front. 'We're not going too close to the traffic are we?' Mel asked.

'No. I'll just stop Max parallel to the road in front of you. You can then stop and see how Smartie reacts,' I replied over my shoulder. My caution was sensible but unnecessary. Mel had halted just three or four yards behind me but I was aware that Smartie was restless. I turned to see Mel trying unsuccessfully to keep her still. As soon as she had sidled up to Max, Smartie noticeably relaxed, followed by Mel. 'She just wanted to keep close to Max,' I smiled.

Mel also allowed the briefest of smiles to flicker across her face. 'Yes, but can we go back now before she gets restless or worried,' she said. She was right. Her first outing on Smartie close to busy traffic had gone better than I could have hoped: it was best to call it a day while we were ahead. The return home was more relaxed in a quick sort of way!

The next day, with that small milestone behind us, brought another hurdle. Jake was not only not progressing but had become a little wobbly on his feet. Apart from that he maintained his usual high spirits but it was the spots of watery blood I discovered on the floor an hour later that set the alarm bells ringing. I racked my brain trying to match the various symptoms to other problems we had experienced with dogs over the years. Then it came to me. We had once seen this in our first Dane Kurt some twenty-five years before. In his case it had been a nasty case of cystitis, soon cured, I recalled, by a course of antibiotics. But Jake had only recently completed a course of them so I doubted that was the way to go. I decided to focus on his diet, removing meat and cereal and just giving him rice and eggs to help him build his strength up.

During the course of the next day his retching had returned with a vengeance and so, realising something more serious was involved, I booked him into the vet's the following morning. Simon Draper's initial diagnosis was that while Jake's heart was strong he was having to work hard and his breathing was becoming more laboured. His mind returned to his earlier thoughts about prostate problems so he decided to give him a sonic scan. He found the prostate enlarged and pitted, pointing it out to Mel and me as we steadied Jake while that strange, noisy thing was being run along his tummy.

'That could explain the blood,' said Simon, 'and also, actually, the vomiting,' he added to our surprise. After further examination Simon asked, 'have you noticed him shaking his head?'

'No,' I replied looking to Mel for confirmation.

'No,' she repeated.

'Hmm. He's got a bit of an ear infection which could be affecting his balance and hence the wobbliness,' he went on. 'Again it could lead to nausea which could explain the vomiting. I'll give him some intravenous antibiotic to knock the ear infection on the head and some anti-vomiting pills to try to help him with that,' Simon added, deep in thought. While he was cogitating Jake threw up all over the surgery floor. 'Let's just see how he goes but if there's no noticeable improvement bring him straight back in. We need to get to the bottom of this.'

While Jake was not sick for the rest of the day we were sufficiently worried about his increasingly depressed demeanour to take him back at five o'clock that evening. While still expressing puzzlement Simon continued to focus on his three earlier diagnoses. 'It could still be any or all of those three things but the heart is the most worrying thing at this stage. We might get the answer by opening him up and having a look but I'm worried about whether his heart is strong enough to cope with the anaesthetic.'

I looked at Jake through new eyes. Suddenly I no longer saw an adult Dane struggling to overcome some unknown illness but an ageing dog, approaching nine, who was becoming distressed and wretched as he lay exhausted on the floor in front of us. It was as Simon went to lift Jake's head that Jake snapped at him, drawing blood from his finger.

Mel and I were shocked. He had never bitten nor attempted to bite anyone before. He had always been the happiest and kindest of dogs. 'He's never done anything like that before,' I said weakly as Simon went to attend to his finger. He gave me a look which seemed to me to convey doubt about what I was saying. Mel picked it up too.

'No, he's never ever bitten anyone before,' she confirmed in a state of mild shock.

'Clearly he's very uncomfortable,' said Simon, slowly shaking his head in thought. 'Something's really bothering him. I think for now I'll give him something to steady his heart, then let's just see how he goes.'

Jake was very low that evening, dragging us down with him. He even snapped at me as I tried to give him some aloe vera. We had always hated the idea of any of our animals being in distress, not least because they couldn't tell us what the problem was. We decided to leave him quietly with Sukie and Angus in the utility room that evening and I checked him every half-hour before going to bed. I woke at 4.00am and went down to see how he was. I found him moribund, lying on the floor rather than on his comfortable bed and totally uninterested in anything going on around him. As gently as I could I got him back onto his bed but he still did not react. 'Oh, Jakey,' I said out loud as I caressed his head, 'what on earth is it? We'll do our best to get you right again but we can't see you suffering like this.' Sukie gave me a bemused look and I stroked her white-muzzled head too.

'How is he?' Mel asked as I got back into bed.

'Not good. I've never seen him like this - just lifeless. I'm not sure he's going to make it. I just wish we knew what was causing it.' Mel, too, was depressed at the news.

'Me too. Until today I thought it was just a matter of finding out what was wrong and putting it right but I think it's really serious,' she replied. We tossed and turned until 6.30 when I decided to get up. As I descended the stairs, turned off the alarm and went through the kitchen to the utility room my mind was literally in a state of suspense as I wondered what I would find. I would soon know whether Jake had made it through the night but tried to prepare myself for the possibility he hadn't.

Thankfully he stirred, still lying on his bed as I had left him. He got up went out and wandered around the garden. After a few minutes he came back in, drank a little water and ate a small amount of breakfast I had prepared to test his appetite. Most of it soon went and he finished the remainder with the other dogs half-an-hour or so later.

A good sign was his increased interest in us but I noticed his breathing sounded a little bubbly. I knew this indicated a general worsening in his condition and shed a few tears as I stood there watching him. He had been a good friend and

I was now having to contemplate his departure. He continued to look more interested, stopping to wash Sukie at one point.

I kept him on a diet of eggs, milk, yoghurt, honey and aloe vera in an attempt to boost his energy without setting off the vomiting again. As he started to perk up during the morning so, slowly, did our hopes. I took him as far as he wanted to walk which turned out to be a full circuit of our five acre field. In the evening he also managed a gentle walk to the top of our small paddock which rose some sixty or seventy feet above the house.

By the evening we were relieved that the anti-vomiting drugs were working but more concerned with his laboured breathing and the increasing fluid in his lungs.

When I checked him last thing before going to bed, he was lying so still I thought we had lost him. But the single flick of the tip of his tail told me we hadn't. For the second night running I said goodbye.

❧

I think it was just two weeks after we moved to Upper Penwithiel in July 1998 that I first became aware of Mel's reservations.

'Do you think we've done the right thing?' she had asked in the direct way she always did. Beating around the bush, in her terms, was presumably only something you only ever did to put out a bush fire!

'Time will tell,' I replied, knowing I would have to play for it - time that is - as there was no way we were going to go through the upheaval, not to mention cost, of moving again so soon.

'How do you feel about it?' she asked.

'Fine. It's all a bit strange but then it's bound to be after living for twenty years in the same house.'

'I suppose so,' she said in that vague way she had of sounding as though she was in agreement when she wasn't.

'Just think of all the things you can do here that you couldn't before,' I suggested.

'Like what?'

'Like being able to get to the coast in half-an-hour,' I said.

'Yes. What else?'

'Like being able to go shopping in Truro whenever you like,' I continued, starting to struggle.

'Yes but I could go to Southampton, Salisbury, Winchester or even Bath before,' she retorted.

'Well you can go to Penzance, Plymouth or Exeter from here,' I said gingerly. I knew what she was really saying was that she was missing Andrew and her friends.

'Yes, I know and I'm not unhappy here. In many ways I've never been happier but...' she trailed off leaving me a little puzzled.

'But what?' I asked.

'Well are you really happy being a bit, well, isolated?' So that was it! It had been Mel who had had reservations about not being near any village or community. In fact it had been one of her first observations on looking at the map on the estate agent's particulars showing the location of the house.

'You know it doesn't bother me at all,' I said cautiously, waiting for her reaction.

'No, I suppose it wouldn't really, would it? You're lucky, being so self-contained. I suppose it's the difference between men and women...'

'Well, it's certainly the difference between you and me,' I grinned. 'And not the only one,' I added a little mischievously. She gave me a look which roughly said, 'can't you take anything I say seriously?'

'As we agreed before we moved,' I went on more earnestly, 'we can have another look at things when we've given it a chance.'

'What do you mean 'look at things'?' she asked.

'Well, if after a while we want to move again we can,' I replied, careful not to be too specific too soon.

'Do you mean that?' she asked, brightening a little.

'Of course, but we've got to give ourselves a chance.'

'When?' she asked.

'When what?' I asked dumbly.

'When will we look at things again?'

'Five years?' I ventured uncertainly.

'Five *years*,' she repeated with an expression which conveyed the fact she had a shorter timescale in mind.

'Well it costs thousands to move,' I said.

'Yes, I know but I thought we'd know whether we liked it here sooner than that.' On the assumption that she already did know, I figured that one of us needed to take a little longer.

'Alright. If by this time next year we're agreed that we want to move we'll start to plan it,' I promised.

'Plan it? And how long after that would we move?'

'A year or two,' I hedged. 'We'd have to play it by ear a bit. It would depend on where we wanted to move and the state of the housing market,' I said loftily, without being totally sure why.

'And where would you like to move?' she asked.

35

'Nowhere yet,' I replied with a grin which I hoped would kill off that particular line of discussion.

'OK but would it be in Cornwall?' she pressed.

'Oh yes,' I said without hesitation. 'We put so much effort into the decision to move here,' I reminded her. 'What about you?' I asked, inescapably opening the issue up again.

'Yes, I think so,' she muttered thoughtfully. 'No, I know so but I can't help wanting to be nearer Andrew,' she continued, 'and James and Justin when we know where they're going to be.'

'But it'll be a while before they know themselves,' I pointed out. 'In fact that's another reason for not being in too much of a hurry. Let everyone get used to things as they are first.'

'You're probably right,' Mel sighed. 'But can we?'

'Can we what?'

'Talk about it again in a year.'

'Yes, of course, darling,' I readily agreed, while thinking to myself that I'd be lucky not to return to or, more accurately, be returned to the subject sooner!

❧

Something unseen and unheard woke me just after four the next morning and my thoughts turned instantly to Jake. I went down and found him little changed and change - for the better - was something we needed to see quickly. He seemed restless so I quietly unlocked the door and went out with him. He moved slowly round to the back of the house, periodically stopping to rest. I resolved that I would not let him continue like that for too long. Simon Draper had given me the times when I could get hold of him at the surgery and, as promised, he fitted me in early that morning.

He had been racking his brain since our last visit and said, 'I'm wondering whether it's something like a heart worm.'

'I didn't know you got those in this country,' I said, rather unsure of the facts.

'It's very rare but there were one or two cases in Cornwall a few years back. From memory they're spread by snails or slugs,' he continued.

'Really?' I asked in total surprise.

'Yes. Of course I'm not saying it is that but I'm just trying to cover all the possibilities. Have you noticed him eating any?' he asked. In my mind I had initially clutched at that particular straw by recalling the huge slugs we had noticed in the garden just after we moved in. But Jake would never consider eating them and I certainly hadn't seen him take any interest in them.

'I don't think so,' I replied, with less certainty than I actually felt because I didn't want to cut off any line of enquiry that could save Jake.

'Let's keep him on the pills he's got for now and I'll give him a diuretic to try to get some of that fluid off his lungs. I'd like you to get a fresh stool sample and bring it in first thing in the morning so I can get it off to the lab,' he said. Pleased that something was being pursued, I readily agreed.

As soon as I got home I went onto the internet to find out whatever I could about snails, slugs and heartworm in Cornwall. To my amazement I found an article written about the very case that Simon Draper had recalled, so printed it out.

By early evening, although Jake had brought up some water soon after drinking he was much brighter so we went on a saunter round the field. Whether it was his idea of a joke or not, it was some one hundred yards from the house that he decided to part with his fresh stool sample. Having nothing with me suitable for whisking it away, I left a large white handkerchief nearby to mark the spot while I rushed in to fetch a container. Had Jake been his old self that handkerchief would have been snatched away to be paraded round me, daring me to try to retrieve it from him. As it was, he just watched, bemused by my strange behaviour.

It was just a little later as I went to let Chan in the back door that I discovered we had a visitor. Sitting on the back step was a large toad. As any self-respecting Basenji naturally would, Chan was doing his level best to encourage the little chap to do something more interesting than just sit there. I suppose it might have been a female though my expertise did not extend to sexing toads - even close to, let alone at a distance! Chan ran up to it, danced in front of it, raised first one paw above his ear then the other before bouncing back and then moving forward to go through the process again. The toad, as any self-respecting toad would, moved not a muscle, preferring to observe the strange goings-on without getting involved.

After letting Chan out again last thing, quite predictably he went straight to the spot where he had last seen his new little horny-skinned friend but stopped short. He then leant forward gingerly inspecting the step with his pointed nose before pulling back and then looking up at me with wrinkled brow as if seeking an explanation. On peering through the gloom I identified my second fresh stool sample of the evening.

3 Letting Go

Over the next twenty-four hours Jake teased us by being in turn brighter and then weaker. The vomiting was becoming more frequent: even keeping water down became a problem. The one thing that made us persist with him was his continuing interest in everything going on around him. He seemed to reach a plateau of stability which enabled us to stop expecting to find him gone each time we checked him.

I delivered his sample to the surgery the next day, in time for the lab's one o'clock collection. However, as the day wore on we could see he was not only no better but slowly deteriorating and so we took him into evening surgery. Because Jake was so weak he had found it difficult to stand on the slippery floor of the surgery and, being a warm sunny evening, we gladly accepted Simon's suggestion that he look at him outside on the grass. We let Jake lie gently on his side.

Simon was clearly very concerned and, because of Jake's weakness and inability to keep down even small pills, gave him injections of diuretic, antibiotic, heart stimulant and wormer. The latter was to treat any possible heart worm while waiting for the result of the lab analysis and was not recommended for dogs, being more commonly used for sheep and cattle. It posed a slight risk which we were ready to take.

It was just as Mel and I were waiting for Simon to return from inside with a phial for the blood sample he also wanted to take, each of us stroking Jake to keep him calm and to comfort him, that we heard a bang. We looked at each other and then across to the car park to see an old red estate that had reversed out of its space, on the opposite side to our Jag, speed away. The woman driving it gave us a glance, curious as to why we were apparently huddled on the ground and, on seeing our own look of anxiety, sped off.

'She didn't hit our car did she?' asked Mel.

'No,' I replied. 'She looked straight at us and she wouldn't have been able to do that if she'd just hit our car,' I added with total confidence, overlooking the fact that she could not have known it was our car!

Minutes later we were on our way, leading Jake slowly back to the car. When we reached it the rear bumper screamed at me. The nearside had been split and some paint scraped off.

'Told you,' said Mel.

'No you didn't, you asked me,' I said, splitting hairs as usual. I swiftly retraced my steps to the surgery and asked who the last client was. They couldn't or wouldn't tell me but said I would need to speak to Mr Draper who had just started his next consultation. It took just a phone call after we arrived home fifteen minutes later to get his agreement to do what he could and another half-an-hour for the lady concerned to phone me with her insurance details.

'I heard a bang but thought it was my Labrador losing his balance in the back as I reversed out,' was her line of defence. Her little mistake was to cost her insurer over £800, more, as James subsequently and insensitively pointed out, than her car was worth.

Over the weekend Mel volunteered for the tricky task of giving Jake further injections of antibiotic, something I know I would have found difficult to do. However, he was just not interested in food, not even his favourite milk and eggs. This meant he had no need to go out though I took him on a wobbly walk up the drive and back which tired him.

We felt able to leave Jake for long enough on the Sunday morning for a short ride up the lane on the horses. There were no surprises except for Mel when we returned. As we reached the bottom of the drive I said, 'it's time you rode on your own.'

Her startled look was as expected. 'What, now?' she asked.

'Yes. You've had a good ride so better get it over with,' I replied firmly.

'Alright,' she agreed, 'but only as far as the Barnweathers'. I'm not going right down to the main road.'

'OK,' I agreed, knowing it was the principle that mattered rather than the distance, and neither of us wanted any setbacks at that stage. As Smartie clip-clopped slowly out of sight round the bend it turned out that I was the one with the real challenge. In short, Max decided to panic as he contemplated the possibility of the love of his life disappearing from it once more. I didn't, as I hoped mine wouldn't take too long to return! Max whinnied, spun, reared and then shrieked, forcing me to wait in the drive in case any traffic went past.

'That was easy,' grinned Mel when she returned five or six minutes later. 'She was brilliant.'

'She always is,' I replied.

'How was Max?' she asked. 'I could hear him all the way there and back.'

'Oh he was perfect. He always is,' I lied.

The good news was that when we took Jake in the following morning, the nurses, who had got to know him, said how much better he looked. We had to agree. Jake's samples had been duly analysed and the results given to us by Simon Draper. 'Well there's no sign of any parasitic infection in the stool but there are signs of a bacterial infection in the blood. I'm shifting my focus to those lungs. I'd like to take an x-ray,' he told us.

I was pleased to be able to make myself useful by not only helping to lift Jake, thinner now but still a weight, onto the table but by being togged up in lead apron and steadying him while the x-rays were taken. These enabled Simon to tell us that while, thankfully, there were no signs of a tumour there were signs of pneumonia. 'We'll hit it hard with antibiotics,' he said.

By midday Jake was far more with it and later ate a little cooked fish and tripe. To our relief his breathing was noticeably easier. By four o'clock he was able to amble up the near end of the field but when I saw him tiring we came back in. There was no doubt in my mind: he had turned a corner.

The next day he was even better: still not well but recovering. While his breathing was no longer laboured he still got out of breath and had to rest but he was happy to walk the full circuit of the field for the first time in days.

❧

Jake was not the only one with mobility problems. James complained to me that evening that his car was showing a distinct loss of power. I went to have a look but could find nothing obviously wrong. Anything less than obviously wrong would have passed me by.

'When did you last get it serviced?' I asked. I didn't quite catch the mumbled reply but the gist of it was that it had been quite a while ago so I suggested he had it done to see if things improved.

When Mel called me to look at Jake the next morning after giving him his antibiotic injection, the urgency in her voice told me he must have taken a turn for the worse. Far from it: he was lying on his back on his bed with all four legs in the air like a puppy. His stripey tail managed a few slow wags as I approached and I managed a quick smile.

It was turning out to be the best day in quite a while. Until, that is, the phone call from James who had been in the process of visiting a number of garages in the area to get quotes for his service. 'My car's completely dead,' he announced with due solemnity.

'Where are you?' I asked. He told me he was a hundred yards from the next garage on his list. I got there twenty minutes later, couldn't start it so went to the garage, part of a Nissan dealership. They were brilliant. The head mechanic followed me back to the car, diagnosed the problem as a split cylinder head gasket, managed to get it started and drove it in. It was fully repaired within a few days for an amount that was far in excess of what James could afford but within a figure I considered to be a bargain in terms of keeping him on the road without any need for us to restart the taxi driving service so familiar to parents of pre-driving teenagers!

Over the days that followed, Jake was up and down: some days we worried while on others we took comfort from the fact he seemed stable but we knew we hadn't got to the bottom of his problem. A vague thought about obstructions in the stomach flitted across my mind, having seen those TV vet programmes where the vet opens up a dog's stomach to find one of any number of foreign objects from rubber balls to knitting needles, the removal of which naturally leads to rapid recovery!

It was on one of his up days that Mel and I felt it was safe to leave him while we went out on the horses for an hour or so. The sheer brilliance of the ride, on a beautiful sunny day which yielded crystal-clear views of Bodmin Moor to the north and the sea to the south, allowed us to briefly throw aside our anxieties about Jake. Being able to revitalise the spirits in this way was one of the major benefits of riding horses.

The others included the character-building that resulted from coping with the unexpected as well as, as the management training gurus have apparently now discovered, developing the skills needed to manage another key individual with a distinct mind of his or her own! In my case the benefits were further enhanced by having to assist Mel, who definitely had a mind of her own, to progress with riding her young Morgan mare who had yet another mind of her own.

For the first time since we had been taking both horses out together, I took the lead in our canter across the field towards home. Usually Mel liked me to stay behind her so as to avoid the possibility of my going too fast on Max and dragging her and Smartie along behind us at a speed she was uncomfortable with. However, her confidence had come on in leaps and bounds and so it was with a 'not too fast' exhortation that she told me to go in front. All was going brilliantly until, despite the wind in my ears, I heard her shriek, 'stop!' I did, of course, and instantly swung Max round to see what calamity had befallen her. It was useless trying to stifle my laughter as I saw Mel hunched over Smartie's neck who had refused point blank to canter through the large puddle Max had just kersplashed through. To my relief and, I suspected, as a result of hers, Mel gave me a sheepish grin from beneath the peak of her riding hat which had just tipped forward a little.

'I think we'd better give her lessons on walking through water,' I chuckled.

'We'd better do something - and it's not funny,' she admonished as she forced herself to frown and pushed the grin off her face lest I did not take the implications seriously enough!

Jake continued to tease us with his three steps forward, two steps backwards progress, though progress it was. We still whipped him into the vet whenever he seemed down. We managed to work into this busy schedule the visit of the three young cats to the vet for their annual jabs in early August. Time, as ever, was passing quickly and had caught us out once more. Was it really a year since we had last taken them?

That evening Mel and I took the dogs round the field together in the deepening gloom. Smartie apparently concluded that we were intruders and started prancing around us, lashing out with her hind hooves, getting Mel quite worried. Until, that is, I took things into my hands and decided to dominate her: the horse that is! Difficult though it might seem to non-horsey people, all that is required is to size up to the horse as though you were several times its size and not vice versa. Mel had never quite become a fully paid-up member of that particular school of thought and continued to grip my arm tightly, throwing the occasional glance over her shoulder as we continued round.

Justin had been working a late shift at Tesco's, usually getting home around 2am, more-or-less since starting there. His logic was faultless. First he got paid more per hour, secondly there was less traffic on the roads and thirdly he would have more time on the beach. I could only assume that that was where he did most of his sleeping! Time, racing again, had soon come round for his first pay day and so it was with some surprise that I found £142 fanned out on my desk when I went into my study first thing the next morning. Next to it was a note with one arrow pointing to the money saying, 'thank you for lending me this,' next to another saying, 'this is the interest,' which pointed towards three large bars of my favourite whole nut chocolate.

It was one of those delicious 'all our efforts haven't been in vain' moments that parents of newly grown up children cherish so much. And he was still a full time student!

When he got up later, though still, it must be said, much earlier than I could have in his situation, he was keen to tell us he had seen a cat identical to Moritz jump up into the hedge in the lane when he drove up at eight minutes past two that morning. 'Are you sure it wasn't Moss?' I asked. Moss was exactly the same colour and sometimes stayed out all night in the summer, despite our usual efforts to get all the cats in at dusk.

'No. He was in the house when I got in.' A strange feeling descended on Mel and me. It was a mixture of 'couldn't possibly have been' and 'perhaps it just might have been'. We knew all the stories about lost cats and dogs finding their way home across many miles and so didn't completely rule out the outside chance that he had been surviving nearby since disappearing almost two years earlier. For weeks afterwards we found ourselves slowing the car and scanning the hedges in the headlights whenever we returned home late in the evening. All we ever saw was the occasional grey squirrel.

'Of course I'm sure,' Justin said indignantly the first time we reopened the matter with him. 'I know the difference between a Burmese cat and a bloody squirrel!' We had to acknowledge that he did, having grown up with them.

Just as we began to hope that Jake was out of the woods, his retching returned with a vengeance. It was back to more antibiotics and anti-vomiting drugs. We began to feed moistened complete food to reduce the bulk and help him keep his food down.

It was just a few days after Justin's 'sighting' of Moritz that, quite independently, Mel and I saw a lilac cat prowling along the hedge at the top of the field. She had seen it from a bedroom window and I had seen it as I walked across the drive. I had also seen what she could not have: Moss was sprawled on the old tree stump by the entrance to the drive. Excitedly we both scrambled up the steep incline to investigate. We could see no sign of a cat until a small unmistakably Burmese type leapt out of the long grass next to the hedge in a futile attempt to catch whatever it had been stalking.

'Cloey!' we said in unison as the disappointing truth hit us.

Dear old Jakey continued to battle away against whatever it was, grateful for the food we were able to get down him. I was happy to take the extra time to help my old friend by breaking down his meals into smaller more frequent and therefore manageable portions. Over the next two days it became apparent that whatever we did had no lasting effect. He would improve a little, keeping down some of his food, but we knew it was less each time. Water and other fluids were getting through but the smaller less frequent stools told their own story. I could no longer stand the trusting but forlorn look he gave me each time he tried unsuccessfully to eat. We even tried 'Complan' at someone's suggestion but to no avail.

We were due to go and stay with Andrew the following weekend and I knew it would not be fair either to Jake or to James, who had agreed to look after the animals for us, to abandon them in that situation. Simon Draper agreed immediately to see us with Jake the following morning. 'We really need to get to the bottom of this quickly,' I explained on the phone.

'Yes, I agree,' he replied. 'It's still a puzzle but bring him in and I'll have a look at him.'

We would have done anything to get back the old Jake, of whom we caught a fleeting glimpse, as I led him out of the house on his lead to get into the car for yet another visit to the vet. He was wagging his tail and the reason for his being so pleased with himself brought us close to tears: he had found a soft toy of Chan's and was mischievously attempting to take it with him, tucked up out of sight in those large soft lips. Slowly and sadly I deprived him of it lest it get dropped and lost on the way.

Once in the consulting room I said to Simon Draper, 'I think it's time to try and establish the root cause of his problems.'

He nodded slowly while sucking the end of one arm of his glasses in deep thought as he surveyed the rather thinner Jake than the one he had last seen. 'Very odd,' you know. 'I did think about some kind of cancer but he just doesn't look cancerous,' he said, to the relief of Mel and me. 'But I agree. We can't keep just treating the symptoms,' he finally concluded.

'It occurred to me that he might have a foreign object lodged in his stomach somewhere,' I ventured, clutching at one of the few remaining straws.

'Well, it's possible,' Simon conceded. 'But I'd have expected a much more severe reaction. This has all been very gradual. In fact he was showing signs of improvement last time I saw him.' I nodded in glum agreement. 'What I'd like to do is 'scope him,' he continued. 'It'll let us look right down into his stomach to see whether anything obvious is causing the problem. I only hesitate because of the effect of the general anaesthetic on a dog of his age, especially when he is so weak,' he went on, looking up at me for my reaction.

I was quite clear in my mind. We had to take the risk: I simply could not bear to see this magnificent animal continue to decline in the way that he had. 'I think the time has come where we must take that chance,' I said, knowing by the slow nod of her head that Mel agreed.

'Right, Mr Cameron. We'll get on with it right away. One of the nurses will get you to sign a consent form and then you can bring him through to theatre.'

We followed shortly afterwards to find Simon and one of his nurses preparing the operating table. 'We're going to need some help to lift him,' said Simon to whoever might hear him in the next room. Soon there was Simon Draper, three of his staff and Mel lifting the thinner though still heavy body of the tranquillised Jake onto the table. I felt strangely detached. Normally I would have been in there helping, if only to reassure my beautiful dog. Instead I watched helplessly as he went under the anaesthetic and, too late, knew I should have been at his head to calm him in those stressful moments. But I knew the moment had passed as I watched him lying there peacefully asleep.

'You can get back home now if you don't want to hang around here. As soon as I've found whatever there is to find I'll phone you,' he smiled kindly.

'How long is it likely to take?' I asked.

'Oh no more than fifteen or twenty minutes.'

'It's not worth our going home then. It'll take us that long to get there,' I explained.

'Well if you don't mind waiting in the waiting room we'll be as quick as we can,' he smiled.

It was a long half-hour before Simon reappeared. I looked into his face for some indication of what he'd found. I saw nothing but questions in his eyes.

'We couldn't get it down,' he said with an involuntary shrug. I looked at him for some explanation. 'The 'scope just wouldn't go in more than about fifteen inches or so. There's some kind of obstruction.' My mind flashed from my foreign object theory to bloat before giving up.

'How can we find out?' I asked, knowing the only answer.

'Well we can open him up but I'm just so worried about whether his weakened body can take the strain,' he replied, begging a question.

All my recollections of those past weeks buzzed round inside my head and I just knew I owed it to Jake to get on with it. 'I think we must,' I said quietly and determinedly, having caught a flicker of agreement in Mel's expression.

'Right, Mr Cameron,' Simon said with renewed determination. 'He's still under the anaesthetic so it won't take long to get in there and see what's going on but, assuming he survives the anaesthetic, his recovery could take quite a while. After all it's a major operation...'

I knew that at that moment I must not fail my friend. 'No, go ahead,' I agreed quietly.

'This could take a while so perhaps this time you'd be better off waiting at home,' he smiled kindly as he showed us out. 'I'll phone as soon as I know what the problem is.'

We both sat in silence for most of the twenty minute drive home which I took more slowly than usual.

'What do you think they'll find?' asked Mel as we approached the bottom of Penwithiel Lane.

'Don't know,' I replied non-committally. 'All I know is that whatever it is we need to know so we can deal with it.'

We sat and drank two cups of tea in near silence. As the minutes ticked by I started to run through all the possibilities. 'It still seems to me that he's got something stuck in his digestive system somewhere. I'm beginning to wish we'd done this sooner.'

The time dragged on for another hour as I began to contemplate the phone call we were waiting for. I hoped it would be something straightforward.

But supposing it wasn't? We already knew it wasn't his liver or kidneys. But it could be his pancreas. While we had come to think of Jake as perennially young, because of his liveliness and exuberance, these last weeks had been a sharp reminder that he wasn't. The phone rang. Instinctively I went to take the call in my study where I hoped I would be able to listen objectively to whatever Simon had to say.

'Mr Cameron, I've found the problem...' he began. My mind raced round the possibilities once more. A feeling of anticipation, suspended somewhere between relief at knowing the answer at last and dread of the possible outlook, swam over me.

'But it's not good, I'm afraid.' Dread began to take over. Maybe poor Jake was going to spend the rest of his days in a half-life controlled by drugs. But at least we'd still have him. Or would we? Maybe he was already... 'Oh he handled the anaesthetic without any problems. In fact I was pleased at how strong he was.' Relief that he was still with us.

'Has he come round alright?' was the obvious next question.

'Well I haven't brought him round yet...' The words ran through me like a cold knife. He was about to ask permission to operate.

Mel, who was standing in front of me, was, by this time, understandably frantic to know what had happened. I cupped my hand over the mouthpiece and whispered, 'he's come through the anaesthetic but he's not come round yet...' and went back to listening mode.

'What I've found is a rather nasty tumour...' my heart sank. '...about the size of a golf ball...' But that sounded operable didn't it? '...but unfortunately it's just where the oesophagus joins the entrance to the stomach.'

'Can you remove it?'

'Sadly, I can't. You see I'd have to remove such a large section of his oesophagus that there'd be no way of rejoining them. Even in a human situation it would be difficult but with a dog, just impossible I'm afraid,' came the unwelcome reply. My thoughts flitted from the possibility of managing the problem back to the reality of what life had been like for Jake recently.

'What are his prospects then?' I asked. 'Can we manage it for a while?' The response was gentle but swift.

'If he was mine I think I'd have to say we have to let him go...'

'You're saying if he was yours you wouldn't bring him round?' The huge swelling in my throat almost choked off the words as I felt my eyes starting to fill.

'Yes. Even if we did bring him round - and it would be easy enough to do...' Maybe we would get him back after all. We'd just carry on looking after him and wait for him to tell us... '...but you have to consider what you'd be putting him through. He'd be very uncomfortable after such invasive surgery...'

That feeling all too familiar to people with animals began to swirl round me. The temptation to bring him home fought it out with the responsibility, which I alone bore, to respect his dignity and quality of life. The brief memory of just two hours earlier when he had wagged his tail with that toy in his mouth brought silent tears to my cheeks and I didn't have to look at Mel. The sniffs told me she was sharing that moment of decision.

Barely able to speak, I said softly down the phone, 'I agree,' feeling as if I was condemning an innocent man to death.

'I'll not bring him round then?' asked Simon.

'No. I'll come in and collect him.'

'Disposal is something we can look after...'

'No, thank you. We always bury our dogs...'

And I knew we always would.

4 Touché

'We've been in Cornwall over two years now,' remarked Mel as we sped over the Cornwall-Devon border in the wrong direction.

'True,' was my only response as I waited to see what her drift was.

'How do you feel when we leave Cornwall?'

'Impatient to get back. Why?' I waited for some indication she was about to disagree.

'Yes, so do I,' she said to my relief. 'I'm looking forward to seeing Andrew of course but I get this funny feeling when I leave. Like I really belong there,' she added.

'Good. If you didn't feel like that I suppose it would be time to move again.'

'Where to?' she asked.

'I quickly glanced at her. I don't know. I don't really fancy retracing my steps...'

'No, me neither, but I just wondered where else you'd like to live.'

'No question. I'd like to stay in Cornwall. It's you we're talking about,' I smiled.

'When I really think about it that's where I want to live. It just seems the natural place to be. But there's no getting away from it. I really miss Andrew.'

We continued in relative silence for a few miles and I recalled my feelings on the day we moved. There was no doubt things had turned out well and all those distant doubts had long since been dispelled.

That evening we had arranged to meet up with Jim and Tricia Carter and Carl and Barbara Wellings, friends from our old village, at Jim and Tricia's house. 'I'm beginning to think we should have stayed with Andrew this evening and seen the others tomorrow night,' said Mel pensively.

'Well, as long as we see both it doesn't matter in what order. I expect Andrew would prefer a night relaxing after a week's work and will enjoy tomorrow with us that much more,' I suggested.

'Maybe you're right,' she sighed.

'Sorry to hear about Jake,' Andrew said, soon after we'd said our hellos.

'Yes, poor chap,' I replied. 'But it wouldn't have been right to put him

48

through any more,' I added wearily. He nodded in agreement. 'It'll do us both good to have a couple of days away,' I said, vowing to myself not to labour the deep sadness we both still felt.

'I thought Sukie would have gone first,' Andrew continued.

'Yes, so did we,' Mel replied sadly.

'Anyway, what have you got planned for tomorrow?' I asked, changing the subject.

'Well, we're having a barbeque tomorrow evening, so I thought the three of us could go and get the barbeque stuff,' Andrew replied brightly. I could see from Mel's expression that she'd like nothing better. But she'd have felt like that whatever we were going to be doing. She similarly caught my expression.

'Come on you'll enjoy it,' she said to me. 'You don't do too badly. When was the last time you came shopping with me?'

'Er, 19, um...'

'Exactly!'

It was as Andrew was looking for somewhere to park outside Tesco's that we caught sight of Tim and Georgie Bruton making their way to their car with a trolley load.

'Stop!' yelled Mel. Andrew complied without knowing why. We both jumped out, leaving Andrew to park.

'How lovely to see you,' said Tim with undisguised pleasure as we ambushed them. 'How are you both?'

We had known Tim and Georgie for almost twenty years. Their children had been at the same prep school as ours but it was not until Mel first saw Jack, their blue Great Dane, in the back of their Volvo outside school one day that the friendship was struck up. Tim and Georgie were also among the genuine friends we had left behind, insisting that we went to supper on our last Saturday in Wiltshire. Being just days before we moved we were already feeling cut off from the many people we knew we were unlikely to see again soon. And they looked after us so well that evening. We really had been sad to leave them.

As sometimes happens with good friends, however, contact had been lost, apart from the ritual exchange of Christmas cards, but our renewed conversation virtually carried on from where we had left off over two years earlier. Andrew soon joined us but the animated babble clearly left him cold as he shuffled from one foot to the other. He too knew them well, having been with us when we overlapped with them on holiday in the south of France one year, as well as having had the occasional swim in their pool.

Tim, being a naturally warm man who everyone who knew him would agree was one of life's characters, drew Andrew into the conversation. But this served to remind us it was time to get on with the rest of our weekend.

'Well, it's been lovely seeing you both,' I said, 'you really must come down and stay with us.'

'Love to. Absolutely love to,' replied Tim. 'And don't forget, if you ever need a bed up here just give us a shout.' Mel and Georgie, by then well into deep conversation on their mutual interest of horses, had to be prised apart. The four of us agreed we had no idea where the time had gone but really would keep in touch in future.

As usual, Mel turned out to be entirely right. I really did enjoy our half-hour or so wandering around Tesco's. It was as though we were back sharing those intimate if routine moments which all families share with their children over the years. Having filled the boot with the contents of a heavily laden trolley - Andrew had maintained the family tradition of living well - we were soon being taken on a 'memory lane' trip round Salisbury. Even in two years we noticed changes but, above all, despite its familiarity it already felt strange to us.

Perhaps the highlight of the weekend was our trip to Monkey World, near Wareham in Dorset. It was not somewhere we would have gone on our own though very much somewhere we would have taken the boys, had it existed, when they were younger. Once again we seemed to be in a reversal of roles! The most interesting thing for me was the psychology involved: many of the inmates, mainly chimpanzees, had been victims of abuse by their human cousins and rescued by the remarkable Jim Cronin, the American who runs the centre with his wife.

There on display were the full range of behavioural problems such as one might see with any human who had experienced such mistreatment - and the treatment was comparable too. Much love and affection, from their human carers as well as from their fellow primates (just what is the link with archbishops?), combined with a gradual introduction to freedom of movement and expression eventually meant new incumbents could look forward to leading a happier life once more. We felt it was worth every penny of the money we spent there to know it was helping these worthwhile people atone for the pathetic shortcomings of the erstwhile tormentors of those wonderful creatures.

'While we're up there,' I'd said to Mel before we left home, 'we could pop in and see the woman who's taken over the Clausentum kennel name from Jean Lanning.' Jean, who had bred both Jake and Mima had told me about this when I phoned to tell her we had lost Jake. It had not taken us long to arrange so there we were looking at a pregnant Great Dane bitch, not far from Andover, on the Monday morning just under a week after losing Jake. I had been more certain than usual that I could not set myself up again for the future pain which the loss of such magnificent animals always caused, exacerbated no doubt by the relatively short time they were with us. Although I had buried many dogs and cats over the years, there was no chance I would ever become inured to it. Laying Jake to rest in the four feet deep hole dug by Steve Masters for Sukie had been especially poignant. Knowing how little time she was likely to have left I decided to leave space for her to be placed on top of him in due course.

The owner of the kennels had been generous with her time and coffee and yet we found ourselves leaving without reserving one of her lovely bitch's puppies. Perhaps it was simply too soon.

It was only when we had crossed back into Cornwall and phoned James to tell him we were on our way that he felt it right to tell us that in the night the horses had pushed over the short piece of post-and-rail fence in the gap in the Cornish hedge between us and our southerly neighbours in order to fraternise with their ponies. When I phoned to apologise after arriving home, I asked, 'how on earth did you get them back into our field?' I knew both could be difficult to catch, particularly Max.

'It was quite easy, really,' came the reply. 'I just waved my arms at them and they turned tail and galloped back.' I made a point of remembering to try that myself sometime!

A few days later Mel and I were enjoying a leisurely ride up the lane, along the track and into the fields we had permission to ride round. A prime condition was that we would not ride through any crops, and one which, of course, we stuck to rigidly. The particular field we were in was full of corn standing some eighteen inches high and had a tractor track running its full length, enabling us to ride through to the next field which was down to grass.

'Keep to the track,' I shouted bossily to Mel who was having a little trouble getting Smartie to canter past a large puddle in one of the deeper ruts.

'I'm doing my best,' came the breathless reply. That was the moment Smartie chose to stop, back up and spin round.

'Lean back, give her the reins and touch her on the shoulder with your stick to remind her you're in charge,' I yelled. It was not that Mel needed me, a complete novice compared with her, to tell her how to ride but at times like that, with a lively young mare taking her full attention, a little back-up helped get everything back on track, in this case literally.

We soon got straightened up, into trot and canter again, with Mel making good progress and me giving her some twenty or thirty yards leeway in front of me so as not to be the cause of any further mishaps. 'Aaah!' Mel shrieked as Smartie turned and then gave a little buck before halting. As if in slow motion, I watched Mel fall forward towards the left side of Smartie and roll through the air, landing spread-eagled on her back. She remained motionless. I groaned inwardly at the thought of the effect that this, her first fall from Smartie, was going to have. Would it simply dent her confidence but strengthen her resolve or would it be back to square one? I instantly recalled the last time I saw her fall from a horse, her previous one, Henry, who had started to make a habit of bucking her off whenever she pushed him into canter. On that occasion she got up, thankfully unhurt, struggled to hold back the tears and crossly led him home vowing never to get on him again, which she didn't. After all the effort she - we - had put in with Smartie I couldn't bear the thought that it would come to nought.

I was, therefore, quite unprepared for what I found when I caught her up. She was lying quite still, giving me fresh cause for concern. Then she slowly started to move but without getting up. I could see she was very gently shaking - with laughter. 'Oh dear,' she giggled. 'That was my fault. I just gripped her with my legs because I was worried about what she was going to do next. I won't do that again.'

'Are you alright?' I asked with a deadpan expression, knowing the worst thing I could do was to join in the laughter. She winced as she got up, straightened herself out and walked stiffly over to collect Smartie who had started to graze some grass at the edge of the track. She was soon back on, to the accompaniment of the odd groan and intake of breath.

'Whoops,' she said, as she indicated the place where she fell. There we could see a perfect indentation of her body shape in the corn.

Increasingly we are using the e-mail to communicate in preference to letters (too slow) or the phone (too expensive) and none more so than the younger generation. So it was with no more than a few key strokes that Andrew asked if he could come down for the weekend one Friday and I replied, 'of course.' He came alone because Amanda was working but enjoyed a relaxing couple of days with his brothers. That sort of informality was just perfect from our point of view - almost the equivalent of just dropping in for chat.

It was just under a week later that fate took a decisive hand, as, we have found, it is wont to do. It was a Thursday when Mel had bought her usual weekly papers, the Cornish Guardian and West Briton. This was only vaguely connected to the longer term prospect of our moving again, within Cornwall, some time. She wanted to keep tabs on what property was around, she said.

'Litter of fawn and brindle Great Dane puppies,' she read out when I finally flopped out in my chair, next to hers, that evening.

'No. Don't want another Dane,' I said firmly.

How often have I tried to summarise in my mind what it is about Cornwall that is so special? How do you put your finger on it? Of course, as with most experiences or feelings, the answer lies within. In the same way that no one can make you happy - as a matter of choice you either are or you aren't - an atmosphere is something you either respond to or you don't, as with a work of art or a piece of music.

The truth is, I suppose, that Mel and I are romantics, with me incurably so. I want to believe in the special qualities of the fishing villages, the coves, the beaches, the cliffs, the moorland and, not least, the people. Therefore, I do believe in them!

The relief in discovering I have not taken leave of my senses, nor lost touch with reality materialises when I discover so many others expressing the same feelings. The Cornish, by and large, dislike having to cross the border into Devon, or England as many see it! They are never quite whole again until they return, crossing the Tamar with its county sign, and heave a sigh of relief at being home once more, whether it be hours or, as is sometimes the case, years later. That is why there are so many Cornish Associations scattered across the globe. Unsurprisingly they are a little jealous of their magic land. They are torn between the inescapable logic that they need an inflow of cash to the economy from visitors, sometimes the need to 'emigrate' to secure a satisfactory standard of living, the effect these can create on the county of their birth and their feelings about it.

There are five broad categories of people who know Cornwall: those who were born and live here, those born here but who live away from here, those who live here but are from elsewhere, those who visit with their eyes, hearts and minds open and the others!

But while it is wrong to over-generalise, my observations are that the others simply come for a holiday and, frankly, wouldn't really know whether they were in Newquay, Brighton, Blackpool, Benidorm or Ibiza. Nothing wrong with that: they just come to have a good time.

All the others are here, visit or want to return for one reason only: because they feel good here. Despite the crowds of August - easy to avoid when you get the hang of it - it is a quiet place. The cities are town-sized, the towns are village-sized and the villages are often just large hamlets. There is crime of course, and being on the wrong end of it is as unpleasant as anywhere else, but it is generally on a lower scale in terms of frequency and severity.

If all this is so, then why is it the perception of some that the Cornish are unwelcoming to incomers? Is it even true? We have not found it so. They are naturally warm but tough, friendly but wary.

Why warm? Why friendly? Because that is their nature, no doubt brought about by countless centuries of independence from the outside world by virtue of being remote from it and interdependence on each other because of the harshness of the environment. Farming, fishing and mining, for so long the county's lifeblood, were the toughest of masters.

Unwelcoming? Only to the idiots who visit and mess things up without a care for the rest of us or who come to live here determined to import the culture and lifestyle of the city or the home counties. Wary? Only because they know people from outside come and go, whether after a week or two's holiday or a year or two's failed dream.

❦

Despite not wishing to be hemmed in by the main roads nearby, the hairy business of crossing one of them with a green young horse precluded for the moment my sharing my ride up to the Moor with Mel. Instead we settled for the comfort of our regular route. We could trot off and on for half-a-mile or more up the lane before being rewarded with our panoramic view to all points of the compass but how I'd looked forward to sharing with her my 'Rim of the World' track with its long, blind curve, sheer drop to one side and views to the south and west. One day, perhaps, but for now the continuing priority was to build on her new found plateau of confidence before attempting any ascent to higher levels of daring.

In fact, as we went out the following Sunday it occurred to me that 'plateau' was perhaps not quite the right word. 'Escarpment' might have conjured up a more accurate image. Her confidence had been building up during each ride out only to fall away again in the run up to the next. But, I comforted myself, the general direction of the jagged slope was still up!

It was because of this that I knew that, despite the incredibly positive way she had coped with her fall the previous time, the colly-wobbles would be back as she put on her riding gear, groomed Smartie and tacked her up.

'Are you OK, darling?' I asked, seeing the need to allow her to release some tension without actually encouraging her to express her doubts: a doubt expressed is a fear in the making, leading, so often, to a self-fulfilling disaster.

'It's nothing really,' she replied through clenched teeth.

'Good!' I replied with as much optimism as I could muster. 'You have the perfect horse there and she's never going to let you down,' I asserted with slightly more certainty that I was right than that Mel would agree.

'I know you're right,' she replied, 'but I can't help wondering whether at my age I've just left it all too late.'

'Left what all too late? You've been riding since you were seven!' She returned a nervous twitch of a smile.

'Is my girth tight enough? Are my stirrups level?' the returning nerves asked.

I knew I had to check them to boost her confidence but equally did not want to fuel the nerves. After satisfying myself all was well, I got up onto Max, turned him down towards the bottom of the drive and, more haughtily than I intended, said over my shoulder to Mel, just a few paces behind, 'I think you can worry yourself unnecessarily about these things sometimes.' I turned briefly to look at her only to catch the slightly disdainful look which seemed to be calculated to remind me of the dangers of overlooking them which I myself had already learned the hard way.

Once in the lane, with due authority I said, 'come on let's go,' avoiding the use of the word 'trot' which, as all riders know, is readily understood and put into immediate effect by most horses! My purpose was what could best be described as fear displacement or just getting on with it. It seemed to work better than I could have expected.

'What a good girl, Smartie,' said Mel, reaching down to pat her on the neck. 'Well she is,' Mel said to me with a quizzical smile when she noticed the slightly self-satisfied look on my face.

'Yes, I know. I've been telling you that since you got her.' The rest of the ride progressed smoothly with Mel even allowing me to coax her into a canter without any mental resistance on her part. 'Well done. Go on,' I encouraged, holding Max back as he sensed Smartie was leaving him behind.

'Don't go past me,' Mel yelled as the canter extended back across the middle of the twenty-acre field, the edge of which we had just trotted demurely round.

'OK, just keep straight,' I ordered, knowing I didn't want too many complications as Max fought to catch up in the only way he knew - fast!

Mel started to wander away to the left of the centre line of the grassed field, still in full, controlled canter. I decided to let some of Max's pent-up energy dissipate by keeping him on the straight line and allowing him to go faster, knowing I would not overtake Mel who was effectively cutting off the corner of the field towards the track home.

With my eyes firmly on Mel, willing her to successfully complete the longest canter she had yet had on Smartie, my mind was not entirely on Max. It was just at the moment that I became aware of his turning his head anxiously in the direction of Smartie that I realised he had decided he had had enough of being on a different bearing. With a determined twist to the left he sharply changed direction to follow her towards the track.

I, encouraged by my less-than-fully-tightened girth, was determined to keep to the centre line. This led, inevitably, to a parting of the ways. It was once again a slow-moving heavy object that came towards me, giving me an almighty thump in my left shoulder as I dived over Max's right.

After the all-too-familiar period of stillness and increasing awareness that not only was I still alive but had the pains to prove it, I struggled to my feet. The last thing I had wanted was to undermine Mel's freshly rebuilt confidence by coming off Max so conspicuously. As ever, Max, having also concluded I was still moving, began to graze nearby. I knew I had to scramble back on board quickly, straighten up the saddle, which was listing hard to starboard, all without letting on I was hurting before Mel had a chance to reflect on how easily it could have been her again. I need not have worried. As I gathered my reins and trotted Max over towards her, gritting my teeth into the phoniest of smiles, she turned her head towards me.

'Are you alright?' she asked with a frown.

'I'll survive,' I replied through steeled features.

'I didn't see what happened,' she said with concern.

'Oh, Max decided to follow you on your short cut and I, well, just carried on.' Mel's frown lifted a little.

'Are you sure you're alright?'

'Nothing a gallon or two of aloe vera won't sort out,' I muttered, ever more aware of the pain in my left shoulder.

'What actually happened then?' she asked.

'Why didn't you keep to the straight line?' was all I wanted to know.

'I was doing so well I didn't want to stop Smartie and she just, well...'

'Headed for the exit,' I said.

'But I still don't understand why you came off.' Then she glanced at my saddle, still not quite centred. 'Was your girth loose?' she asked, surely knowing the answer.

'Might have been.' With my humour evidently coming out on top she could contain herself no longer.

'I think,' she began with a broad grin, 'you can worry yourself unnecessarily about these things sometimes,' before laughing louder than I was able to.

❧

'...fawn and brindle puppies, KC reg, from show winning stock, super temps, family can be seen...' Mel read out from the Cornish Guardian, as casually as she might read out what was on the television that evening.

'No,' was all I said as I looked up from my own paper.

'It can't do any harm to look...'

'It can't do any good either. For one thing we said we'd never put ourselves through the misery of losing a Dane again, for another we've still got poor old Sukie and it wouldn't be fair to put her nose out of joint and I doubt we'd like them anyway.'

'What makes you say that?' asked Mel, cocking her head to one side.

'Well, who do we know who breeds Danes in Cornwall?'

'Well, no one but that's not surprising: it's years since we were showing so we wouldn't know anyone anyway!'

'No but we know the type of dogs we like and we probably won't have heard of the breeding...'

'But we won't ever know unless we find out.'

Finally I folded my paper and put it on the table next to me. 'You mean you want to phone up and find out what breeding they've got behind them. And then how many dogs and bitches of each colour...'

A weak grin began to spread across Mel's face which she tried to suppress before it got out of control. 'Well, that way we could find there was nothing we wanted and then forget about it,' she announced with her own impeccable logic.

'But we'd forget about it even quicker by doing nothing,' I said, trying to pull down the shutters on that particular line of discussion. It would have been fatal to admit it at that point but Mel had succeeded in getting me to conjure up a picture of a litter of fawn and brindle Dane puppies. It wasn't difficult since we had had one of our own some twenty years earlier. But I also had an instant recollection of Jake and his sister Mima as puppies some nine years previously and the time had gone so quickly that they seemed to have been with us no time at all.

'You're thinking about it though, aren't you?' asked Mel, the grin finally winning the battle.

This time it was me trying to keep my face from straying from the task of presenting a serious exterior. I, too, found I was losing the battle. 'But what about poor little Chan? It would be grossly unfair now he's settled to introduce him to something smaller only for his self esteem to be shattered when it grew to several times his size.'

'Nonsense,' said Mel, warming to the possibility of a luscious victory. 'He'd get used to it gradually. It's not as if the change would take place over night.'

'I'm telling you now, I'm not interested in any old Dane puppy.'

'Course not.'

'It's got to have the American bloodlines we like,' I insisted while slowly becoming aware of the scale of my retreat and impending defeat.

'Or Swedish.'

57

'Same thing really.'

'When shall I phone then?' Mel asked solicitously.

'When we've decided we want one. And I'm still not sure,' I added in a vain attempt to back-pedal. The truth was that I was still feeling the pain of Jake's and Mima's loss and knew Sukie was nearing the end of her span. A mental battle was taking place in my head. On the one hand I wanted to wait and see how I felt after Sukie had gone. On the other we had never been without a Dane for over twenty-five years. But we had never felt any of our animals could be replaced and so I began to waiver: perhaps it might be nicer to have a puppy while Sukie was still with us...

'But they might all go quickly and then we might not be able to find one for a while.' Mel had hit that particular ball back at me in the game, set and match sort of a way she had discovered over the years.

'Alright. There's no harm in finding out but ask all the right questions about what's in the pedigree,' I instructed, in a last ditch attempt to hold on to the initiative which, in truth, I had never actually had!

'Would you even recognise the names?' she asked, cruelly twisting the knife.

'Go and get on with it before I change my mind!'

It was only minutes later that Mel returned to the room to tell me that while some puppies had already been ear-marked for their new owners there were still fawn and brindle puppies of both sexes available.

'But are they any good?' I asked.

'Oh, they sound lovely,' Mel oozed. 'Super temperaments and both sire and dam are show winning dogs. Jeanette Callan, the breeder, has got the dam and we could see the sire which is owned by a friend of hers in Cornwall.'

'I suppose we'd better go and see them then, but don't forget, if we don't like them that's it. I'd rather wait for the right one,' I replied.

'I thought you'd say that which is why we're going to see them tomorrow,' Mel announced triumphantly. 'And before you say anything, it's after the stock market's closed so you can't object.' I thought about it but stifled my response.

'We need to decide on whether we want a dog or bitch and a fawn or brindle,' I declared with a fleeting ripple of excitement at the thought of choosing our first Dane puppy after so many years. 'What do you think?'

'I think it's down to you. I chose Chan so it's only fair for you to choose the Dane,' Mel replied. My thoughts gathered pace and I gave voice to them.

'Well we've always said we'd never try to replace any animal with one of the same sex and colour so I suppose it should be a fawn dog or a brindle bitch,' I mused.

'I'd really love a brindle bitch,' Mel said, before biting her tongue. 'Sorry, your choice,' she quickly added.

'But you said you couldn't have one again after Clara,' I reminded her, referring to the beautiful bitch we had had to have put down at just fourteen months because of a rare muscle-wasting disease.

'It's so long ago now. I always told myself I would have one again one day,' she explained with misty eyes.

While I considered this briefly, I was soon focusing my mind on the idea of a dog. 'But with such a large breed we've got to have a dog,' I said with a male logic that sailed over her head.

'Why?' she asked.

'Well, I've always wanted a really big Dane and none of our dogs was ever that big really. It's just an ambition of mine to have a really super large dog one day.'

'Well, it's your choice,' Mel conceded.

'And we're definitely not in the market for one of each,' I said with a defiance that served only to challenge her to entertain the idea for a split second.

'No,' she responded in all seriousness. 'I really don't ever want to have too many.'

The next day we cruised down the A30 and took the slip road off by McDonalds towards Fraddon and then made our way through the lanes to Mike and Jeanette Callan's house, home of the Tyak Great Danes. Before we opened the car doors we could hear the unmistakable deep 'oof' of a Dane, as yet still out of our sight. Then another and then several!

Jeanette appeared at the gate, needing no knock at the door or ring of the bell to tell her we had arrived. As usual there was a two-way exchange with her wanting to check our credentials just as we did hers. Very quickly we established that each knew Danes very well and, indeed, a number of mutual acquaintances such as Ron and Freda Lewis, owners of the Walkmyll kennels, and Jean Lanning, well-known for her Clausentums.

After a cup of tea we were soon out in the big puppy kennel surrounded by puppies. It took a few minutes for the confusion to give way to an objective assessment. We had already explained that I was choosing and wanted a fawn dog but had also said that could change if I preferred one of the bitches to any of the dogs. I also knew that colour was secondary to overall conformation and temperament.

The overwhelming sensation of finding myself among so many puppies was not unlike getting your eyes accustomed to a change from brightness to darkness or vice versa. Very quickly I found myself narrowing the choice down to a fawn dog and a brindle dog. The fawn, which I could hold with his weight resting on my left forearm, his legs dangling over it and his chin cradled in my left hand, while I stroked him with my right, was very affectionate. But I had always found dark brindles very attractive. The only way to choose was to ask Jeanette to remove the others, by now up to all sorts of mischief and oblivious to the implications of our visit. They were making the most of our attentions having no way of knowing we would soon be gone!

As I looked down on the two dog puppies, each with beautifully chiselled heads, the darkest of brown eyes and black masks, my final selection made itself on the basis of body length. The shorter fawn it was to be! Mel clearly approved.

'He's absolutely beautiful, darling,' she said, handing over to Jeanette the brindle bitch she had been surreptitiously holding on to.

'You prefer her, really, don't you?' I asked, narrowly failing in my intent to avoid drawing attention to the love-in that had been quietly taking place behind me.

'It would be lovely but no, I've got my little Chan at home and we agreed it was your choice.'

'We could have both, I suppose,' I said thoughtfully before deciding that for once we would stick to our resolve. 'But I'm not sure it's the right thing to do.' Quite apart from anything else, the sudden thought of two puppies to rear and, not least, to house-train rapidly dispelled the very thought.

Mel's eyes met mine while Jeanette's averted themselves as we attempted make up our minds. I looked at the small, warm body, settled on my arm, and the kind look in his eyes quickly settled matters. 'This one, definitely,' I said.

'He's a really nice puppy,' said Mel. 'I'm sure he's just right,' she added, failing miserably in her attempt to ignore the bitch puppy which Jeanette was still holding and which had turned her attention to bashing her chin with a small stripey paw.

'Are you sure?' asked Jeanette who, like many before, was slightly uncertain what conclusion our confusing communication had been heading for.

'Yes, this chap's the one,' I replied, hardening my heart once-and-for-all against the brindle dog puppy at my feet which was trying so hard to regain my attention.

'We'd better go inside, have another cup of tea and sort out the paperwork,' said Jeanette briskly lest any further indecision took hold. She returned the two brindle puppies to their dam and litter mates. Once indoors she said while waiting for the kettle to boil, 'I usually don't let them go until they are at least eight weeks but I know you know what you're doing so, although they're only seven, I'm happy for you to take him today if you'd like to.'

For once Mel and I had no need to exchange glances. 'We'd love to,' I replied without hesitation, feeling the excitement inside me leap at this little bonus. The burly little chap wasted no time settling into the new game of terrorising Jeanette's adult house dogs. It was at that moment that our conclusions about the wonderful temperaments of Jeanette's Danes was confirmed unequivocally.

The adults, of varying ages, were as patient and gentle with the boisterous little interloper as could possibly have been imagined. This said much for the way they had been raised, all being encouraged to get on together. With no hesitation whatsoever, both Mel and I fell instantly and hopelessly in love with Paddy, their huge, gentle, dark brindle dog whose kind dark-eyed expression told you he would never harm anyone or anything unless, perhaps, it was a stranger up to no good, when all bets were probably off!

'Good,' said Jeanette. 'I'll get the pedigree and insurance certificate organised.' We went on to discuss the puppy's diet and she kindly gave us a plentiful supply to tide us over until we were able to stock up in bulk, as we had got used to doing over the years. A cheque was handed over and we waited while Jeanette went off to find us some newspaper for the short journey home, 'just in case.'

Despite the number of Danes we had owned over the years, there was nothing like the exhilaration of a new puppy. I was sure it was something to do with the fact that as they had so much growing to do we knew they would not be tiny puppies for long. Very quickly we would be into the leggy stage then the bolshy adolescent period followed by a gentle maturing, beyond which we knew, all too soon, we would see a greying of the muzzle, a slimming down of the body, and then a weakening of the muscles until once more old age, if we were lucky to have them that long, would steal them away. It was certainly true that they rapidly secured a very special place in our lives which, eventually, we had learned not to take for granted.

But for now we had the comfort of seeing that trusting little dog, our first Cornish Great Dane, curl up on Mel's lap ready for the journey to he knew not where for the next part of his barely-begun young life.

❧

On the Saturday, two days and numerous puddles and piles later, we began to turn our attention to the September rally of the Jaguar Enthusiasts' Club. For the first time since we had arrived it was being held in the beautiful grounds of Lanhydrock and it was that Sunday. Just a few miles from Upper Penwithiel, it was the nearest such gathering to home and so we knew we had no excuse not to be there, apart, that is, from the need to consider what to do about Zennor. We had decided the new addition to the family needed a Cornish name that would befit him both as a small puppy and the large, strong adult we hoped he would eventually become. What better name than that which also happened to belong to such a rugged and most beautiful part of the county.

While it was true to say that we had an initial jolt on being so rudely reminded of the constant attention required by a Dane puppy, he did settle in very quickly. So it was, on the Saturday morning as Mel and I discussed how long we could leave Zennor the next day that it came to us, or, more accurately, Mel.

'He's no trouble, really, is he?' she muttered over breakfast.

'Who? Zennor? No,' I replied.

'But the biggest surprise is Chan,' said Mel. 'I thought his little nose might be put out of joint but he seems to have accepted Zennor so well.'

'For now,' I replied.

'For now?'

'Well, yes, because Zennor's still small enough to walk under him,' I explained. 'He can lord it over him. But it won't be long before it's the other way round.'

Mel considered this thoughtfully, not entirely sure of the implication. 'But it could so easily have been a problem from day one,' she went on.

'I guess so,' I mumbled as another thought entirely crossed my mind of its own volition.

'That sounded thoughtful,' she analysed with her usual clinical precision about such things. 'What are you thinking?' she asked, inclining her head so as to get a better look at what my face might be giving away.

'Nothing,' I replied dishonestly and, therefore, fatally as I struggled to keep a deadpan expression in place.

'Are you thinking what I'm thinking?' she asked allowing a smile to creep across her face. When she asked this it usually meant her intuition had struck home with the same deadly accuracy as any self-respecting heat-seeking missile. I knew I'd been rumbled as she made a wiggling motion with her forefinger as she drew it across the front of her face. It was the same shorthand she had used almost exactly twenty-seven years earlier to refer to the incessant tail-wagging of our very first Dane, a brindle boy called Kurt, in the seemingly endless period of three weeks from when we had first seen him to the day we could finally take him home. It was our way of saying 'isn't it lovely we're going to get him soon?' or something similar. I could stifle a broad grin no longer.

'We're totally mad,' I said, knowing everyone but she who mattered most in my life would unhesitatingly agree.

'But it's nice though, isn't it?' Mel said, with neither of us yet saying anything about what had simultaneously hit us.

'Are you sure that's what you want?' the voice at the other end of the phone asked half-an-hour later.

'Oh, yes,' I replied. 'Should have decided it sooner,' I conceded.

'Well, you might not believe this but I had a feeling you might do this,' she continued. 'In fact I said as much to Mike.'

We arrived at Lanhydrock a little later than planned, partly to minimise the time we would have to leave Zennor. In fact, the usual picnic went by the board and the time we spent looking at the array of different Jaguars, augmented by those of our visitors from the Devon region of the club, watching the driving test and generally chatting was cut short by my saying to Mel at 3.30, 'it's really time to go.'

Just thirty or forty minutes later we got out of the car to a familiar cacophony.

Ever since his arrival, little Chan had slept in his travelling cage at night, partly to protect him from the cats - claws and eyes being best kept at a distance from each other - but also to protect the cats. Despite his affinity, indeed amity, with them when we were present, he seemed to assume they were fair game whenever we left him alone with them. Turning them on their backs and nibbling them around the neck and tummy seemed to be the best fun.

Since Basenjis are well known to live life according to a set of rules all of their own we should not have been surprised to discover that while he hated being cooped up in the cage while we were around, he preferred the security of it at night.

This happy state of affairs was to change from the very instant that Zennor arrived. We knew that Danes hated to be cooped up and the realities of a yet-to-be-house-trained puppy of that size dictated that he be left to sleep without being caged. That was the catalyst to change Chan's own views on the matter. He had been truly brilliant in the way he had accepted the altogether more floppy, clumsy approach to play adopted by a young Dane but the other side of the coin was that he objected to being shut up at night when there was still so much playing to be done with his new friend.

Knowing the importance of sleep to a rapidly growing Dane puppy I just had to take the tougher line and ignore the howls of anguish that began to rent the air as I ascended the stairs last thing at night: from Chan, now keen to escape from his cage and from Zennor for no reason other than his new friend was unhappy!

Even so, a degree of tranquillity had settled on the household by the Sunday after Zennor's arrival.

This was to be short-lived however. It was around 6.00pm that night that we began the process of introduction once more. It was Marmalade who now had the task of getting to know a strange little tri-colour dog with pricked ears and no bark and four furry creatures who lived high up in the kitchen and who leapt about it, usually without touching the floor, except for poor old Daisy, that is. Her leaping days were over; she could just scrabble onto a higher level out of reach when required, though usually her well-tried tactic of bluffing it out on the floor with a succession of fierce growls worked well enough! However, the task of getting to know the flop-eared, bouncier, altogether less delicate dog took next to no time at all because just three days earlier they had been part of the same little pack. Yes, Marmalade was the name Jeanette had given the brindle bitch we had persuaded her to let us have despite her having decided after we had taken Zennor that she might hang on to her herself!

Bedlam was soon the apparent result. Zennor had someone familiar and of his own size to play with and with whom he could gang up on the larger, swifter incumbent. Chan, on the other hand, rapidly rose to the challenge of bossing two awkward customers where earlier there had been just one. The cats, meanwhile, could be forgiven for edging closer to a state of paranoia: what on earth had they done to be condemned to a life with this bunch of ill-mannered hoodlums?

❧

In the days and weeks ahead, things were not always quite stable. Chan increasingly struggled to cope psychologically with the fact that both newcomers, while great fun and a perfect foil to his reversion to puppyhood, were rapidly catching him up in size. What he didn't know, and we did, was that situation had some way to run.

He objected more and more vociferously to being caged at night and so it was with heart in mouth that I took the decision last thing one night, without consulting Mel, to leave Chan loose with the Danes. Next morning there was total silence from the kitchen as I turned off the alarm. But this, I soon realised, was the result of three pairs of ears tuning themselves into my approaching footsteps, momentarily distracting them from their very busy time of playing in a heap on the floor under the table.

Cloey, Moss, Dandy and Daisy very rapidly settled to the new regime, helped by Mel's idea of leaving open the window between the kitchen and conservatory so they could escape to total peace and quiet whenever they wished.

Sukie, whom we had kept quite separate from the puppies so as not to put her nose out of joint or, more importantly, so they could not make a nuisance of themselves with her, was content to be with Angus, our old American Cocker who, in turn, needed a quieter life as his sight continued to deteriorate. This was the direct result of his allergy and we were resigned to the likelihood that he would be totally sightless one day. Sukie herself continued with her slow but ragged decline, sometimes better, sometimes worse.

The contrast with the Dane puppies could not have been greater, with the youngsters' unsteadiness from the increasing demands made by their rapidly growing bodies outstripping the ability of their limbs to adequately support them while Sukie's unsteadiness was a one-way street in the opposite direction. In short their lives were in front of them and hers was behind her.

Nevertheless we felt she had enough time for us to introduce the puppies to her before they got too big because we had set our faces against ever having two separate packs with all the chaos that can induce. As we expected, the outcome was a non-event with Sukie acknowledging the existence of the pups without wanting anything to do with them. In fact Zennor, having none of the quiet and laid-back Zen approach to life suggested by his name, took it upon himself to show Sukie just how friendly he was, rushing to play with her when she lay down in the drive for a rest from her exertions. She let him know in no uncertain terms what she thought of such disrespect and nipped him on the ear. This was enough to ensure he and Marmalade kept their distance afterwards which, we concluded, was no bad thing.

The still-warm sunshine allowed us to let the puppies romp outside several times each day, punctuated by the regular snoozes they needed to permit the necessary growth. One afternoon when Mel had been keeping her eye on them as they slept on the lawn she answered the phone only to discover when she looked for them that they had gone. In a panic typical of any young mother whose toddler has strayed further than it should she rushed off to find them. 'Come and look at this,' she called through my open study window. 'Quickly, without making a sound,' she added.

I followed her up the drive to the field gate where both Zen, and Marma as they had already become, were sitting next to each other and looking up in total awe at Max and Smartie who were standing the other side of the gate, heads gently lowered to check out the credentials of the little newcomers. Then, when Max got close enough to sniff them, Zen suddenly scuttled off down the drive, casting worried glances over his shoulder: Marma stayed put and, without actually enjoying the experience, saw it through!

We knew from our experience of generations of Danes to savour moments like that. All too soon they would be fully grown and, at the very least, in awe of nothing! And there were other sweet memories in the making too, such as on the occasion of their second jabs and first check-up at the vets. The veterinary nurses had all craned their necks round the consulting room door, amidst 'oos' and 'aahs', to see these two lovely little dogs which I struggled, with Mel's help, to confine to the table top. As soon as the formal proceedings were concluded, we stood chatting for a few minutes, just long enough for both pups to curl up together for an impromptu doze after their little ordeal before we scooped them up to yet more appreciative noises from the nurses. Whatever else transpired we knew they would probably never again fit on that table together.

It was about a couple of weeks later, in late September, that Sukie gave us the biggest scare so far. One morning she just couldn't get up from her bed without help and even then fell twice before finding the strength to go out. I followed her out where she collapsed once more, looking quite dreadful: her very spirit seemed to be draining from her. I knew her time had come. In tears, I told her I loved her and that I would see her again one day, before thanking her for eleven-and-a-half years of companionship and love and going slowly indoors to phone the vet. An appointment was made for 3pm that day and a deep gloom closed in on Upper Penwithiel.

At least the sun was out and I was able to let Sukie go out and enjoy her last hours in peace. She spent most of her morning asleep on what had become her favourite spot on the cobbled drive. I satisfied myself that they were warm enough not to be a discomfort and left her, returning at increasingly frequent intervals to see she was alright and, yes, to talk to her. More than once I spotted Mel doing the same. It was just after 2pm on one of my checks that she slowly stood up and walked towards me, gently wagging her tail. I went to fetch Mel. 'Come and look at Sukie.'

'She suddenly looks a lot better,' she said.

'That wouldn't be difficult,' I replied. Mel gave me one of her knowing looks. I continued, 'I don't know what to do now. How can I put her down when she's like this?' Perhaps, I thought, Mel would gently prod me into reality, reminding me of Sukie's age and my promise not to let her suffer so I prepared myself for what I had set in motion.

'You can't,' said Mel firmly, to my surprise. 'We always reckoned they told you when they'd had enough and she seems to be saying she hasn't yet.'

'Shall I cancel the vet?' I asked, uncertainly. She stroked Sukie's head, smiled at me and nodded. I hoped I was about to do the right thing.

❧

'Touché,' Mel said with a grin when I told her James and I were going out to do some fencing! Ridiculously, as I then knew, I had hoped the Dane puppies would rapidly learn the house rules, including the one which stipulated that they should always come when called and absolutely never go through the hedges into the road or through the fence into the field. What had proved to be gaps far too small to let an adult Dane through were not up to the challenge of much smaller versions. And, of course, once these new rules were learned, namely that it was actually good fun to scramble through to the other side, there was no stopping them. Hence the lorry from Duchy Timber which unloaded rolls of stock fence, bundles of round wooden posts and buckets of staples.

James and I soon agreed a modus operandi which he declared unfair but which, I reminded him, gave him a very fair chance of repaying in some small way our continuing investment in him. He was to wield the sledgehammer while I fixed the stock fence, otherwise known variously as sheep fencing or pig netting, to the posts he had driven in, with the staples. In just a few hours we had the entire garden surrounded. When let loose to test the efficacy of our work the puppies spent only a fraction of the time trying to escape as they had when they could! Instant peace and security reigned, for the time being.

Zen and Marma's growth continued apace and all too soon they were the same size as the Dane puppy sculpture we had acquired some years earlier. Inevitably I spent some time patiently getting them to pose for a photograph next to their bronze friend. Soon afterwards Jeanette and Mike Callan paid their first visit to satisfy themselves all was well. It was with a mixture of bemusement and amusement that we waved them off later to the accompaniment of two Dane puppies, standing with their front feet up on the gate, whimpering longingly after their departing car. We then knew they would never forget Mike and Jeanette.

It was later that week that I was disconcertingly held up in the middle of Bodmin by a train! An old cream and brown Pullman coach was being transported by road from Bodmin General, the old station now used only by the privately owned and funded Bodmin Steam Railway. I first caught up with it as the low-loader it was on started reversing towards me as part of a complicated manoeuvre to get round the mini roundabout and head towards the A30. It was probably the most exciting local event of the year.

It only slightly delayed my progress in getting Marma to the vet for tests following suspected cystitis. In text book fashion, not previously achieved with any of our dogs before, she performed on cue and donated a small sample to order in the middle of the consulting room. The vet was impressed!

Very soon after that James went off to his first job interview 'up country' while Justin prepared for his last year at college. Mel prepared for winter by storing the garden furniture away.

'Come and see what I've found,' she yelled, waking me from a day dream in front of my computer screen as I joined the stock market in one of its short dozes. I came to with a start, knowing of old that such commands were often attached to some dire consequence or other of something she or one of the boys or animals had done.

'What is it?' I asked slightly breathlessly as I skidded to a halt by the back door.

'Look!' she said, pointing to a small pool of water on the patio.

'Who did that?' I asked, bemused that she should think what was obviously another contribution from one of the bitches was of such urgency.

'*I* did, emptying the base of the umbrella,' she explained, still leaving me none the wiser. 'Look what came out,' she continued. I followed the direction of her pointing finger to see a minute newt lying passively and totally unconcerned in the puddle.

5 Cornish Hairdryer

October came in and swing-top rubbish bins went out. What prompted their departure was not only the ability of our lovely three-month-old Dane puppies to get at the rubbish by standing on their hind legs and sticking their noses into the bins, but the propensity of Marma in particular to extract herself in a panic when we approached and run off with the detached upper part of the bin round her neck like a garland.

We had had to cope with all these growing phases many times before but never have we had two identically-aged puppies up to the same mischief: it was not trouble doubled but squared! And the egging on by a little Basenji whose very silence let him off the hook, as though he was an innocent bystander, didn't help.

A few days after we had followed Justin back to Bournemouth with all the odds and ends of his belongings which wouldn't fit in his own car - something which had never been necessary with Andrew and James in their college days - Mel was off to one of her half-way days out in Exeter with her old friend Tricia Carter, Exeter being halfway between our old house and the Cornish one.

The whole idea, undoubtedly in Tricia's mind when she suggested it, was to take Mel's mind off the emptiness which she felt, in sympathy with the house I suppose, whenever the boys were all away. It was the day after her outing that it was to become even emptier when I knew I could no longer put off the cold, sad but necessary decision to call the vet in to gently send Sukie on her way. The professionalism, combined with the simple human kindness, of the young female vet and nurse enabled Mel and I to say goodbye, unashamed to shed a silent tear, without in any way distressing Sukie. We had, anyway, shed many more tears in anticipation of that stark day in the weeks and months that preceded it.

Afterwards we felt the almost forgotten familiar sense of relief that we had done the right thing. Sometimes in the past there had been the feeling that perhaps we could have held on a little longer, confused with one that maybe the decision should have been taken sooner. At eleven years and nine months of age we were certain the timing had been exactly right.

Following just seven weeks after our unexpected loss of Jake, we were finally able to fill the hole dug so many months back by Steve Masters.

Because Sukie had lived such a full and long life, our sadness lifted sooner than it had with our earlier dogs which we had lost that much younger, too often unexpectedly. In a way, that freed us up to concentrate on our new additions. The annual Jaguar Enthusiasts' Club lunch at Jamaica Inn was soon upon us again and we invited our friends the Gilberts back for tea. They were keen to see the Dane puppies, especially their younger daughter, Laura. The real scene-stealer from her point of view, however, was little Chan. There is undoubtedly something in the nature of Basenjis that appeals to youngsters: my guess is that it has something to do with a shared naughtiness in the case of younger children and rebelliousness in the case of teenagers. There was no doubting the wistfulness of Laura's smile and wave at Chan from the rear window of her father's Jag as it turned out of our drive for the journey home.

After they had gone and we had stabled the horses for the night I decided, on a whim, to walk the dogs round the field for the first time. The Danes were still too young to go on extended hikes because of the need to conserve their energies for growing but they had shown increasing curiosity about what lay the other side of the five-barred gate, so I indulged it.

The sight of young Danes lolloping along so awkwardly, legs and ears flying out at uncontrolled angles never leaves you. Nor does the shared wonder of exploring new sights, smells and sounds. Add in the antics of an athletic little Basenji literally running rings round them and you have a picture you know will stay with you. After just five minutes I rounded them up for the return amble, easier said than done because of their reluctance to leave the exciting new world they had just discovered.

That brief excursion was enough to stimulate in me the idea that a little lead training for the Danes was overdue. I had always started that at about four months in the past, just to get them used to idea before they discovered they were big enough to exert an equal and opposite force at the end of the lead. I had recently abandoned the idea as far as Chan was concerned because the whole concept of allowing anyone else to interfere with their democratic right to roam where they wish is totally foreign to Basenjis. Any thought on my part of exerting even relatively little and opposite force had met with a stubborn, heels-dug-in resistance on his part!

However, I was soon to face a quite unexpected obstacle in my early attempts to lead-train Zen and Marma. It could best be described as foot-dragging brought on by hurt feelings. Never had I seen such expressive eyes in any dog as those two had. They seemed to be saying, 'what are you doing to me. I'm only a puppy. Surely you don't intend to be so hard on me.' I just gave up and decided to leave it for another day. The last thing I wanted to do at that stage was put them off being walked on a lead. Was it a conspiratorial look of, 'that was easy,' which

70

I noticed being passed between them when I finally hung up the lead in the utility room?

❧

In the same way that, subconsciously, Cornwall had exerted its magnetic attraction on Mel and I over many years, until, finally, we had given way to its persisting force and moved here, West Cornwall reminded us that it too continued to beckon.

'I've decided that's where I'd really like to be,' Mel said as we were grooming the horses one Sunday morning in preparation for a ride.

'Hmmm,' was all I could say to that. I knew moving too soon would result in the costs eating into our equity.

'Is that all you've got to say?' she asked.

'Well, in principle I agree, though we mustn't forget how much time and effort we put into the decision to move here,' I reminded her. 'It's convenient for the station when I need to go to London or the A30 whenever we want to visit the boys or vice versa.'

'I know,' she replied. 'That's the trouble. But whenever I get past Truro I just feel that's where I belong.'

'I know what you mean. Somehow I just feel that's where we'll end up. I can see myself when I've totally retired and finally put my feet up just being able to go for walks along the cliffs or beach...'

'...and amble along to the pub,' Mel said, picking up my line of thought precisely.

'But where exactly would you want to live?' I asked.

We continued this line of conversation all the way out and all the way back. Our conclusion was that once James had settled himself in his career and Justin, who was crystal clear about what he wanted to do, had graduated the following year, then we could seriously consider a further move.

'There's nothing to stop us looking,' Mel said, giving me one of her hopeful sideways glances, as we ambled back down the lane, with Max grunting at each stride down the hard slippery surface of the hill.

I gave Mel one of my exasperated looks which she knew was a sign I was close to capitulation. She clinched it with one of her smiles. 'No, I s'pose not,' I muttered into the space between Max's twitching ears.

'When? Saturday?' she asked. I replied inaudibly. 'What was that?' she asked leaning towards me and peering into my eyes.

'I said if we must,' I replied not entirely truthfully.

'Good. You can take me to Rinsey first and then we'll have a look

71

round,' she concluded with a smug, triumphant look on her face. After we had untacked the horses, sponged them down and rugged them up before putting them out into the field, we stood for a few moments looking over the gate at the departing horses, less full of themselves after their exercise.

'Of course, we would have to find somewhere with a decent field,' I said vaguely. 'I never want the horses to be cooped up so they can't get up a good gallop,' I added as the two of them wandered up to the top of the field to see their friends next door.

'No, I agree,' said Mel.

'And the dogs liked their romp round it last week too. They're not going to get any smaller, either.' Mel gave me a questioning look.

'You don't want to move at all really, do you?' she asked.

'I didn't say that but it's just got to be right. I mean this has most of what we want, doesn't it?' I reasoned.

'Yes, but it's just not in the right place.' Sensing a reopening of the debate she thought she had so recently won, she switched conversations. 'After we've showered you can take me round the field with the dogs. I'd love to see them running free,' she said.

We pushed ourselves up the field behind the dogs half-an-hour later, Mel's hair still wringing wet: she always left it a while before drying it with her hairdryer, as I couldn't help recalling from the very first time I ever took her out as an eighteen-year old. She had been waiting at the end of her road, damp tresses framing her face: she had simply always done it, to help it set the way she wanted. 'Aren't you cold in this wind?' I asked.

'Yes, but we'll soon be back indoors and I can dry it,' she replied. Fifteen minutes later we emerged from the wind which was always blowing harder at the top of the field. 'Look at this,' she said as she looked at herself in the hall mirror and gently pulled at the ends of her hair. I did and saw that it had totally dried in a style I knew she wouldn't be happy about.

'You look like a starched Afghan,' I exclaimed, trying not to laugh.

'Permed is the word you're looking for, I think,' she said.

'Either way you've got the Cornish hairdryer to thank.' She gave a look halfway between puzzlement and mock annoyance. 'The wind,' I explained.

The following Saturday took us to the home, west of Truro, of our friends Chris and Hugh Roberts whom we had met at the Jaguar Enthusiasts' Club. Hugh had built up an expertise in restoring Jaguars that had led to his opinions being sought out by fellow members on their progress in rebuilding, for example, an E-type and also as a senior judge at concourse competitions. Chris was one of those extremely able people who constantly took on new challenges. She was the female version of the busy man: as the saying goes, if you want something doing, ask a busy man, or, in this case, woman! She had been asked and had consistently proved the saying true.

On this occasion, however, she had invited around thirty members, both Cornish born and bred and the rest of us, for an informal lunch to celebrate the marriage of Terry Chapman to Margaret. It was a very friendly and relaxed occasion with all the women taking their own contribution to the lunch, making for a wide choice for each course. This was to be the first of a number of such events.

A couple of days later Mel had a phone call from Trudy Connolly, the yard manager at Monnington Morgans near Hereford where Smartie came from. They were having a special clinic, or teach-in, there just before Christmas and wanted us to swell the numbers and, of course, to take Mel and Smartie on to the next stage in their work together. Trudy even offered to come and collect Smartie, suggesting that she also took Max for company for Smartie on the journey. Why, I could even get some saddle-seat training in on him. Quite what Max would make of this American riding style I didn't know. He was probably too well versed in the English style to respond to it, though I had on occasion slipped into it since having had it drummed into me when I was riding Finn, the Morgan gelding, in parallel to Mel's earlier training. He seemed quite oblivious to anything being different and continued to accept telepathic commands as usual!

How could we refuse such an offer? We didn't, and began to look forward eagerly to December.

Having finally remembered to get the chimney swept, somewhat later than usual, it was time to order the logs. We had been disappointed with the dampness of the previous year's and set about finding a new source. Neighbour Sue Little, as ever, proved a reliable source of information and very soon Bernard Libby delivered the best load of logs I'd ever seen. Not only were they perfectly cut to the right size for our woodburner, having been asked to specify my requirements on ordering, but they were seasoned hardwood and totally dry. The size of the load, more than enough for the entire winter, made it excellent value for money. In expressing my delight I offered to recommend him to friends and neighbours.

'Oh no, please don't do that,' he replied. 'I've got enough trouble coping with my present customers. I was in two minds whether I could fit you in but seeing as how I used to deliver here when the Bullocks were here, I decided it was alright.' A penny spinning in my head finally stopped and dropped. Bernard was the man Ben had told us about the day we videoed the house after he'd accepted our offer. Ben had not put Bernard's name on his list of local suppliers and services left for us when we moved in but now we had found him! We continued with our chat about the years he had been supplying logs to people in the area and how infrequently he was able to put up the price for fear of losing his customers.

I tried, unsuccessfully I think, to convince him that with the value-for-money he was providing he could increase his price in excess of inflation each year until he had caught up with other prices in the area. After he'd gone I found myself reflecting yet again on a valuable lesson in living. He had seemed a very contented man, as were so many around us who had spent their entire lives here as, indeed had their fathers and forefathers. Bending to, let alone trying to take advantage of market forces was not a priority: being happy to provide what his customers wanted and to secure a living was what mattered. In short, I suspected he had no trouble sleeping at night.

❧

Mel had moved way beyond each ride out being a milestone. Indeed they were becoming routine. However, no two rides are ever the same and something interesting usually happened. It was the following Sunday, on our totally relaxed amble back down the lane, that Mel and I had an unusual little challenge. As ever, Max, on account of his longer stride, had edged a pace or two ahead of Smartie.

'Hey, slow down,' Mel said, in a voice slightly raised from the conversational level normal on that part of the ride. That told me something wasn't quite right. I turned, expecting to see her stopped or, worse, going backwards as Smartie, still a very young horse, messed around. But no. Very simply, Max had swished his tail, catching it in the cheek-pieces of Smartie's bit and was, effectively, towing her along. Far from protesting or pulling she seemed as content going along with this new approach as any circus elephant asked to hold the tail of the one in front with its trunk!

The small challenge came in disentangling them without dismounting: the coarse hair of Max's tail was wedged very firmly between the two adjoining pieces of metal: the only quick solution was to tug gently, breaking off the last few centimetres of hair. Neither horse batted an eyelid though I noticed Mel wince, less in sympathy with Max's tail than in anticipation of a possible urgent requirement to get off!

James' progress in tracking down his first real job was more rapid than he had been expecting. While having the sense to turn down any he wasn't totally happy with, he was quite sure when the right opportunity came. He was to join an international household products company, boasting many well-known brands, as a graduate trainee in product management.

While, almost inevitably, it meant finally leaving the family home in Cornwall, he had had two years to prepare for it. He was to move to a different part of Wiltshire from whence we had moved two years earlier, in the M4 corridor in fact, in return for which he would for the first time receive serious payment! Our own feelings were unavoidably mixed. We knew that, aside from his spells away from home at university, this really was a final, permanent move away from us. However natural and, indeed, desirable, Mel and I could not help but reminisce about his life with us. But we knew the move represented his final growing up and the culmination of years of effort and study, leading on to much greater things, we had no doubt.

The growth of the Dane puppies led to the first oval plastic bed we had bought for them to share becoming too small, necessitating another trip to Trago Mills in search of the next size up. Since Chan had taken to sleeping in their bed, we let him keep the smaller one. This didn't stop him, however, from taking up residence in the new, larger bed when it arrived, leaving the younger, though by now bigger, Dane puppies to conclude they should continue to squeeze into the old one!

I had had my share of negotiating over the years, ranging from spats on pay with a union to massive amounts going into large company pension funds. These all prepared me well for the little matter of agreeing a suitable price for the disposal of our excess effluent when Dave Burridge's driver informed me that because our two tanks had yielded no less than 1500 litres, the charge would have to be increased beyond the standard one based on 1000! A brief discussion with Dave produced a satisfactory compromise, during which I learned of his forays into Russia and the Ukraine at their invitation, via the local council here in Cornwall. Not only was he able to contribute valuable knowledge and experience to them but he was amazed to discover one or two areas where they could teach us a thing or two. The world was undoubtedly getting smaller!

Why was it, I often asked myself, that animals were such an important part of our lives? I suspect that in both Mel's and my case it was connected with our being only children. There were two consequences of that, it seemed to me. First we were both self-sufficient, and not only quite capable of surviving lengthy periods on our own but occasionally had to have such time to ourselves.

Secondly, having had no constant companions around our own age, as young children we had both liked the idea of having a pet to share our time and our thoughts with. Mel had grown up with a cat from Cornwall, in a delicious reversal of Derek and Jeannie Tangye's situation where they brought a cat from London to live in Cornwall. Mel's, a beautiful marmalade colour from a farm near Helston, had arrived in London by train, the last inch or two of his tail missing as the result of an incident as a tiny kitten. She had also had a Corgi but he had mysteriously disappeared to the vet, never to return, while she was at school one day. Apparently he had showed signs of an unreliable temperament though he had never been any kind of problem as far as Mel was concerned. It was to be many years before she quite came to terms with such a loss for which she had not been prepared.

In my case, I had suffered more or less total denial of the company of any kind of pet. The only one we had ever had was an eight-week-old Alsatian puppy, as the breed was known in those days. I was about three or four and can still recall his making a muddy paw print on my light blue felt slippers. We were constant companions. My recollection is that it had been Dad's idea and Mum had gone along with it reluctantly. Following some misdemeanour or other, probably associated with the mess he created, he was only with us for two weeks. With hindsight, that unexpected loss of so new a friend who had so quickly wormed his way into my young affections, seemed as dramatic a loss as I could have expected to have experienced at that age. After that there was the hour during which I had, with their permission, borrowed and smuggled indoors the kitten belonging to my nearby aunt and uncle. This little deceit went unnoticed until the frightened and disorientated little chap deposited a typically smelly little pile in a corner behind an armchair. Then there was the time, when I was around six that our teacher asked for volunteers to take home the class tortoise for the Christmas holiday. Surely, I can recall reasoning, Mum could not object as he would be in hibernation and no trouble at all, so I shot up my hand. 'You had better ask your mother first,' had been the teacher's response. On that occasion it had been forthcoming but the amount of companionship afforded to me during those few weeks, despite my frequent gentle nudges of his shell to see if he was awake, had been nil!

It was just after we returned home from our honeymoon in 1971 and were slowly getting used to the new routine of married life that Mel and I became conscious of the emptiness of the house we both returned to from work each night. The investment of a small sum in a potted plant or two made an immediate and most unexpected difference. We were returning to a house with a living thing waiting for us! True, the one in the front window showed little sign of recognition when we climbed the steps to the front door and no affection whatsoever in return for the care lavished on it, though, in those days, the idea of talking to them had not yet become a recognised practice. But it was a start. From there it was a relatively short step to acquiring our first cat - two, in fact, both Burmese. This was because, we were told by the breeder, they would be company for each other and, therefore, quite able to be left while we were out at work, whereas one alone would be miserable and, she said, she would not sell us just one. Not only was she right but that theory was to explain why, down the years, we had never restricted ourselves to one of any living thing, including children!

How far off those days seem now, when the forerunner of the Millennium Dome at Greenwich, a rather less impressive Dome of Discovery on the South Bank of the Thames, was the focal point of the recovery of the tired, though reinvigorated young people of my parents' generation after the war.

But does all this mean that those of us who love our animals have somehow abandoned the human race in favour of them? This seems to be a common misconception, particularly among people who do not share our love of animals, categorising us as unsociable - even anti-social - oddballs. In fact, come to think of it, it is those very people whom I would not be too sure about myself! No, while we have found it to be the case that animals on average tend to be more reliable than people on average, for example never striking poses, always uncritically returning the affection given, indeed even offering it when it hasn't been given, we would certainly not divide our friendship between animals and humans in that way. Rather we would like to think we have a range of good friends drawn from both species!

Looking back over the years, I can see how our view of animals has evolved from the simple friendship of our long ago childhood, through the useful accessory to the family stage when the boys were growing up, right up to the fully paid-up member of the family status ours now enjoy. Show me someone who subscribes to the school of thought that animals don't have souls and I'll show you someone who has not gone through that long process. The soul is what we have seen evaporate from an animal dying in front of us: it is the spirit, or very essence of who they were, just as it is with people.

❦

It is a popular conception that a major benefit of cats is their propensity for keeping down the mouse population. No one seemed to have instructed Moss in such matters, however, as he had so far yet to appear at a door or window proudly displaying a catch. That had always been the case as far as Daisy was concerned too. Perhaps it was a lilac thing, though, come to think of it, Moritz, our lilac Burmese boy who went missing never to return, was no mean hunter! It obviously wasn't a difference between the sexes either so I had to admit to having no idea why cats could be so different in that respect.

This left us with Cloey and Dandy who had started to compete with each other for our approval it seemed. Hardly a day or week went by that summer without one or other of them depositing a small body just inside the conservatory. Usually, but not always, it would be dead though hardly ever, we noticed, if it was a shrew. In that case Mel or I would creep out when the cats weren't looking and help it escape into the thickest part of the laurel hedge.

With the colder weather approaching as October drew to a close, one small mouse arrived fit and relatively well, courtesy of Dandy. As soon as she dropped it, presumably feeling the warmth of the Rayburn, it clearly took a decision to stay. It was last seen diving for safety behind the dresser under the baleful gaze of two small Great Danes and the quizzically interested stare of a rapidly growing up Basenji. No further trace was ever found to our bemusement.

A possible explanation presented itself a week later when another live mouse was brought in by Cloey. As soon as she saw me she dropped it. Though very much alive, it decided not to run for fear of drawing attention to itself. This gave me time to find the dust pan in order to scoop it up and take it out to restore it to its freedom. Too slow! Marma beat me to it and to my utter amazement swallowed it whole, as casually as any human despatching a small canapé while in conversation over a drink. It just vanished in a split second. When I looked in her mouth there was no sign of it, though a slow swish of her tail told me she was quite pleased with her unexpected Freddie Starr-style snack. Far from being a one-off, it was to become something of a party piece for her!

While the Danes continued to grow fast, they were far from half their ultimate height and so had to be nurtured with care. Too much of the wrong food and they would grow too rapidly, risking some distortion in bone growth with permanent consequences. Too little and they would fail to reach their full potential size. Physical shocks to their joints was also something to be avoided at all costs. Damage at that critical age could result in bone growth being inhibited with the awful outcome of twisted or misshapen limbs.

It was with my heart in my mouth, therefore, that I saw Marma balanced on the edge of the metre-high dry stone wall between the house and the barn one evening after being fed and let out. As soon as she saw me she advanced slowly towards me, tail waving to proclaim her pride in having found such an interesting new game. Knowing what was going to happen next, I rushed forward and caught her just as she leapt and before she could damage those delicate pastern joints. She was even more pleased to find I had joined in. I deposited her gently, just too late to stop Zen, who had emerged from behind a rhododendron, following suit. He did not have the strength at that age to withstand a crash landing and so crumpled into a heap as soon as he reached the cobbles. Far from being hurt, he got to his feet, shook and ran round to retrace his steps to do it again. I chided him and made him go back. I knew we had a long wait to see whether he had done any lasting damage.

Above us a thick plume of grey-white cloud, suffused like shot silk with the deep orange-pink of the setting sun, slashed the deepening blue evening sky. It gave the appearance of a belching furnace chimney. Standing deep in our valley,

I could only wonder at the magnificent sunsets to be seen from vantage points further west. Would we one day live somewhere like that, where we could even see the sun setting on the water?

The onset of gales and prolonged heavy downpours in the days that followed told us winter was upon us. Chan tiptoed round all water and mud as if it might dissolve his feet: Zen and Marma waded into any puddles they came across and delighted in getting as much mud on themselves as possible, happily bringing much of it into the house. There seemed to be more that divided these two very different breeds of dog than united them!

6 Great Escapes

Mel had always relished her ability to escape over the years. Whether from the confines of the house when the children were growing up or later when she was rattling around in it on her own, she had managed to get away from it all by riding, going shopping or attending various keep-fit classes. Now that she had me to bump into throughout the day, her occasional days in Exeter where she met up with Tricia or, more frequently, her days in Truro to have her hair done were important opportunities to get away for a few hours.

While the house always seemed strangely quiet to me on those days, I, too, relished the chance to organise my days exactly as I wanted. Usually this meant luxuriating in doing everything at a leisurely pace or not at all if I thought it could wait.

It was on one such day, when James had also gone off shopping for clothes for his new job which he was due to start soon, that I delayed putting the horses out until I'd walked the dogs, the lovely sunny November day I had got up to having already deteriorated into a much murkier, wetter affair. At the top of the field my usually inspiring view was quite depressing as I watched the mist of penetrating drizzle swirl like smoke among the trees in the valley below. The dogs were no more enthusiastic than I was to hang around any longer than necessary and so, for once, they needed no encouragement to turn for home before any serious rain arrived.

I went through the gate and after Zen and Marma had followed me into the drive I turned to look for Chan. A Basenji through and through, he was either not where you wanted him to be or actively going about his usual purpose in life which was to try and work out the opposite of what you wanted him to do so he could do that. Following the others through the gate was, as usual, definitely not on his agenda. It was at that point that he obviously said to himself that it was the perfect time to walk round the field again, go and wind up the horses, still in their stables, or, more likely, revisit the scene of some mischief I had minutes before driven him away from!

How I wished on that occasion I had been able to spot him up to his usual naughtiness. Instead when I turned and scanned the field with my eyes I saw precisely... nothing. Where was he? I retraced my steps all round the five acre field but he was nowhere to be seen. The field even *felt* empty: I just knew he wasn't in it, despite the fact that the many undulations in its surface meant there were always parts of it out of view wherever you were standing. I went round again, calling and whistling, hoping that, for once, he would come to me. There was no sign of him or any clue as to where he had gone.

I had trained myself to cope with all eventualities over the years without panicking, even describing a personal strength in my annual appraisal form one year as my being panic-proof! 'Don't panic,' I would say to myself as the first line of defence, rapidly followed by, 'when's the time to start panicking?' On that occasion I rallied some logic. I knew where he could not have escaped: no Basenji would go near anything prickly, for example. That ruled out much of the boundary of the field with its impenetrable hedges of gorse, hawthorn and brambles, leaving me to focus on the old overgrown gateways and small gaps used by red deer in the area. Then my system failed. As I contemplated Mel's return later and my attempts to explain that I had somehow lost Chan, the first wave of panic hit me. I went round the field again, calling and whistling much louder, deciding I didn't care if I did startle the neighbours.

The only neighbours that turned out to be very startled indeed were the sheep in the field to the north. Ah, sheep! I just knew Chan would be in there running round in circles trying to round them up as I had seen him do with the horses. But no. The sheep were grazing peacefully in the drizzle as I knew they couldn't if there was an obvious danger in their midst.

It was just as logic returned and I started to work out my priorities for the next stage of the search that James returned. He could see I was getting increasingly edgy and started applying his own mind.

'Surely the most likely place he'd have gone is through a hedge into a neighbouring field,' he concluded.

'Yes,' I agreed, 'but if so he's in no immediate danger. But what if he got out into the lane? He could be hit by a car or, worse, find his way down to the main road.'

'Hmmm,' James said thoughtfully. 'So why don't you go up the lane while I go down it to see if he's there?'

'Good idea, but he'll probably run away if he sees either of us. Still, it might set our minds at rest before we start thinking about trudging across the fields.' After ten minutes or so of calling and whistling in all the hedges and gateways for a quarter of a mile either side of Upper Penwithiel, we both got back, glum faces telling of our lack of any success.

'God knows what your mother'll say,' I thought out loud gloomily.

'You stay here in case he comes back and I'll go and look in the big field at the top.'

'But there's no way you can get into it,' I sputtered with uncharacteristic pessimism.

'Want a bet?' came the characteristically optimistic reply.

James' departure into the dim damp distance left me alone with my thoughts once more. Chan could already be some way away and completely lost. Still not a year old, he had little chance of surviving with his thin, smooth coat geared up for the tropics rather than the Cornish winter. I had to do something so phoned the few houses in a radius of a mile. None had heard of a Basenji and were none-the-wiser after my brief description. 'If he's a hunting dog, maybe he'll start chasing sheep, then he could be in trouble,' said one neighbour. 'Better warn the chap who's got the sheep next to you. There's some as would shoot a dog on sight.' That I didn't want to hear so made sure the farmer concerned was aware.

'He wouldn't actually chase sheep,' I asserted confidently. 'Just sort of circle them and round them up. But he's only a puppy,' I added in the hope it would secure some leniency if he was caught in a field of sheep.

It was just getting dark when Mel phoned to say she was stuck in a traffic jam on the A30. For once I was pleased at the extra breathing space it gave me. 'What's new?' she asked, as she always did. For a split second I thought. Should I tell her now so she was prepared for the fact by the time she got home? For one thing it would be a shock whenever I told her. For another, there was a faint if dwindling chance Chan would turn up.

'Never mind darling. See you when we see you,' I replied as cheerfully as I could.

'Oh, is James back?' she asked.

'Yes,' I replied.

'Did he get the clothes he wanted?'

'Not sure,' I grunted.

'You must have noticed if he came in with some bags,' she asserted as only she could.

'Um...' I said vaguely, hoping the question would fade away.

'Typical man,' was all she said. 'Traffic's moving alright now. Be home in about a quarter of an hour.'

That at least gave me time to rapidly think about what else I should do, apart from composing what I was going to say when she got home, so as to soften the blow. In that time I phoned three local vets, the RSPCA and two police stations, each time having to run through my potted description of this unusual little dog. In the end I resorted to a comparison with a Jack Russell which seemed to satisfy them.

Minutes before Mel swooped up the drive, James arrived back, drenched through, his combat trousers doing a sterling job of camouflaging the streaks of mud that seemed to cover his lower half. As I picked out his features under the newly lit-up security light, I detected a self-satisfied grin. In his arms was an equally soaked and muddy little Basenji, shaking from head to toe.

'He must be frozen,' I concluded.

'It's not so much that as fear,' James said. He answered my puzzled expression: 'when I found him he was standing shivering with fear behind a gate on the far side of a field full of sheep. I could see he wanted to come through but he was obviously terrified of the sheep!'

My relief was overtaken by joy when Mel drove in, got out and came over to us. 'Who's taken you for a walk in the rain, then?' she cooed at Chan as she took him from James. 'He's shaking,' she said. 'You are cruel, taking him out in this,' she admonished gently.

'Wait until you hear what really happened,' said James with a wicked grin.

Chan spent the entire evening curled up asleep on Mel's lap.

The time was fast approaching for James to effect his own escape - from home, from Cornwall, and from, well, childhood. This time we all knew it was a permanent parting of the ways. Of course the reasons for it were entirely positive: he was going to make his own way in the world in a career of his own choosing. But time began to hang heavily on us as the day approached.

It was with a strange feeling of déjà vu that Mel and I planned to take him out for the day before he left, much as we'd done before his abortive departure for Salisbury two years earlier. This time, however, having just had confirmation that he had attained his Masters in Management and Marketing, he was going with a definiteness of purpose that had been lacking before.

It was a day or two later that he went off again to shop for clothes. Later that morning I popped into Bodmin to get him a roller ball pen as a small going away present - I knew it wouldn't be high on his list of priorities! I saw him coming down Bore Street towards me with a sheepish grin on his face. He had been looking for some new trousers but decided to go to Plymouth instead. We stopped for a brief chat before going our separate ways. Then it hit me. I had quite taken it for granted that he was around and had not therefore been unduly surprised to bump into him. But in just over a week he'd be gone and then there would be no question of a chance meeting like that again. A very important era was about to end.

So was another. In a way that only the younger generation can, Andrew announced to us his split from Amanda - by e-mail! Mel and I were very sad for both of them. Having no idea what the future held for them we simply hoped that whatever it was they would both find happiness again.

There was no let up in the wet weather that week with local flood warnings and, in Lostwithiel, floods. It was hardly surprising therefore to find that the day out we had arranged with James was going to be wet. What better place to experience the full force of the weather than Land's End, where James decided he'd like to go. It wasn't just that the rain when we arrived was truly horizontal but it was freezing too. Somehow we fought our way against it to walk along the cliff-top before seeking refuge in a cafeteria. In season it would have been uninspiring: out of season and on that dismal day it was depressing. The lunch was not quite what we'd had in mind but we did get the chance to recover the feeling in our faces and hands.

'I'm really enjoying my last day out in Cornwall,' James announced with a rueful smile, 'but I was hoping to enjoy the fresh air and exercise.'

'We'll drive back along the south coast and stop somewhere for a walk later,' I suggested.

'Somewhere we can stay vertical, preferably,' he said.

For obvious reasons, Mel was a little subdued that day but on the way back she pored over the map in search of somewhere we could spend part of the afternoon together before making our way home.

'I've got it,' she suddenly said enthusiastically.

'What?' I asked, still mentally scratching my head.

'Logan Rock.'

'What's that?' James asked.

I explained that I'd heard it was a huge stone of some fifty or sixty tons so finely balanced on another that it was possible to rock it. When we parked the car by the Logan Rock Inn in Treen it was still raining. A small sign pointed us along a footpath across the fields towards the sea. The wind was gusting rain around our faces and mud was splattering up around our lower legs. Normally we would not have put ourselves through such discomfort knowing we could return on a better day. However, we knew we would not be returning with James and so we battled on down the last steep slope towards the rock. Mel and I exchanged glances. James picked up the gist of our communication.

'You don't really want to go any further do you?' *We* did but our bodies didn't. 'It's OK, I'll be quicker on my own,' he smiled. We each gave a weak smile in return.

'Are you sure?' asked Mel.

'Yup. Won't be long.' James half ran, half galloped down the steep path and then up again the other side until he was a small figure in the distance.

'He did that quickly,' I observed with admiration.

'He's young and fit,' Mel sighed wistfully. My mind wandered. Oh to be able to do what he was doing with such obvious ease and relish.

'It reminds me of when he was a boy,' I said. 'He always enjoyed that sort of thing. So did Andrew and Justin. I can see them now in the adventure playground at Wilton House.'

'Yes, I remember...' nodded Mel in my direction as I half stood and half sat on a rock, resting my hands on my knees, slightly out of breath after the trek across the fields. '...as if it was yesterday.' Soon James was heading round a ridge high up on the rock, looking for the best way forward. 'I hope he doesn't slip on those wet rocks,' she added.

'I don't think there's any danger of that. He's leaping around like a gazelle!' I replied.

'Yes, but you know what he's like. Frightened of nothing. Remember his mountain bike crashes?'

'And his argument with a spring board.'

'Exactly,' said Mel from beneath a frown that flickered briefly at the thought of the stitches he had had in his scalp. Looking back to where he had just been we could no longer see him. 'Where's he gone?' she asked rhetorically.

'He's probably found the route up somewhere.'

'Where exactly is the rock anyway?' she asked.

'No idea,' I replied with a small shrug. It was some fifteen minutes before we saw James' tall figure again, leaping down from rock to rock. Minutes later he was back, having run practically the whole way up the steep slope towards us. He was fresh-faced and wet with rain and sea spray.

'You're soaked,' said Mel, relieved to see he had not obviously come to any harm.

'Did you find it?' was all I wanted to know.

'Not sure. I couldn't see anything that was obviously it but asked a man and woman in walking gear. He waved vaguely in an upwards direction on the far side of the rocks. I went up as far as I could but there was a sheer drop into the sea. As it was so slippery I decided not to risk it.' Despite her efforts to disguise it, Mel took a small intake of breath.

'But did you a see a stone that looked as though you could rock it?' I asked.

'Don't think so,' replied James. We were all a little disappointed and James was cross with himself for the rest of the afternoon for not finding it.

'Sorry you had a fruitless trek,' Mel said on the way home.

'It's OK. I'll come and look for it when I'm home again some time,' he said brightly. He never has.

Later we read an explanation of the fact that the stone stopped rocking in 1824 after being dislodged by a small naval detachment after a drink or two too many. They were ordered to restore the rock to its original position. They eventually did but it rocked no more!

We were becoming increasingly worried about the puppies' growth, particularly Zen's. Both had got to the gangly stage, with front feet turned outwards instead of straight to the front but Zen had also become weak in the quarters, almost as if he had become too heavy for his muscles to support him. After consulting with old friends Ron and Freda Lewis we switched to a different complete food. The problem, they thought, sounded like an excess of protein. 'You don't want more than twenty or twenty-two per cent. Most of the feed for puppies have far too much for the giant breeds,' Freda said with her usual authority.

We switched as soon as the new food could be delivered at a cost around double what we had been paying so we needed it to work for two reasons.

The day for James to depart for his new life in north Wiltshire was soon upon us. To give him time to find somewhere to live, his company had agreed to put him up in a local hotel for a month. We offered to go with him so as to avoid the horrible sensation for him of arriving somewhere strange on his own and, we would have to confess, because we wanted to see where he was going to be. When they heard about the arrangement both Justin and Andrew, in collusion, told us they'd be there too. Lunch, it seemed, was on me! The result was that what could have been a glum occasion for Mel and me turned out to be fun and it was so much easier for us to bid our farewells when we were leaving them all together.

We got home to a very empty house, except, of course, for four dogs and four cats!

It was just forty-eight hours later, when phoning James to see how things were going, that I elicited from him the concern that he might become a workaholic. This, it turned out, was prompted by his early observation that most people in his office started work at 8.30am and were still working at 6.30pm. Stifling my amusement at the very thought of his concern after so short a time, particularly after his year of relatively relaxed working hours in Asda in Cornwall, I gave him a little talk about the realities of life in a demanding job and what counted for normal pressures working in a marketing environment: there were always going to be tight deadlines to meet. This 'excitement', I reminded him, was one of the key reasons he selected his career following the results of the psychometric tests his career counsellor had given him almost two years before.

It was just under a week later that we received yet another of those phone calls every parent of a young adult dreads. Justin, then twenty-one, managed to put a nasty unwanted dent in the front of his car in Bournemouth, just after returning to college for the winter semester. It turned out that while waiting to enter a busy roundabout, the car he had been following moved forward then stopped unexpectedly and he didn't. Yet again, he had a lucky escape, was unhurt and the car's damage was liveable with.

The two Dane puppies also had an escape which turned out to be lucky. Having been well and truly thwarted by the impregnable fence James and I had put up, they decided to climb the small bank inside the entrance gate and launch themselves over the fence next to it and onto the driveway down to the lane. We hadn't seen them go but had soon missed them on account of their quietness. The means of their escape was quite apparent as there was a hole through the holly part of the hedge and muddy footprints on the cobbles. They had got no further than the post-box where they were carrying out a forensic search of the area with their noses.

Once again, after returning them whence they came, I had to make urgent additions to the fortifications, checking the whole perimeter of the garden for potential breakout points! I found a gap deep in what I had previously regarded as an impenetrable hedge and got viciously attacked by holly and brambles as I made sure that even that well-hidden gap was plugged with stock fence.

Just a day or two later even this was found flattened as our two little darlings left no stone unturned in their implacable drive to escape. Yet more wire, staples and posts finally turned this small stretch into a bomb-proof barrier.

It was bright but windy the following day when Mel and I crossed over into Devon on an unusual mission. We were headed for a small airfield at Dunkeswell near Honiton. This was where Andrew proudly told us he would be making his first parachute jump, in aid of Marie Curie Cancer Care. If he raised more than the required amount in sponsorship he got to make a tandem free fall jump.

Having had great problems overcoming a fear of flying myself some thirty-five years earlier, my heart was in my mouth as I contemplated standing on the ground and watching my eldest son jump from the open door of a plane, knowing I could never contemplate that myself. Mel's anxiety was less personal, having never had any fear of flying, but was the simple concern of a mother for one of her precious offspring. In the end I had overcome my problem in the weeks before our trip of a lifetime to Australia in 1984. I had been taught by a clinical psychologist that the secret was to breath diaphragmatically so as to disperse the build-up of adrenaline that was causing the problem. This explanation was so simple and matter-of-fact that I accepted it, tried it and found it worked so never had a problem again.

Our purpose in being there was not only to give Andrew moral support but to share in what was promising to be a very real achievement of his own. It was he, after all, who had had to be gently pushed along the ramparts of the castle on St Michael's Mount with his eyes closed so as not to see the sheer drop below when he was eleven. In the event it turned out that it was he who was giving support to us by reassuring us that not only was he calm and relaxed but actually excited about having the opportunity to do it!

The usual hour or so's wait while the jumpers had a brief period of instruction became protracted as the bad weather closing in put everything on hold. It was the combination of wind and poor visibility that threatened the safety of the jumps due to take place. We found our emotions being tugged in opposite directions. A small part of us was relieved at the prospect of any risk receding as the likelihood of a jump that day declined. On the other hand it would be an anticlimax for us after our journey up that morning as well as a major disappointment for Andrew, indeed a denial of his chance to demonstrate his courage in making such a jump.

It was therefore with a curious mixture of relief and renewed anxiety that we saw the low cloud vanish and felt the wind drop. The jump was on again after all! The call came for the day's contingent of volunteers to make their way to the 'departure lounge'. We were able to follow and watch as the small group were kitted out with suits, helmets and harness. There was a spread of ages, of both sexes, most but not all first-timers.

Andrew was resplendent in bright red from head to foot and in very high spirits as I got him to pose for a few photographs. Eventually it was the turn of his small group to be led out to the light aircraft that was to take them to a height of about ten thousand feet. One look at that made me mutter to Mel, 'you wouldn't get me up in one of those!' It wasn't the fact that it was a small aircraft - I had been in several during my few years involved in business in the Channel Islands - but that it had no door on one side. As the small machine wound itself up for the dash along the runway, I imagined sitting in it as Andrew was. My heart would definitely have been in my mouth as I contemplated the very moment of ejecting into nothing minutes later.

Once aloft the plane took some fifteen minutes to drone its way up to its allotted height. We began to wish away the wind and low cloud that had seen fit to return at that precise moment in the proceedings. As the small insect circled high above us for another ten minutes, its sound barely audible above the wind, we began to contemplate the extreme let down of a cancellation at that late stage. Mel and I and supporters of the others on board periodically strained our eyes against the brightness of the sun behind the thin cloud. 'There's one,' said the girl friend of one of the young men we had watched getting ready earlier. All eyes turned heavenward in the attempt to identify the jumper. All they could make out was a tiny silhouette.

Our task was to be slightly easier in that respect as Andrew was not only in red but the tallest of all, including his instructor, to jump that day. As each pair emerged from the side of the plane my thoughts leapt on the assumption it was Andrew. I really was going through the, to me, agonising process of leaping into the unknown.

'No, that's not him,' said Mel in answer to my unasked question as the second pair went. 'That's him, I'm sure,' she said excitedly when the third pair, harnessed together, emerged, rolled over and then fell for some seconds, which seemed like minutes, before their parachutes finally opened.

'How do you know?' I asked, unsure, having been wrong twice already.

'I just do,' Mel replied emphatically. While not wanting to miss taking in the full spectacle with my naked eye, neither did I want to miss the chance of a good photographic record of the event. I waited just long enough to be sure it really was him before raising the camera with its big zoom lens to my right eye. It was at that precise instant of recognition that I felt my chest swell with the same pride I had felt at James' graduation in Swansea more than two years earlier.

The different stages of Andrew's childhood flashed through my mind bringing me up short at the overdue realisation that he was not only a man but a man of character and courage.

'I'm so proud of him,' trilled Mel. 'It's funny but as soon as I knew it was him all my worry lifted. I'm so glad we came.'

'Of course,' I grinned back through my camera strap as he finally got close enough for a good shot, just before he and his instructor landed, like some giant two-headed arachnid!

We strode over to greet him after he had been unclipped from his instructor and had released himself from the parachute which it was someone else's job to capture and refurl. His face was flushed with a combination of the effects of exhilaration and the icy cold wind.

'That was brilliant, really cool,' he grinned. His speech was quickened by the volume of adrenaline still rushing through his system. 'I want to do it again,' he pronounced without waiting for the question hovering on my lips.

'Really?' I asked.

'Oh, yes,' he replied eagerly. 'As soon as I can afford it.'

'We're so proud of you,' said Mel as she gave him an enthusiastic hug. She also had in mind the charity Andrew had just raised a couple of hundred pounds for. Quite apart from her own friend who'd been stricken by breast cancer, Andrew's best friend had also lost his mother from the disease at a young age. It was unstated but we knew he had quietly raised it with them in mind.

As had already been arranged, he returned to Cornwall for a few days with us, followed by James and Justin the next day. Andrew was rightly proud in describing his intriguing tale in great detail to his brothers that evening. James' eyes in particular lit up in interest at the prospect of another challenge in the offing but we all knew that day had definitely been Andrew's.

❧❧❧

On the Saturday evening it was another of those occasions when our sons insisted that Mel and I defied the onset of creaking bones, in my case, and aching muscles in hers: we were going ten-pin bowling in Plympton! As ever, it was an evening of intra-family rivalry. There were two keenly contested results: first, to win and, second, not to come last. After toying with us to begin with, James soon struck out, literally, in the lead. But he wasn't the only one to get strikes that evening - we all did, just not as many. But the biggest strike awaited our return home. That evening the TV aerial and phones were taken out by a lightning strike for the second time. On this occasion, however, my deployment of a surge protector, at some cost, saved the computer. I was most impressed when phoning the manufacturer for a replacement a day or two later to be told there was no charge. When I queried this I was simply told, 'it's done its job sir, so we replace it free of charge.'

The storm had raged through the evening and threatened to continue into the night. On a visit to the stables last thing, the sound of hay being steadily chomped as I approached reassured me: the horses were quite unperturbed. The same could not be said for poor Zen who lay curled in a tight crescent on his bed, muzzle resting on front paws, the whites showing as he rolled his eyes at each thump of thunder!

The next day, Sunday, our old friend Rodney Bamford returned to replace the amplifier on our TV aerial, on the boundary about a hundred yards to the west of the house. Shortly afterwards the three boys were gone again.

My final task in November was to visit the offices in Shropshire of the company of which I was a director, via an overnight stay in Bredwardine. Away for barely twenty-four hours, my return was amply rewarded by the appearance in the drive of a small tricoloured Basenji, with an inquisitive - almost accusing - expression on his face, who had come out with his mistress to greet me. He then proceeded to follow me everywhere for the next few minutes. Shortly afterwards I sat in my study opening my e-mails with two rather large Great Dane puppies curled up at my feet wondering where I had been. Mel, too, fussed around me, telling me what had happened in my absence and soon had a sumptuous meal on the table. No man could want for a greater welcome.

7 Second Degree

In came December and out came milk teeth: the Dane puppies were finally emerging from their teething phase, every bit as uncomfortable for them - and disturbing for us - as for any human baby. In this case, however, they took it out on the nearest object rather than a teething ring, despite being supplied by Mel with various hide dog chews and rubber toys. They seemed to prefer the kitchen table legs!

That was not the only indication of time passing. Both puppies continued to grow apace but Zen's front legs, while straighter, still gave cause for concern and his quarters were so weak he could not help sitting down each time Marma pounced on him with her front paws. It soon became apparent that she did this deliberately, enhancing her increasingly obvious status as leader of the pack - after myself and Mel of course - though I would not be so unsubtle as to put the last two in a particular order! For some reason Mel took exception to my description of her as top bitch!

The extremely lengthy wet period continued: the ground was so sodden that all the water running off the fields above us came straight down without being absorbed, through our drive and into the lane. I made a mental note to check that any future house we might move to in Cornwall must also have this feature of being on a slope and not at the bottom of one: watching the water go by was infinitely preferable to having it collect around us!

Jeanette and Mike Callan made a second visit to see how Zen and Marma were progressing. I explained my reservations about Zen being apparently too big for his own strength and Jeanette, too, was a little puzzled but thought he would probably grow out of it. She thought she might ask the opinion of Avril Thorndyke, a successful breeder and exhibitor of Danes we remembered from our own showing days who was now living in Cornwall. She, apparently, had once had a similar problem with one of her big male puppies. What was without doubt was the fabulous temperaments of our two and the fact that they both recognised Jeanette instantly. Once more when they had driven out into the lane to return home the two pups cried at the gate!

It was as I travelled up to London for my December board meeting that I came up against the first severe consequence of the prolonged heavy rain. Part of the railway line between Plymouth and Exeter had been washed away and the resulting delay and coach link led to my normal four hour journey turning into one of six! The icing on the cake was that we got to Reading seven minutes earlier than the revised arrival time with the amazing consequence that we were held there for seven minutes to keep us to the original revised time, as it were. It could only happen here!

The day after my return home yielded the second severe consequence, in the form of a frantic phone call from Mel. She had gone to do a major shop at Tesco's in St Austell when the continuing rain was relatively light. There was a cloudburst while she was in the shop and when she drove home in the dark along the main road she hit a huge puddle at the bottom of a hill which hadn't been there earlier - the puddle, that is, not the hill which had been there all along and still is! The outcome was a bent exhaust pipe between the manifold and catalytic converter, causing a leak accompanied by impaired performance and increased noise. Luckily the huge cost of putting it right was covered by the insurance though, on second thoughts, after the large excess and subsequent loss of no-claims bonus I probably ended up paying for most of it after all!

One disadvantage of Zen's and Marma's rapid growth was their ability to be able to see and, worse, get at items of interest which had previously been out of their reach. This first became apparent when we returned to the kitchen early one evening, having left them for ten minutes while putting the horses away for the night. A rather nice little basket full of apples which had been sitting on the dresser was on the floor in minute pieces with the apples scattered to the four corners of the room, each with a small piece nibbled out of it. A rapid review led to the repositioning of everything which we thought could now be at risk.

A few days later Justin returned home from college for Christmas to face our usual request to produce our Christmas cards. He had long protested that he was a designer and not an artist but once again we prevailed: the result was not only better than anything we could have bought but had the added attraction of being unique. Naturally a small sum exchanged hands adding to the depleted student pot at such a critical time of year. The relief a few days later was palpable when he discovered the flat battery in his car was not terminal, so to speak, but the result of the excessive demands of the huge speakers he had acquired and installed in his boot that term. He reacted coolly to my own humorous comments on the situation which related to the power of the speakers far exceeding the output of the poor little Ford's one litre engine.

Jeanette returned shortly afterwards bringing Avril to have a look at Zen. She was in no doubt. 'He's just going to be huge,' she said. 'You must be very careful not to over exercise him or you'll ruin him. But don't worry. I think he'll be alright if you keep him wrapped in cotton wool.' The passing image was brief as I took on board her comments.

'You mean no exercise at all?' I asked.

'That's right. Just restrict the area he can move around in and let him rest a lot. It'll be worth it in the end.' I had no doubt about it but it wasn't just Zen I was thinking of. Marma was still very active with none of Zen's problems. Who was going to explain to her that she was no longer going to be able to play boisterously with her brother?

My long held mental picture of one day owning a really *Great* Dane was beginning to shape up as a real possibility so I needed no second telling. From then on a more sedate life for the puppies beckoned.

That was more than could be said for us. A day or two later Dandy arrived on a windowsill outside the sitting room just as it was getting dark. For once she had taken a leaf out of Moss' book, as the mouse she brought in for us was not only alive but totally unscathed, aiding its successful attempt to escape as soon as she dropped it. Mel and I, at first watched but soon helped by Justin, began the process of lifting each chair in turn. As soon as we found the small terrified creature it shot under the next one, eventually disappearing under the TV stand. Dandy, so obviously active in catching it in the first place, then decided it was far more interesting watching our futile efforts than joining in herself.

We settled on the idea of reinforcements and brought Cloey in to help. We didn't bother with Moss who we knew would just curl his feet up under him to watch us in comfort. The last we saw of the mouse was when it dived under the hi-fi cabinet. I was most concerned at its failure to reappear after we moved the heavy piece of furniture, imagining it living on the plastic sleeving of however many yards of wiring were inside it. Certainly it had made its last appearance that particular evening! If cats could laugh I know they would have been doing so then.

❧

It was 8.00am when I looked up at the electric-blue sky, open-mouthed in wonder. It was marbled with a myriad of small puffs of cloud, each lit up with crimson-pink light from the sun rising from below the line of black conifers on the sky-line to the east. It was my time of day for checking the drive for any piles left by the dogs. We always kept buckets and shovels handy in strategic places for the purpose, half filled with diluted Jeyes fluid, and I had to replenish them. An hour or so later, after the dogs had been let out, I noticed that the fluid had disappeared from one up by the barn. Although I felt certain they wouldn't have touched anything so pungent smelling and foul tasting, panic led me to conclude that one of the Danes had drunk it. I checked, heart in mouth, for any signs they had and kept checking throughout the morning.

A report on the local TV news told us, as if we might not have noticed, that Cornwall had had only nine days without rain in the last three months. The only thing which we had not noticed was those nine days! If it had been in Noah's day, the whole area would have been deafened by the sound of nails being hammered into thousands of arks under panic-driven construction.

Later Dandy earned her keep for the day by catching the mouse in the sitting room when it ill-advisedly poked its head from under the TV stand. I rushed to pick her up, the small creature gripped between her teeth still very much alive. As I went to take her outside to drop it where it could escape she decided instead to prolong the game by letting it go while still inside. There followed some minutes of frantic activity with Mel and I lifting each chair in turn in the sure knowledge that Dandy would rearrest it on sight! Knowing her propensity for devouring live mice we had even drafted Marma in as back-up. In a moment of confusion, when I thought Mel had hold of the chair while she thought I had, we managed to drop it on Dandy who niftily reversed out of the way with a squeal, thankfully unharmed, while Marma focused her attention on the cat. If mice could laugh that one certainly would have from the safety once more of the hi-fi cabinet.

When going up to the barn in the afternoon I spotted a small milky-coloured puddle draining onto the nearby grass: there was to my huge relief a hole in my bucket! My faith in the sense of the Danes, at least in that respect, was reinforced.

❧

Mel and I, like most parents, had taken great interest and delight in the way our sons had developed over the years. It was fascinating to try to attribute this or that behaviour or characteristic to one of us, one of our parents or grand-parents and to determine which others were environmental, that is down to the way we had brought them up or they had been taught at school. It was never easy to be sure whether a blaze of temper here or an unacceptable action there was down to their copying one of us or taking after Uncle Cyril or someone!

On balance we were pleased to discover that by their early to mid-twenties we had three tolerably civilised, caring, accomplished and responsible adult sons.

It was different with the animals of course but not that much! Smartie, after all, had been a last resort for Mel. Having suffered at the hands, or should it be hooves, of one or two rogue horses in the past, culminating in her loss of nerve, the whole rationale in buying a six-month-old foal was that it had not been ruined by poor handling or training. In short, Smartie was going to be as well or badly behaved as we were able to make her. Of course it was also right to ensure the right hereditary factors were present, hence our emphasis on her temperament, courtesy of her ancestors!

She was now fully grown, well behaved and trustworthy in all situations so Mel was well satisfied with the outcome. Smartie had been tested in numerous situations and it was a credit to both her and Mel that on the one or two occasions that horse and rider had parted company Mel always quickly accepted responsibility. For my part I was not entirely convinced the flat cutaway saddle was entirely blameless.

This is not to imply that the end result was some kind of dull, immaculately behaved Dobbin-like creature - far from it. She was bright, lively and inquisitive to the point of being a nuisance at times but she was trustworthy and sensible, always seeming quite shocked whenever anything went wrong on a ride.

Max, of course, had been like that for most of the time I had owned him. His only little foible was that small things would sometimes worry him or even make him jump but he had never been responsible for my ridiculous acrobatic antics on the occasions the earth had come up to hit me! Naturally, as a big horse not absolutely certain where his four corners were at any one time, he had stood on my foot once or twice - a not-to-be-recommended way of assessing a horse's weight. To be fair he was always mortified on hearing the various expletives that found their way to my lips on those occasions. This is not to say that he was clumsy - he wasn't. In fact he could be amazingly nimble: watching nigh on three-quarters of a ton charging full tilt down a one in two slope and stopping on a sixpence at a fence was impressive. No doubt all this had as much to do with his early German schooling as the hereditary kindness of most large horse breeds. An endearing little requirement of his was that all doors or gates he was being asked to go through should be fully opened first: if they weren't he did the necessary with his nose before passing through.

The cats too had matured as well as we could possibly have expected but each with his or her own special characteristics. Daisy, in her dotage, was as soft and loving as ever but just more frail. Certainly her grit in standing her ground against all comers - young Danes and Basenji alike - was as much sheer experience as inbred Burmese courage! Cloey, the smudge-faced chocolate tortie was a law unto herself, not least because of her swishing tail. Far from being something she was to grow out of, it became her trademark. It was not a temper-related thing but just a communication thing. It said, 'I might be a bit smaller than the others and strangely marked but I'm just as important.' And she was. Independent too. Not for her the warmth of a convenient lap but rather an aloof vantage point from which she could observe what was going on. Certainly she purred instantly when you picked her up but just as quickly she would make her escape. It was usually her that came in last each evening and it was always her we could see darting along the hedge at the top of the field in search of something interesting in summer. Sometimes she would proudly present the household with the prize of a half-eaten mouse or, sadly dead, bird.

Her slate-blue half-sister Dandy was different again. While a little standoffish in the company of the others, when she was on her own with you she clambered all over your lap, rolling first this way then that so as to make sure you appreciated the time she was so graciously lavishing on you. Her trademark was a most mournful miaow which she emitted like a marker beacon as she wandered round the house in search of someone as if to say, 'it's only me but I'm lonely. Where is everyone?' She, too, hunted from time to time, usually arriving on the window sill outside the sitting room with whatever it was still alive and able to rapidly escape as soon as we freed it. She never seemed sufficiently moved to go after it again.

Her lilac brother Moss was developing into the real character of the three younger Burmese. Not for him any timidity in the presence of the over-attentive young dogs. If you can't beat 'em, join 'em seemed to be his philosophy. He was always ready to show his trust by stretching out with them in front of the fire, retreating only when one of them took him too literally and started to play over-roughly. Even then he would re-enter the fray moments later when he began to feel he was missing something. Although he would go off each day when the others were let out, he never took hunting seriously. He was simply curious and was as interested in stalking the horses from a vantage point in the barn as anything else. He could sometimes be spotted creeping along the top of the partitioning of the stables for a closer look. He sometimes had to be admonished for scratching the valance of our bed if he managed to creep in unnoticed but it was always with a heavy heart: he was permanently happy and playful. Even when he announced his arrival in my study on a rainy day by skidding with wet feet across a newly printed out sheet from my computer, my crossness was always short-lived. He would somehow deflect it by studiously playing with an elastic band he found in the 'bits and pieces' tray on my desk.

Chan, while fully grown for a Basenji, was falling further and further behind in the height-from-the-ground stakes. How could you explain adequately, to remove that permanent wrinkled frown of bewilderment, that the ability of the Dane puppies to pass under him had been reversed permanently? Instead the growls we had come to associate with worry became cries for help whenever his threats to Zen, on raising himself to his full height, were increasingly ignored. Somehow we would have to help him come to terms with this new, unwelcome from his point of view, order. He continued good-naturedly, however, to prize Moss as an honorary canine or was it the other way round?

One advantage his relatively small size did give him was the ability to jump onto a lap. It was something he came increasingly to exercise as a right. Mel loved it, having always hankered after a small dog. While Angus was fairly small he had always been a fairly aloof little dog, as American Cockers can be: aloof though not unaffectionate. Those two, in fact, tended to ignore each other which was a blessing since Angus was continuing to lose his sight and could ill afford to fall out with anyone. The Danes, however, seemed strangely intrigued by the little black dog who happily went about his business and they didn't mind at all when he occasionally bumped into them by accident. Zen in particular began to be almost protective to Angus, not least because he got worried by the aggression of Chan. Angus was a kind of ally, albeit one who was unlikely ever to take up arms in his defence!

Marma was already developing her character. When sleeping she often took up what appeared to be a somewhat promiscuous position, lying on her back and legs apart but quite dead to the world. When awake, however, she was quite unmistakably the boss. Zen was kept very much in his place by her. She was quite ruthless in exploiting his weak quarters and would bowl him over if he tried to compete with her. The combination of her bossiness and Chan's aggression caused us to worry he might develop an inferiority complex so we found ourselves trying to boost his ego whenever the others weren't around! We also knew we had a more important reason to protect him: his still-rapid growth meant his bones were not only not fully formed but relatively soft. We performed dog psychology gymnastics in our efforts to bolster him mentally and physically while allowing Marma to fulfil the natural role of leadership she had taken upon herself.

Despite Zen's shaky self-image, he was nonetheless developing his own endearing little foibles. He seemed to have spiritually inherited directly from Jake the propensity to 'talk'. This was always a sign of pleasure which he exhibited when he realised something nice was in the offing such as a meal or a walk. It went something like, 'wo-wo-wo,' on a declining scale! It was then that he also began what was to become the established behaviour of sticking fairly close to me on walks round the field. While this was clearly for the purposes of self-preservation at that stage in his life, it enabled us to form a good working relationship: I knew he would never be difficult to control.

After a further successful attempt at catching what was already being referred to as the indoor mouse, Dandy carelessly let it go again. It was to be some time before it made its next appearance.

We made our next appearance at a graduation ceremony, this time in

Bath. James had got his desired degree result and we, together with Andrew and Justin, were there in support. Mel and I were delighted that the other two boys had decided to join us, especially Andrew who had not, so far anyway, taken a degree himself.

It was a more mature and confident James who once again strode on to the platform to accept his certificate which, as before, was a dummy one because the real ones had yet to be produced. As well as pride I felt a strange, distant emotion, one which echoed that I had experienced at the age of twenty-two when friends of mine had emerged from university. It was a feeling of having missed something I shouldn't. It was momentary, of course, but still there. I wondered whether any similar thoughts had flickered across Andrew's mind.

Following a relaxed and noisy meal in a nearby pub we all scattered once more to our respective points of the compass.

Dandy, we discovered the next day, had no compass or, at least no sense of direction when up a tree, that is: Mel came in from the garden, cradling her in her arms to announce that while hanging out some washing in the rare sunshine she had heard a commotion behind her. She had turned just in time to see Dandy slither backwards off a bough of the cherry tree and down through its branches to the ground. She nursed a few grazes and bruises on her chin and legs for a few days afterwards, hiding herself on top of the kitchen cupboards. I had no idea cats were not naturally good at climbing trees!

Christmas was rapidly upon us once more and Father Christmas got locked in a stable on the 23rd December! He was not so much tending to his reindeer but mucking out after the horses when he heard a metallic clunk. His little dog had accompanied him up to the barn where he had acquired a fondness for racing round and round, up onto the stacked bales of hay and into and out of the stables. He had closed the door of the stable he was working in, unbolted, to stop the small Basenji getting in the way or, more accurately, making off with the future contents of the barrow! The clunk had been the arrival of the kick-bolt on the outside of the door at the bottom of its bracket. After uttering a few very un-Father Christmas-like words I was forced to lean over the door and use my horse pooper-scooper to hook the lever up and effect my escape.

It was on Christmas Eve that Marma effected her own escape. After being unable to find her in the garden we hunted up and down the lane before Mel spotted her, nose to the ground, zigzagging her way up the field, quite oblivious to the horses. After coaxing her back to the safer environment of the garden, I set about finding the means of her exit. I found no gaps at the bottom of the several hundred feet of stock-fencing James and I had so lovingly installed some months before. Unbelievably, the only possible gap, barely big enough for her to squeeze through, was at the end of the five feet high stone wall running between the house and the barn. It was just twelve inches wide at the narrowest point and she would have had to have persisted in walking along the ledge for about forty feet to find the gap behind a dense shrub that enabled her to get out. Yet again, out came the gloves, hammer, staples and roll of fencing to block off what I now knew was the only remaining gap in our defences. As I peered over my shoulder, I found Marma inches from me watching, no doubt with wry amusement, as I set to.

It was not quite a white Christmas unless, that is, you lived on the top of Dartmoor. Snow was clearly visible in distant Devon from the Cheesewring near Minions on the top of Bodmin Moor when we went with the boys kite-flying in a freezing wind on Boxing Day. Clearly impressed, they decided to head off for Dartmoor two days later but this time to their relief and ours we stayed in the warm!

Then the snow finally did arrive on 30th December and we rushed up to the Cheesewring to take a look at a white Cornwall. The Moor itself lay under about three or four inches of snow, changing the view from the top dramatically. No longer was it an area of desolate scrub or heathland: it was now a scene from the Arctic. Further afield, such as the area around Upper Penwithiel, the snow was thinner, perhaps only a quarter of an inch or less. Even so the picture and the atmosphere were captivating. We savoured it knowing how rare it was. The boys, then twenty-five, twenty-three and twenty-one decided they were really fifteen years younger and began to enjoy it much as they had done so many years before with snowball fights, sliding down slopes, falling over at the bottom and then rolling downhill until they were white all over. Mel and I merely stood there, arms round each other and smiling at the thoughts of times we thought had gone forever.

On returning home we found that time had indeed gone forever: Cloey had finally outwitted the open-faced kitchen clock. Not only was the pendulum still once more but it was lying beneath the clock on the worktop as were the hands, pointing at nothing in particular!

8 Follow Me!

We are born to be either leaders or followers, we are often told. In my experience this is an over-simplification. It all depends on the circumstances. For example, there is no question that Marma is the leader of our little dog pack, after the humans of course. She always has been and would seem to bear out the 'leaders are born' theory. But there was no doubt that little Chan had his moments. I noticed one morning when I'd gone to let the dogs into the utility room from the garden for their breakfast that the Danes were nowhere to be seen. Chan was right there, however, and on seeing me begin to fill the bowls with food he ran out again. I went to see where he'd gone. He had shot round to the back of the house where, it turned out, Zen and Marma were waiting.

I watched as he 'told' them what was going on. Almost immediately they followed him round to the other side of the house and into the utility room. It was no one-off feat as he was to perform it again many times. I even began to use him to go and get them though it has to be said I needed to be able to demonstrate that there was a good reason - like food or a walk - for his doing so!

Just as the first day of May in Padstow heralds 'obby 'oss day, so the first day of January there means it's Darkie Day. It celebrates the arrival and liberation of slaves in the harbour generations earlier. In fact an MP, either too dim-witted or lazy to look into it, declared it racist and asked for the name to be changed a few years ago. It took the one black local resident at the time to explain that the festivities are the very opposite! Proud tradition won and on the 1st January, and Boxing Day, a band leads a group of singers and dancers, faces blackened, round the town. What they are doing is commemorating the joy expressed by those slaves so many years ago when they arrived in that most unlikely, for them, of destinations.

It was those unexpected sights and sounds which greeted us when Mel and I took James and Justin, Andrew having already returned to Wiltshire, for what we thought would be a quiet look round on a Bank Holiday. I really envy the Cornish their centuries-old traditions: it creates a feeling of security and belonging missing from most modern life in towns and cities these days.

On returning home, dear little Chan showed us his versatility. The first thing we always did on arriving back was to let the dogs out. He had developed his rounding-up skills into driving-out skills, nudging and worrying his larger but younger friends out of the door!

Then it was Justin's turn to pack and return to Bournemouth. That left James still with us for a few days before returning to his part of Wiltshire. He was clearly still in two minds about living there and so, while he was home, he went to investigate a marketing job on offer near Bodmin. Mel and I had a pact not to interfere or influence him in any way. While, as any parent would, we quietly hoped our son might live in Cornwall again, it was paramount that he took such a decision in what he judged to be his best interests. It was no real surprise to discover that after his interview he was offered the job nor that he had concluded it would not be a good career move. In our heart of hearts we knew he was right.

While his decision was not directly connected it did make ours easier. For some time we had been mulling over the possibility of moving further west. We were as certain as Justin so obviously was that his career in graphic design would take him away from Cornwall. He was due to graduate in July so we put Upper Penwithiel on the market with a view to repeating the trick we had pulled off on our move away from Wiltshire three years before. We aimed to move as soon as his college days came to an end just as we had done with James when he graduated. We did not want any feeling of uncertainty about home to get in the way of his final months' work. Predictably he took it all in his stride.

When we eventually exposed to all three boys our reservations about putting more miles between them and us, their reaction surprised us, though perhaps it shouldn't have. We had been really concerned to avoid doing anything which diminished their motivation to visit us. We need not have worried as they helped us to be more philosophical and put things into perspective just as we had done for them over the years.

'It might take us an hour longer to get to you,' reasoned Andrew, 'but we'll be much nearer to places we want to visit so we'll spend less time driving around Cornwall when we do come down.'

It was so logical, if true, that we both heaved a sigh of relief. 'Are you sure about that?' I asked, to test his assertion.

'Yes, of course. I'd rather be nearer places like Penzance and St Ives. And we'd still not be too far from Newquay and Truro.'

'Anyway,' added James, 'what's important is where you want to be. I'm happy to visit you wherever you are.' This, I knew without even glancing at her, would have moistened Mel's eyes. It did mine.

Sensing the effect of his brothers' reactions on us, Justin finished the job: 'we're going to be doing what we want and live in the best place for us so why shouldn't you?'

Days later we were due to be visited by a representative of one of Cornwall's prominent estate agencies to give us his valuation, paving the way for a final decision on our part.

While washing down the drive as I waited for him to arrive, I spotted Moss strolling across it in front of me, not a care in the world. Until, that is, Chan noticed him and went after him to investigate...followed by Marma and, in turn, Zen. Chan's interest then became rather more proprietorial causing Moss to glance casually over his shoulder. He then leaped effortlessly onto the small dry stone wall between the house and the side lawn, tail erect with the tip gently twitching. Chan skipped up behind him, followed slightly less confidently by Marma and altogether more clumsily by Zen. I stood in the late January sunshine, mouth falling open in wry amusement with hose pouring water aimlessly into a nearby shrub, at the wonderful sight of a Burmese cat followed, in single file, by a Basenji and two Great Danes, the last of which was picking his way gingerly along the eighteen inch parapet towards the gate into the lane. I watched, wondering what was to happen next, when Moss, feeling Chan's breath up his rear, nimbly hopped up onto the gate post and teetered across the double gates. On turning to see Chan stopped in his tracks but frantically trying to work out how to continue the pursuit, he seemed to toss his head contemptuously before effecting an elegant exit onto the safe ground the other side of the gate. The Indian file, so orderly up to that point, then disintegrated as quickly as it had formed. It was a sight I knew I would never forget in the years ahead, probably long after they'd gone...

The valuation was pretty much in line with what we had paid in 1998, adjusted for the house price inflation that had taken place since and so our course was set. We instructed the agency to proceed to put Upper Penwithiel on the market.

Later that day Dandy yet again brought us a very fit and healthy mouse. While waiting on the windowsill outside the sitting room for Mel to let her in, she dropped the mouse which survived the four foot drop to scuttle off into the nearest hedge. Dandy's priority had switched to being in the warm so she did not pursue it. A day or two later we found her chasing a live mouse round the sitting room. Was it yet another of her gentle catches or could it possibly be, we wondered, the same one which had defied our attempts to capture it a few weeks before? This kind streak was clearly genetic because a week later Cloey brought a small young bird, not long fledged, into the conservatory. As ever, the gift, presumably for us, was dropped inside the door. Before Mel could yell for me to come and deal with it, it shook its feathers and, somewhat uncertainly, flew up and away out into the garden while Cloey helped herself to some food from her bowl in the kitchen.

It was around this time that Chan developed his highly attuned approach to escaping from the kitchen practically every time we opened the door. Despite our efforts to outwit him by nipping through the narrowest of gaps so as to complete the manoeuvre in the quickest possible time - not so easy when clutching a mug of hot tea - his strategy of varying his direction and speed continued to win the day. Just as you cottoned on to his basic tactic of hiding under the table, positioning himself for the opportunity and shooting through your legs as the door opened, he would change to hiding on the small bottom shelf at the end of the kitchen units next to the door so as to be through the gap before you even looked for him! It was to be a running battle for many months before he eventually accepted your wishes to stay, well, for most of the time.

This is not to say that the Danes were angels: they were not. Marma, in particular, had proved difficult in a number of ways. Her speciality at that time was to be attracted to and then chew plastic. It was after she had started to chew the indicator repeaters on both sides of the Jag that I got cross. I knew that lashings of creosote on a fence stopped a horse - even a Morgan - from making a meal of it and so it was that the little orange box-shaped covers on the car took on a slightly browner hue from that point!

It was into February, with the snowdrops at their peak, and, in fact, on Andrew's birthday that the effect wore off and I found the chewed-up remains of one of the covers in the drive. I discovered that, as with any component with the Jaguar name on it, the cost of a replacement was painful. From then on the car was to be kept in the garage at all times.

It was the same day that, after Cloey threw up the remains of a chewed and swallowed mouse in the sitting room, we had reason to be grateful for Marma's strange eating habits. With no encouragement from us she showed she could despatch such remains just as quickly as she could a live one. But the next day, when I found that the corner of a worktop in the kitchen also held some attraction for her, out came the creosote again. This was to be another ongoing battle over the months. Zen, we knew, would never be the instigator of such uncivilised behaviour but we suspected that Marma egged him on so as not to be the only one in trouble! Of course the reason, while totally unacceptable, was the ongoing teething phase but one which, thankfully, we knew wouldn't last.

Mel had drummed into me over the years we had owned horses many common sense precautions. These ranged from always tying up a horse before attempting to put on its rug or pick out its feet, to never standing too close behind it in case it decided to hoof you or putting yourself in a position where it could tread on you: you should never sit on the ground when attending to its feet or legs, for example.

Suffice it to say I had gradually ceased to see the need for any of these safeguards, knowing as I did the gentle and careful nature of Max. To this day I have never had reason to regret placing my trust in him in this way. It was, however, this dropping of the guard in relation to more critical preventative measures, quite unrelated to the behaviour of the horse, that did result in little mishaps. For example, it was my laxity in not tightening the girth sufficiently on two previous occasions which had led directly to my parting company with the saddle. And so it was my slackness in leaving Max's head-collar on while he was loose in the barn that day that resulted in an incident so minor that it was funny, though on another occasion it might not have been.

I had been pottering around in the yard in front of the barn and was vaguely aware that Max had been watching me curiously with those huge benevolent brown eyes of his. Then after a few minutes I also slowly became conscious of the fact that he was standing unusually still. I went into the barn to investigate. In one of the supporting poles, some five-feet-six from the ground, was an old nail hammered over many years since. Max, bless him, had contrived to get the noseband of his head-collar (made of webbing) hooked under the head of the flattened nail. The odds, I knew, were against it. Calm as ever, he waited silently and still while I released him.

Dustbins soon hit the top of our agenda. We had been well aware of their attraction to a young Basenji in earlier months but had taken comfort from the fact that the combination of using the clips on the lids and 'discouraging' Chan whenever we caught him at it - ie yelling at him - seemed to have made it a thing of the past. But we had reckoned without his instinctive need to communicate with his younger giant friends. The first signs were obvious enough: we found the odd dustbin lying on its side. If we were untimely in our discovery then we also found the contents lying alongside it. If we were really unlucky we found them strewn all round the garden. After waiting too long for Marma and Zen to grow out of the habit - it being mere coincidence of course if we ever found Chan aiding and abetting them - there was only one short term solution: we had to keep the bins in the barn, protected by the metal field gates which were fitted across its entrance.

The two drawbacks of course were that we had further or, more accurately, Mel had further to go to deposit the rubbish in the bins and to move them every Wednesday to the bottom of the drive for the bin men to empty them. It was shortly after this new regime, in fact, when Zen decided at last to show us his mettle. The dogs happened to be out the next time the bins were due to be emptied. The noise of the truck naturally drew them away from whatever mischievous business they were up to. Marma, as the dominant one, started the process of barking as she usually did.

Then one of the men ambled towards the gate to say hello to them. The intensity of Marma's barking increased as he edged nearer to the gates and she backed away from them! Then Zen broke the habit of his lifetime so far and acted like the young adult male he was becoming. He not only started barking meaningfully for the first time but stood his ground and then advanced on the hapless man who, seeing his strategy of making friends crumble before his eyes, retreated uncertainly. I had watched this from a distance: having gone out to call the dogs away, I had decided to see what happened. After all, their prime role after being companions was to deter strangers and I did not want to discourage Zen's instinctive behaviour at that crucial point. If I had, his morale would have been shattered for ever!

In fact, it wasn't only the bins that had to seek temporary refuge in the barn. Being deprived of the more up-market Jaguar plastic, the dogs - well mainly Marma - had turned their attention to any plastic they could find on the boys' cars whenever they visited: we had managed to cram all three in the barn on more than one occasion. Then we also had to take care whenever we brought the horses in or out. A stray hoof here or there could easily create a need for a visit to a bodyshop and I don't mean for a wash down with ecologically friendly shampoo!

21st February brought news of the first outbreak of foot-and-mouth disease, in Essex. Mel and I instinctively knew that we had to cease riding out the horses immediately. It was not that there was any outbreak near us nor that there was any real danger of our horses picking it up from our field or the lane if there had been. But the Trevithicks next-door-but-one had a field full of cattle and the farm whose fields we had been given permission to ride round sometimes had cattle in one of their fields so we knew that we had an obligation to play safe. It was to be a day or two before we realised that not only was it a good idea to reassure both on this aspect but that it was appreciated as a small sign of moral support during what was going to be a very worrying time for them. I knew it was going to be another little challenge for Mel. Along with her other beliefs about horses - chestnuts are mad, mares are difficult, young mares are impossible for example - was one which said that horses which get insufficient exercise become uncontrollable. While Smartie was no chestnut, I knew without asking that the local farmers would not be the only ones to experience anxiety in the indeterminate period ahead.

In the same way as friends and family had queried our reasons for moving to Cornwall in 1998 so they wanted to understand why we were planning a move further west. Was it simply a question of sentimentality? Did we just want to live nearer to where our love had blossomed almost thirty years before? Not really, was the honest answer. Indeed the area we knew best around Ashton was not what we had in mind. The truth was complex: yes, we wanted to live nearer the sea. Why else come to Cornwall? But we didn't necessarily want to live on the coast. There were three good reasons for not wanting to: wind, holidaymakers and price! What was inescapable, however, was the draw we still felt to what can best be described as the Camborne - Helston - Penzance triangle.

No, it wasn't because we wanted to be in mining country, despite the quaintness of old engine houses - the worry of subsidence was too big a factor. It was a heady combination of wanting to be close to a good local community: no ghost village consisting largely of holiday cottages for us thank you; of wanting to live in a picturesque unspoilt landscape, and yet to be able to get to attractive coastline in, say, ten minutes. And of needing to be close to good riding of course.

Why hadn't we gone there in the first place? Mainly because we had had to view our original move as something of an experiment. If things hadn't worked out we had had the option of moving eastwards again. In particular we were very concerned about the effect on our immediate family. In the event, that had largely been beneficial: it had helped our three boys stand on their own feet as well as ensuring that not only did we see them for longer periods than we otherwise might but the time we shared was what is rather offputtingly referred to these days as quality time.

So, we concluded, the time had come to follow our instincts. Originally we had taken satisfaction from the fact that we had avoided the holiday hotspots and we needed to ensure we did not make that mistake this time. We were able to narrow our choice down to a very small area in west Cornwall, knowing it would also narrow our chances of finding the right house in the right timescale. Maybe we would fail but we knew we had to try: and we did have a second choice of area to fall back on. Where? For now that must wait!

The neat trick of getting our papers delivered by the postman, one which had satisfied my natural propensity to find ways round, over or through challenges thrown at me, hit an unplanned obstacle. The Royal Mail decided to start the daily delivery routine earlier just as the local newspaper distributor decided, probably by default, that it would delay its own deliveries. At a stroke this succeeded in ensuring that each morning the usually welcome noise of today's paper hitting the mat was replaced by the more disappointing, and frankly useless one of yesterday's news arriving! This was progress?

The only positive outcome was that I was driven to search the internet which yielded most of what I wanted at www.ft.com for free! Mel was not so happy at being cut off from her less pink version of the day's events and so the other positive outcome, of having no paper bill for the first time in thirty years, was outweighed by the cost of petrol required for her more frequent visits to Bodmin.

It was around this time that the full realisation of the effect of two large dogs reaching adolescence at the same time hit us, or rather the garden. Their fascination with the pampas grass we had inherited with less than total enthusiasm led to its gradual demolition, blade by blade. First it was an endless game of hide-and-seek through and around its base and then wholesale death by the deliberate extraction of leaves and stems one by one though, to our slight disappointment, the plant lived to fight another day - and is still winning the battle for survival!

One of the first houses we looked at had an indoor pool. A pool had never been on our list of priorities, not least because everyone we had known who had had one had told us not to bother. This was because of both heating and maintenance costs and the time taken to keep it clean and usable. But we had to look if only because the house seemed to offer everything else we needed at a reasonable price. And Mel, predictably, soon began to warm to the idea of a daily swim, something we had always enjoyed together when on holiday.

As might have been anticipated, the perception of getting a lot of house for the money was instantly dispelled on sight and, indeed, on site! The house was just fifty yards from a busy road, despite our enquiry of the agent on this point having been met with the answer that it was five hundred yards back. There were other features of the house not to our liking: they could loosely be described as too 'dingly dellish'. Also the pool had seen better days and would need money spending on it.

While we were therefore happy to walk away from it, for some reason the attraction of a pool remained with us, without quite making it onto our list of 'must have' requirements!

9 Timing is Everything

Our first visit to the already world-famous Eden Project since the incredible 'biomes' were opened to the public was poorly timed, being on the hottest day of the year so far. While it was still only early April, we were able to experience the Tropical zone at a time when the temperature controlling mechanisms were forced to go through their paces. While I found that zone more interesting than the neighbouring, still developing Mediterranean zone, what I found most interesting was the engineering. The metal framework of the supporting structure was awesome and the automatically opening vents controlling the air temperature completed the overall impressiveness of the project.

The timing of the arrival of our swallows on the 21st was no better, coinciding as it did with a light ground frost. I could only guess at the mild disappointment or bemusement on their tiny faces as they huddled together in the small brown purses attached to the roof timbers high up in the barn. It made me ruminate on the factors that caused them to head for their summer home at the precise time they did. Was their instinctive decision temperature-driven or simply time-driven? No clear answer came to me!

The contemplation of that question led me on to the even more puzzling ones of how they acquired the stamina to travel such long distances and the satellite-navigation accuracy needed to return to the same spot each year. Again one can only be awe-struck with wonder: I vowed never to take such a regular and commonplace event for granted nor my good fortune in being able to observe it at such close quarters. I knew that whatever transpired in the years left to me, I would always relish such simple experiences.

The first viewings of Upper Penwithiel were just getting underway when our already slightly dog-eared garden suffered a new blow or, more accurately, pounding. It was 7.30 in the morning when I looked out of the kitchen window. Still bleary-minded I did a double-take when I realised the two horses I could see grazing seemed nearer and larger than normal. The very simple explanation was that this was because they were not in the bottom part of the field but in the garden! The GARDEN?

I shot out, instinct taking over as I vaguely contemplated the disaster that could unfold if the postman should arrive unusually early that day. Dogs are a well-known occupational hazard of mail delivery, but horses? And one of them 17-hands! Luckily I had yet to let out the dogs otherwise the resulting bedlam would have been complete. As it was, I merely served to inject, let's say, a degree of anxiety into Smartie and Max as they looked up to see me rush out of the back door. Startled, they ran round the side of the house. Smartie collumped up the cobbled drive making a bee-line for the open gate into the field. But not Max! He accelerated to full gallop along the side lawn and vaulted the low dry stone wall by the entrance to the drive, somehow clearing the metal hatch to the cess-pit. The consequences had he landed on it didn't bear thinking about.

Using a variety of wild arm gesticulations familiar to all horse owners I managed to drive them both back through the gateway into the field and slam it shut.

'Very impressive,' grinned Mel from her observation point at our open bedroom window. A more serious expression formed on her face when she asked, 'how on earth did they get out?' I shrugged as I walked thoughtfully back into the house. I knew I had probably been the last one to go through the gate when I walked the dogs the previous evening but I simply couldn't believe I could have breached the one golden rule close to the heart of all animal owners - that of always closing gates behind you. The trouble was, I concluded, this was such a subconscious action after so many years that I couldn't actually remember closing it...

When Mel came down I knew we would have to try to get to the bottom of it. 'The trouble is,' I confessed, 'I think I must have been the last one to use the gate but I just don't remember closing it.' I waited for the repercussion of disapproval I knew I deserved. It didn't come.

'It's easily done,' she said to my amazement. 'It's just instinctive isn't it? I sometimes have to check things I've done automatically, simply because I can't remember doing them.' I hoped my conscious effort to stop my jaw dropping wasn't too obvious. 'What?' she asked, stifling a little smile.

'I can't believe I didn't get it in the neck,' I said somewhat sheepishly.

'Just be more careful. What would have happened if the gate to the lane had been open?' I gulped at the thought. From then on the field gate was checked meticulously each time it was opened, usually by me when walking the dogs.

The next morning I went into the kitchen to make a second cup of tea for Mel who had just come downstairs. I caught her singing 'happy birthday'. She saw my puzzled look. 'It's Daisy's birthday today,' she grinned.

'Yes, of course,' I replied, not being sure of the exact date but, for once, being absolutely certain of her age. We had speculated over the last year or two about how long she'd live since we had noticed her spending a greater proportion of each day asleep. Of course the arrival of the kittens had definitely given her a new lease of life but we had in the back of our minds that it might be a final burst we were seeing. But no, she had made it to eighteen, making her not just the oldest cat we had ever owned but the oldest animal.

I scooped her up, noticing how light she was. The lack of activity had led to a wasting of her muscles though she was still able to jump to any height up to about four feet. We told ourselves that if the day came when she could no longer do that it would be unfair to let her carry on: it was important to us that she should still be able to continue doing all the things cats do. I peered into her eyes and they were dimmer now but as I ran my forefinger along her neck the ensuing purr was as strong as ever. I hoisted her to her favourite position with both front paws over my left shoulder and her head against my neck. The purrs continued contentedly.

It was moments like that which suddenly made me aware of the passage of time. When we first bought her Andrew was eight, James five and Justin three. Yet that time had sped past with indecent haste, hardly giving us time to adjust to all life's changes. A comfortable, happy feeling engulfed me when I recalled the central role Daisy had played in our lives. There was absolutely no doubt: she was a fully-fledged member of our family but, I wondered, for how much longer? I brushed aside the parallel question which this thought caused to briefly flash through my mind about my own longevity. My fifty-six years was more than three times Daisy's great age!

It was the very next day that it happened again. I had let the dogs back in and opened the gates to the lane for the postman at about 7.45am. I was setting up my computer for the day when I heard the familiar yet chilling sound outside the window of metal on stone. I leapt from my chair and rushed out of the front door to see Smartie's tail vanish round the end of the house. Despite the ultra care which I had been exercising in closing the gate to the field, they had got out again. I had to defer the mental inquest already underway in my head in favour of the physical priority of securing them, knowing that, this time, there was no barrier between them and the outside world.

I chased after Smartie both to try to corner her in the relative safety of the back garden and to check my assumption that Max had been in front of her. To my great relief he was and she had merely done what she'd always done and followed him. This time it was me that cantered the length of the side lawn, vaulted the wall and pulled the gates firmly shut in the certain knowledge that Smartie, exercising her usual curiosity, would not be far behind me.

I turned to find her about to leap the wall herself. The suddenness with which I turned startled her, sending her back towards Max who, laid back as ever, was happily grazing the greener grass of the back lawn. The main panic over, I turned my attention to getting them back in the field. My slightly more relaxed mind couldn't help noticing the large hoof-sized dents - in Max's case tea plate-sized - which covered all the lawns. I dismissed early thoughts about how to get rid of them as they both started work on some of the small shrubs I had planted in the banks round two sides of the back garden.

By the time Mel had appeared, unable to disguise the look of horrified amazement on her face at such an early repetition of near-disaster, I had called upon all my horse psychology resources to successfully guide them both back up the drive and into the field with no contact whatsoever.

'How did you manage that without headcollars?' Mel asked.

'Who needs headcollars?' I replied, turning my mind back towards the little matter of how they had escaped .

'Did you shut the gate properly last night?' was the inevitable question she asked next.

'I know I did,' I said thoughtfully as I leaned over the gate to watch the horses wander off up to the top of the field, the excitement over. 'I shut the gate and rattled it like this to check it was closed,' I explained. Then I saw it. The jaws of the heavy duty gate catch had widened to the extent that the 'tongue' of the catch was no longer able to stop the latch passing between them. A firm pressure against the gate was all that was required to open it. All a horse had to do to open it was lean on it! This was why field gates were usually fitted to open into the field so that pressure against them was against the post. In our case, because the land rose so steeply behind it, the gate would not have been able to fully open inwards.

A few deft clouts with a club hammer was all that was required to put things right as well, of course, as a careful check each time I went through the gate. And all this was done in dressing gown and slippers!

It was after a spring which had seemed less sunny than usual that I chuckled at another brilliant piece of timing. In early May, Perranporth, on the north coast, intriguingly opened a new sun dial, the largest in Cornwall. I was delighted as I couldn't imagine many sun dials were opened these days. To add to my fascination we were told it was calibrated to tell Cornish time which was some twenty minutes behind London. There was an increasingly large part of me which relished the differences between Cornwall and the rest of the world and this was another small blow in the pursuit of that very worthy end!

We had got used to our farrier doing an excellent job of shoeing our horses but we had our eyes opened when we were invited by him and his wife for a drink one evening at their attractive farmhouse up on Bodmin Moor. Not only did he attend to horses' feet but he also made carriages for his own use - he was very much into driving, restored miniature cars (with as much care as any classic car enthusiast), repaired clocks and, for good measure, pottery and ceramics. He really had me worried, though, when he showed me a computer with its back off. 'I'm trying to figure out how it works,' he said in all seriousness! In his spare moments he had also restored and decorated the house. I came away feeling quite inadequate.

In the days that followed we noticed that Daisy had started to lose weight. There was no apparent reason for it but I took the precaution of giving her small amounts of aloe vera. It was to no avail as she quickly became painfully thin, even making little Cloey look large. We were at first concerned then rapidly alarmed. Within twenty-four hours she had stopped eating and would only lap a little milk or water. She spent the whole of that evening sleeping contentedly on my lap. Whenever she woke briefly she rewarded me with a strong purr.

That night I moved her bed into the conservatory, fearing that her new extreme weakness would make her vulnerable if she got down onto to the floor where the dogs were. I gently laid her on her side where she looked up gratefully at me before resuming her sleep.

When I came down in the morning she was in exactly the same position as I had left her and I knew she had left us, at the grand age of eighteen years two weeks and a day. What timing. We laid her in the space I had subconsciously earmarked for her above Jake and Sukie.

By way of total contrast it was on the same day that Perry Como died. Both had given us magic moments.

The next day we were naturally sad but this feeling was tinged with gratitude that Daisy had led a reasonably trouble-free life. As a bonus, her final decline had been rapid and devoid of suffering or any loss of dignity.

We had long told anyone who had been interested that we thought we owned the only Morgan in Cornwall. This was less a boast, idle or otherwise, but more a stratagem to flush out anyone who knew differently as it would be nice to be in touch. It was Mel who finally nosed out the information that there was indeed another Morgan owner in Cornwall, namely Heather Smee who not only owned Briarpatch Morgans near Townsend but bred Morgans. Mel had pre-arranged a visit with Heather for that day and so our minds were moved on from the sadness to what turned out to be a very pleasant and relaxing day among our favourite breed of horse.

It was a lovely warm May day and we were impressed with the tranquil, unspoilt beauty surrounding their little corner of the county. Not only did Heather and her husband surprise us with a little picnic lunch by their small lake after showing us their horses but her small granddaughter presented Mel with a posy of buttercups.

I was fascinated to be given a rundown on her husband's latest business venture which was running a worm farm. It seemed he had struck a little vein of gold in meeting the demands of both farmers and fisherman. While I always understood the ecological importance of the small creatures, I had no idea of the requirement for such a service.

It is difficult to sum up the delightful atmosphere of that day; it was a little like 'A Year in Provence' meets 'Darling Buds of May'.

❧

Marma was certainly not going to be outdone in the timing stakes. A month or so earlier than we had expected she decided to have her first season. There were no obvious warning signs and certainly no indications that she was in any way growing up! Although we had supported her in her natural assumption of the role of queen bee she had yet to reward us with any semblance of a responsible attitude. If there was mischief to be indulged in she was always the ringleader.

But now, for the next three weeks, she would have to be separated from her brother and Chan. They joined Angus whose disapproval at having his peace so rudely shattered was palpable! All of them behaved impeccably during that time. Chan, not too surprisingly, resorted to scratching the door to the conservatory to ensure we were aware of his general disapproval. But we resisted the temptation to resort to caging him as other Basenji owners had suggested we would eventually find unavoidable.

However, the biggest surprise was Zen. We naturally expected him to work out that there was a bitch in season despite our efforts to ensure they did not so much as catch sight of Marma during her purdah. Usually it was given away by the scent left on the ground but while he occasionally showed interest he did not become fretful. He didn't even go off his food like most dogs do. The only sign of anything being amiss was a slight loss of weight.

Marma herself seemed not to miss the others, unsurprisingly in view of the concentration of attention she was receiving. The principal effect on us, ignoring the inconvenience of keeping them apart and feeding and walking them separately, was simply that we missed the companionship of the two young dogs. We consoled ourselves with the knowledge that we would not have to go through it again as we planned to have Marma spayed three months after her season finished.

It was at the height of her season, when we had to be most meticulous in maintaining her isolation, that the unexpected happened. Did she manage to get loose with the dogs? No! But just after we heard news of a rare earthquake being recorded in Cornwall - at no less than 3.5 on the Richter scale - Marma became frightened to go into the kitchen. Was it some mysterious animal sensitivity to subterranean shock waves? Probably not. We concluded that it was more likely that she had been shaken by the crash that must have accompanied the breaking of crockery and glass that we later discovered had taken place when a shelf collapsed in a cupboard. Was that itself, perhaps, caused by the earthquake? No, it was simply caused by a gradual overloading that had taken place, exacerbated by the arrival of a number of new mugs and heavy glasses acquired to replenish those broken over many months 'by the dishwasher' and I do not, of course, refer to Mel! It was to be some days before Marma went past that particular cupboard again without giving it a suspicious wide-eyed glance.

10 I See No Ships

'Sorry, you must have the wrong number,' the voice at the other end of the phone replied earnestly.

'Are you sure?' I asked ridiculously and understanding for the first time why people sometimes asked that. First I was sure I had dialled the familiar number correctly and secondly I was impatient for my curry! I had watched that day's general election results coming in and, once more, had been cheated out of the usual suspense of waiting for the outcome in the early hours of the morning by another landslide.

'Quite sure,' affirmed the pleasant and friendly Cornishman, a little older than me I guessed.

'You're not the Indian restaurant, then?' I asked, casting my mind back to the earringed hard-of-hearing local man serving in another Bodmin Indian restaurant. After failing to catch our orders first time it had led James to quip that he'd better order something that was easy to hear.

'Definitely not,' he answered good-naturedly.

'You don't sound very Indian, actually,' I conceded, smothering a grin.

'No, I'm not Indian at all,' came the unnecessary confirmation with an undisguised chuckle.

'Sorry to have troubled you.'

'Not at all.'

I have found that in unhurried Cornwall there is time for such pleasant passing of the time of day. Indeed it is almost a prerequisite! To have hung up without any further exchange of words would have been verging on the impolite.

Our erstwhile neighbours, Julia Warburton and her father Dixon, having moved up onto the Moor, had wasted no time in searching out the pubs up there. Apart from the Cheesewring Hotel near Minions they had also got to know the Crow's Nest in a tiny village called, coincidentally, Crow's Nest! As they had recommended it to us on more than one occasion we decided to give it a try when Andrew, James and Justin descended on us to celebrate James' twenty-fourth birthday.

I'm always delighted to make new discoveries, particularly when, as in this case, it was clearly a local pub for local people. Certainly there was no shortage of visitors from nearby towns such as Liskeard and Bodmin as well as a trickle from further afield but the atmosphere was very much one of a pub catering for locals rather than visitors. The acid test is whether you can comfortably slot in, joining in conversations round the bar when appropriate. Naturally we received the odd questioning glance but, while not originating locally, we were soon accepted for what we were: a local family out for a special meal.

The village, as with many in Cornwall, had a strong mining background as well as having an agricultural community around it today. The pub's atmosphere was heavy with this history with horse brass and old photographs adorning the walls. Naturally it also had its own ghost though we didn't meet it that night. But why 'Crow's Nest'? The nearest coast is some miles away! Apparently the word 'crow's' really means cross - and the village lies on a crossroads. The picture of a ship outside the pub serves to confound the story but perhaps that just adds to its charm!

Days later we found ourselves relaxing for a couple of nights away at our favourite hotel, the Nare near Veryan. It was our thirtieth wedding anniversary and, given that we could not leave the animals for long, was as good a place to celebrate as we could think of. Even then we were dependent on Justin delaying his return to Bournemouth for a few days to make it possible. Such is the need for forward planning!

As it happened, we arrived on Tuesday which is the traditional night of the week that the proprietor holds an informal drinks party for guests at 7.00pm. We remembered first meeting Mr and Mrs Gray on one such occasion in the past. As Mr Gray had since passed on it was the redoubtable Bettye Gray who greeted us that evening. Into her eighties she still went on a skiing holiday every year. She is undoubtedly the matriarch of probably the foremost family of hoteliers in Cornwall. Members of her family have extensive hotel and catering interests, particularly in and around Newquay. Her book, 'Oh my dear life!', gives a fascinating insight into the building of these interests from the early part of the last century with her life running like a thread of gold through those years of amazing success.

As ever, she was charming and stimulating as she signed my copy of her book: she explained that she had handed over the running of the Nare to her grandson Toby Ashworth. I found it difficult to imagine her taking a back seat though it occurred to me there were such things as back seat drivers!

There is already clear evidence, however, of fresh thinking with the eventual addition of the Quarter Deck restaurant, reflecting his interest in sailing as well as his erstwhile career in the navy. There are also clear signs of the old ways being continued where these meet the requirements of the hotel's discerning guests!

The next day we walked to the top of Nare Head. Once there we sat quietly for a while observing the familiar, peaceful, though ever-changing, scene surrounding us. We were never quiet for long, however, and chatted non-stop on our descent.

We stopped and talked to a couple around our age from London who were walking up from Carne Beach. They told us that each year they returned to Cornwall for their holidays to walk the next section of the coastal path. So far they had covered the north coast and the south from Land's End to where we met them. They were confident of finishing the job now that they had walked most of it. I cringed mentally at the thought of just tackling the section they had still to cover!

When we returned to the hotel later, we phoned Justin to hear the news that Moss had disappeared shortly after our departure the morning before and had not been seen since. My immediate thoughts were opposing. I said, 'no need to worry yet. He's stayed out for the night before. It's that time of year, really.' I thought, 'but Moritz disappeared just as suddenly and we never saw him again.' I knew that both Justin and Mel were thinking the same. 'Let's leave it another twenty-four hours before we start to worry.' In reality we already had.

The following day we returned home after a punishing journey of some twenty-five minutes. There was still no sign of Moss. Justin was clearly very concerned, feeling in some way responsible.

'Don't worry, it's not your fault,' said Mel. 'We've always had cats staying out at night in the summer.'

'But not for more than one night,' he replied miserably.

'Frankie stayed out for a week once,' I chipped in.

'Oh, yes, that's right, he did,' said Mel, slowly recalling the incident some six or seven years earlier.

'A week?' asked Justin with surprise tinged with relief that perhaps all was not lost.

'Yes, we concluded he must have got locked in somewhere. Someone's shed or garage probably,' I added as I, too, found memories seeping back into my brain. When he did finally return it was as suddenly as he had disappeared. I went down one morning and, as I plugged the kettle in, there he was on the windowsill outside miaowing to be let in just as if he'd been on a five minute walkabout. True, he was thin and dehydrated but he was back and, by letting him catch up on lost food and sleep gradually, he had fully recovered in a few days.

Somehow this made us all feel better - for all of a minute when we faced up to the fact that Moss was still missing and knew we had no idea whether we would see him again. All our normal optimism had rapidly faded when we thought of Moritz.

'All we can do is contact neighbours and go and look for him. Apart from that we'll just have to wait,' I said. I rang round all seven houses within about a mile as the crow flies. None had heard of or seen him.

We knew Justin's unhappiness was compounded by the fact that he was having to return to Bournemouth that evening, leaving us with the problem. However, we all brightened at the thought that he was going back to the students' ball and then the results of his three years' efforts culminating in his graduation.

'Can I borrow your old DJ?' he asked as he was packing.

'Well, you can,' I replied thoughtfully, 'but will it fit you?' I replied, conscious, as he was, that both Andrew at 6'0" and James, 6'4", had borrowed it without complaint in the past and not forgetting that originally it had been made to measure for me! With him standing at just 5'10" or so I envisioned the need to at least amputate the legs - of the trousers that is, not his!

'Only one way to find out,' he said over his shoulder as he raced back up the stairs two at a time. He reappeared at the top of the stairs minutes later looking fairly immaculate. 'They're OK,' he announced. I looked at the bottoms to try to work out how he'd contrived to get them to fit.

'Are your legs longer than I thought?' I asked. Without saying a word he pulled back the bottom of the jacket to reveal a waist as high as you often seem to see on gentlemen of a certain age, halfway between hip and armpit! 'Are you sure they're alright?' I asked doubtfully through the grin I found myself unable to stifle for much longer.

'Yes, of course,' he replied with mock indignation. 'It's just a kind of fancy dress really, isn't it?' I supposed it was when I thought about it. He retreated to his room for a minute before emerging once again. 'Problem solved,' he grinned. This time he gripped the knees of the trousers and shook one leg at a time at me at the top of the stairs. 'Look!' I could see he had rolled the bottoms up on the inside so they looked a perfect fit, well almost, with the waist round the equator rather than the arctic circle this time.

'You look lovely,' oozed Mel as she always did when one of her sons sought her opinion.

Minutes later he was on his way.

'Don't worry about Moss,' I said as he slowly went down the drive with his window open. 'In this wonderful weather he's probably having a fabulous time,' I said. I'm not sure any of us was convinced.

'He did look super,' Mel said after waving him off down the lane. 'I hope I get some photos of him.' I had a feeling she might.

We had had our house on the market for three months and while several people had viewed it and expressed interest, we were losing confidence. Worse, we had seen nothing that interested us or met our admittedly fairly rigid requirements. After discussing matters, Mel and I agreed we would not keep the house on the market beyond September. It was my unshakeable belief that leaving a house on the market for too long damaged its value. People either concluded that there must be something wrong with it or, just as bad, expected to be able to make an offer lower than the asking price. We also agreed to switch to a new estate agency set up by experienced emigrés from the firm we were currently with. This, we reasoned, should refresh the campaign to sell it.

The agency concerned confirmed our asking price was reasonable - another of our little concerns - and took us on.

It was that time in the morning when I open the gates for the postman that I met Mel coming back from the direction of the lane. I had trudged down the drive lost in the mental pattern of routine without realising she had gone. It was her broad white smile that hit me first. Then the reason for it. In her folded arms was the large, floppy, unmistakable figure of Moss.

'I was on my way back from posting a letter when I just saw him sauntering up the lane.' If we caught the postman he was happy to take the occasional item of post from us though he had hinted before that we should post it in the box outside! Often, however, we didn't hear him until he had gone.

'He looks alright,' I said, giving Moss a quick once over with the fingers of my right hand.

'Yes, I've checked him and he seems fine. He's not even thin, so wherever he's been he's been looking after himself.' She hugged him to her face, beaming with delight. I was equally pleased to have him back, as if a missing member of the family had returned. Only then did I realise that, in his absence, I had switched off my emotions, fearing he had disappeared like Moritz nearly three years earlier. The relief when I switched them on again was huge.

Never again did I get cross with him for leaping about in my study, knocking things flying or just embellishing every piece of paper with muddy pawprints when it was wet outside. Yes, his hallmark was his clumsiness just as it was for many males, including Max, Zen and, er, me!

Both Cloey and Dandy made their own fuss of him, busying themselves with washing him after he had taken his fill of food and leapt onto the highest kitchen cupboard where he reclined majestically. He soon slid into a deep and prolonged sleep, exhausted. We knew we may never discover where he'd been.

Someone else who became exhausted was James. While he had now settled well into his career and no longer harboured doubts about it, he was worked hard by his company but, as anyone who has ever worked in marketing knows, that comes with the job. However, the combination of demanding work, long hours and having to look after himself, including doing his own washing and feeding himself which, after his hour's journey home each night, probably left something to be desired, led to a bout of glandular fever. I had never seen anyone afflicted by it before but it was truly debilitating. His doctor in Bath, where he shared a house, told him to expect to be off work for two or even three weeks. After a couple of days failing to get himself better Mel persuaded him to come home: we both knew that his recovery would be all the quicker if a few home comforts were available, not the least of which were some proper meals!

After our suspicions were confirmed that a run-down immune system was almost certainly to blame we prescribed a course of aloe vera. James was initially sceptical and not encouraged by the bitter taste but the rapid turnround in just two days allowed him to return to Bath clutching his own small supply. The glandular fever cleared completely in a week and has never returned.

In Bournemouth, Justin was reaching the end of his graphic design degree course and was increasingly excited: about his final project, which could best be described as moving graphics which he generated on a computer, by the potential he saw opening up for his career and by a forthcoming exhibition in London which would enable the students to get themselves known by potential employers. He was soon in a race against time not only to complete his project so it could be marked for his degree but also to get it onto tape or disk for the exhibition. His enthusiasm was extremely infectious and we looked forward to his graduation with our own excitement.

In fact it was on the day that Justin was in London that we received yet another lightning strike. Once again my computer was protected by the surge protector I had invested in, though, rather like a bee using its sting, it died in the process! Again, the investment turned out to be a good one because not only was the computer unharmed but the manufacturer once more replaced the protector without charge. While the phone and fax escaped for similar reasons, the phone line was put out of action and the alarm system was terminally damaged, just as my home insurance claims record had been taking a turn for the better!

Two days later we had a rather disappointed Justin phoning us with the news of his 2.1 degree. We knew he had been hoping for a first and certainly had done nothing to discourage his ambition - indeed we thought he was right to set his sights on it - but we were swift to rescue him from his high expectations. Not only had he successfully graduated but had done so with a good grade. It was the future opening up in front of him that now commanded his attention and what a future it was going to be!

At the end of that week we were off to Bournemouth ourselves for our third graduation ceremony. More accurately we were off to Wimborne Minster where the degrees were to be awarded. Mel and I had been there two or three times over the years but it was the time we took the boys to see the miniature village there that swam back into our minds that day. It must have been some fifteen or sixteen years earlier, we calculated. It seems to be visits to places on such an infrequent basis that underscores the passage of time. It really did seem like yesterday or, at most, the day before that we had bought them all ice creams and poked our heads into the Minster itself.

On Justin's graduation day we were there as of right as, more particularly, was he. It was a great day. Justin seemed to have amassed a group of good, happy friends who were all intent on enjoying themselves and they certainly did. By far the greatest part of the gown hire charge must go, I guessed, on the refurbishment of the mortarboards which seemed to spend as much time in the air or on the ground as on any head!

As a bonus the sun was out and the peal of bells from the ancient tower topped off the atmosphere of celebration. Afterwards we all returned to the college for a cream tea and champagne. The highlight for us was seeing an exhibition of the (now) graduates' work which in Justin's case included his moving graphics: we found them moving indeed as we marvelled at just how far he had come in those all too short three years. It seemed his peers also rated his particular piece highly, judging by the applause they gave each time it was shown. We, naturally, concluded we had bred yet another little masterpiece!

11 Toast To A Cat

Just over two weeks later our nest was emptied earlier than we had expected. Justin went off to stay with Andrew en route to a week's work experience in London. As a new graphic design graduate he had a novelty interest for design companies wanting to check on the techniques being currently taught by one of the foremost design colleges in the country. Naturally Justin was seeing it as a two way street as he got into his stride in seeking his first career opportunity.

Mel and I had long considered the eventual arrival of the time when we would finally be living in our house on our own for the first time since Andrew's arrival in 1975. While we had always expected that it would be a stark, poignant turning point in our lives we hadn't reckoned on it being such a drawn out affair with James, for example, spending a year with us in Cornwall between degrees! This time we knew it was to be deferred once more for a month or two or however long it took Justin to find a permanent job: we knew that with his natural enthusiasm it wouldn't take him long.

It was he, after all, who had asked me why I was being so pessimistic when I once told him he could become a millionaire by the time he was thirty-five!

So, Mel and I decided to use his week away as a practice run. We booked a table at our favourite little fish restaurant, Trawlers in Looe, and enjoyed an almost Mediterranean atmosphere one evening in late July. We had been enjoying a very warm spell and this had enabled us to indulge our imagination a little.

When he returned, Justin seemed a little uninspired by his week. He had found the firm's requirements less than stretching and altogether too mundane compared with what he had been doing. I helped him come to terms with this by employing him to revamp all our private and business stationery: boring work but it was paid!

Basenjis were as different from Great Danes as they were from cats we concluded. Apart from not being able to bark, Chan just seemed to operate on a different plane from the Danes. They were reasonably amenable to doing what you wanted whereas he appeared to prefer the alternative of doing the opposite. While sometimes boisterous they could be kept under control: he was totally independent of everyone.

It was, perhaps, his cat-like behaviour such as the way he washed himself, climbed on things and, indeed, his lack of a bark that enabled him to make such good friends of the cats. But from their perspective he was still a different species. It must have been the more than usually blurred edges between him and the cats that allowed them to start seeing the Danes in a more benevolent light. What else could have given Moss the confidence to lie down between Zen and Marma on the rug in the sitting room one particular night?

It was one of those fleeting but memorable moments. All three were blissfully dozy together with the Danes being many times Moss' size and equally unfazed by his presence! Then, just as quickly as he arrived, when he got squeezed a little too uncomfortably by them in their sleep, he slunk away. Needless to say, Dandy and Cloey remained aloof and at a safe distance.

That was not the only memorable moment that evening. Later, after dropping a jumbo-sized peanut down the side of my chair, I was fishing around for it under my cushion when my fingertips brushed something soft and furry. Imagining it to be one of the cats' old catnip mouse toys, I pulled it out. It was indeed one of the old cats' toys but this mouse was not catnip but real. The perfectly preserved but perfectly flat and lifeless form was presumably the indoor mouse who must have emerged from the hi-fi unit or TV stand and hidden under the wrong cushion just as I was about to lower my not inconsiderable weight on it!

While we had yet to receive an offer on our house we had sufficiently strong interest from one couple around our age, to feel the need for more urgency in finding our next house. In fact we did find a house right in the middle of our preferred part of Cornwall. It had everything we wanted with rooms of the right quantity and size and was set in glorious quiet countryside. The continuing very warm weather give it, too, something of a French atmosphere, assisted no doubt by the superb open-air pool. The house was not architecturally inspiring but it was low in maintenance requirements, as was the garden, being mainly laid to grass. Its biggest drawback was its lack of land.

We were to get sufficiently interested to make an offer on our first visit subject to our being able to negotiate the purchase of a few acres from the farmer owning the surrounding land. The owner was not sufficiently moved by this to accept. Having failed on a number of occasions to acquire some land from the farmer himself he was not sanguine about our prospects of doing so. That served simply to increase my determination to succeed where he had failed!

I returned to the village a couple of days later, intent on tracking down the farmer. I asked at the first house I came to after driving past the one we wanted to buy. Yes, they knew the farmer but could not or would not say where he lived. They directed me to a nearby house where a relative lived, they thought. It turned out to be his mother's and sister's home. After hearing enough of my story to convince them I wasn't up to no good they gave me his phone number.

When I rang later that evening he was naturally caught off guard but told me no land was for sale or ever would be as he was passing it onto his son. He wanted to know, however, what we wanted it for and seemed more amenable when I told him it was for horses. I later decided to write to him so I could cover everything I wanted to put to him without his feeling pressured.

I followed this up with another phone call a few days later to get a more mellow response along the lines that it might be possible to release a small parcel of land if the price was right. While careful not to get into negotiation too soon, I hinted that I had in mind a price in excess of twice the agricultural price without being specific. It turned out he had in mind no more than two acres which, together with part of the two acres which made up the garden, would be barely enough for two horses.

To keep alive my bid I wrote again suggesting he might like to consider how much land he would sell me for £5000, £10000, £15000 and so on. I hoped that by negotiating land for money rather than money for land he would feel in control of the process and be less defensive about selling.

I told him my purchase depended on it but that if I didn't buy the house someone else might who had no need of any more land, depriving him of the opportunity of getting such a good price for, perhaps, some years. This seemed to grab his attention and he promised to think about it. I said if I didn't hear I knew he wasn't interested. He replied that he would definitely phone me when he had had a chance to think.

In parallel our potential purchasers wanted to return for a fourth visit. So far we had had the wife and teenage son, the wife and husband, the wife and a builder and now the wife wanted to bring father-in-law who would be housed in the cottage. I drew the line at this and said when they were ready to make an offer they would certainly be welcome to. The reason for my reticence was that they had first promised our agent they would make an offer when they had put their house on the market which they hadn't when they first looked. Then they said they would wait until they had sold their house. Now they were saying they would rather exchange contracts on their sale before committing themselves.

I felt I had to know how serious they were before going any further, not least because of my efforts to acquire the house we had found together with the land.

It was early in September that Andrew and James came down to see us for a few days. We took them to west Cornwall on one of them and enjoyed an excellent meal outside in the still warm sunshine at the Halzephron Inn at Gunwalloe. Afterwards, on the way to a go-kart track to give their adrenaline an outlet we took them past the house we were trying to buy. They were not sure what to think until we mentioned the pool at which their enthusiasm seemed to perk up. Mine perked down when they challenged me to a race on the kart track. I had joined in many times before, even putting myself in danger in the line of duty as a father, not least when James decided to go over the top of me when he couldn't get round me once! My real problem was simply that of being unable to see clearly when my glasses were shaken by the vibration.

Just after my return from a board meeting in London, Marma delayed her appointment with the vet to be spayed by the single most effective ploy at her disposal. She came into season again. Being only three months after the last one it was three months earlier than expected. This meant having to delay at least another six weeks. It was, however, quite in character for her to defy us in this way!

When I ordered the logs from Bernard Libby again, I spoke to his wife who was most apologetic about the fact that they had increased their price for the first time in four years by £5 a load, where a load was a small lorryful! I decided not to repeat my suggestion of a year earlier that they should increase it in line with inflation every year like the rest of the business world! This would be more advantageous to them and would probably go unnoticed by most of their customers.

I was now well used to seeing the stock market react to events in the world: a profit warning from a major company here, a sharp increase in inflation there or a drop in unemployment could all knock the FTSE 100 index or its constituent shares off course in an instant.

I had just returned from walking the dogs round the field when Mel called urgently to me from the kitchen. 'Come quickly!' I lurched in through the door to see what calamity had hit her while I was out. 'Look...' She nodded towards the television. 'A plane has just crashed into one of the twin towers of the World Trade Centre in New York.' My mind saw the smoke and flames billowing from the live pictures and rapidly considered the chances of such a freak accident. I also vaguely and instinctively wondered in the back of my mind what effect, if any, it would have on the stock market. After dismissing the likely effect on insurance shares as relatively small because of the spread of risk I came back to the reality with a jolt. Real people must have just died in that accident and I felt slightly ashamed at the way I had reacted.

'I suppose it was going to happen one day...' I began. Then, live, I saw the second plane hit. 'They were no accidents,' I immediately exclaimed, the full horror and implications washing over me. Then anger shot through me as I contemplated the mentality of those who had taken such calculated action against innocent people. We all felt angry - Justin was with us at that moment too - and impotent. We were watching scenes of pure terror for those involved and yet could do nothing.

Then I had to think about the effect on the stockmarket simply because I knew it was about to cost me quite a sizeable sum. I didn't want to be so mercenary at such a time but I could not simply stand by as money disappeared into thin air. To my amazement the reaction was relatively small in those early minutes. I started to sell some of the more sensitive options while I waited for things to become clear. Then they did and the markets plunged. Not only was I too late but I became strangely philosophical. My reactions had been almost instinctive which is what I had learned to become. But the effect on me suddenly hit me as being as nothing compared with that on the people in New York. I decided to abandon any further attempt to salvage money from the wreckage so to speak.

We all watched the blanket coverage on TV for some hours, tossing over in our minds and occasionally giving voice to thoughts as to what it was all about.

It was a day or two later that I e-mailed a director colleague in New York. I had realised that the effect on anyone in that city at that time was bound to be traumatic. My words were inadequate but the reply sent a shiver through me. He described the moments before the first crash when the plane flew just a few hundred feet over their office building.

A more direct effect on me was when my online trading system went down. The central operating system was run by a company in New York and their building was close to the Towers: they had been hit by a power cut. Once again I saw this in perspective and was duly awe-struck by the system coming back up in a matter of hours. I sent an e-mail expressing gratitude and support. This world of ours was certainly shrinking fast...

❧

The Royal Cornwall Show was severely affected in 2001 by the foot-and-mouth outbreak. Not only was it postponed from the usual June to September but, with no livestock there, it was a very different event. While the general atmosphere was as pleasant and genial as ever, the heart of the show was missing.

That did not stop everyone from making the best of it and enjoying themselves. The highlight for us was undoubtedly the display by the King's Troop. The speed with which these amazing military horses cantered flat out across the arena towing their heavy gun carriages was truly inspiring. The guns firing twenty feet in front of us were truly deafening!

Perhaps the most poignant moment in that bustling day was when we were all invited to stand silently for three minutes as a mark of respect for those affected by what had happened just two days before in New York. I never knew how long three minutes could be. Such diverse thoughts ran through my mind: gratitude for being alive and a prayer for action to be taken to prevent those currently engaged in terrorism from doing anything like it again, with the minimum possible effect on the innocent. Two wrongs will never make a right but that particular wrong needed to be eliminated, I thought.

It was around that time that I started my preparations for what was to be a major upcoming event: Mel was approaching her half-century. I drew up a list of friends old and new, from Wiltshire and Cornwall, and sounded them out on their availability on the Saturday before Mel's birthday in January. Nearly all replied straightaway that they would be there. Where, though? I considered the Nare first. While that was not so easy to get to, especially for those from up country, I knew Mel would love it. Unfortunately the room I had in mind was not available. It was being refurbished and was, in fact, to become the new Quarter Deck restaurant. After browsing through the Yellow pages it suddenly hit me. I had always wanted to try the Carlyon Bay Hotel, ever since, that is, I discovered some years ago that my then chairman was the owner or was it one of the owners?

Not only did I find them professional, and enthusiastic to help put on the best evening they could, but the quoted price for a menu that could be selected from on the night was extremely competitive. I had never got on with the idea of choosing in advance a three course meal for consumption two or three months later.

Marma had so infuriated me one morning when we were walking round the field that I ended up losing Chan's lead. Ever since he had strayed across two neighbouring fields and got lost as a puppy I had carried a small retractable lead in case I ever needed to prevent him repeating his escape trick. I had never needed it for that purpose as he seemed to have been chastened by the experience. I had reason recently to sometimes put him on it to try to break his habit of going round the field again just as I wanted to take them in. But the lead was in my jacket pocket that morning and was the first thing which came to hand when Marma ignored my command to come while rooting around in the muck heap. It sailed through the air, and went straight past her. She obscured my view and so I didn't see it land. Despite the assistance freely given by her and the other dogs in looking for it, it was to be some days before it finally came to light when I was emptying the barrow while mucking out the stables.

The same lead was in trouble again a few days later after I had clipped it on to Chan's collar when we were completing our walk to prevent him doing his lap of honour. The problem was caused by Max taking a closer interest than usual in the small black, white and tan dog. Chan threatened the unwelcome complication of getting the chord wrapped round and round Max's legs as he started to do what came naturally to Basenjis and attempted to round up the huge horse!

I had no option but to let the lead casing fall to the ground to allow Max to simply step over it. Far from walking off as I had hoped and leaving me to recover Chan, Max decided he really wanted to investigate what he had seen me drop to the ground. Within seconds he had the lead case in his mouth and proceeded to amble slowly away from me with one very confused little dog in tow!

I was telling Mel the story while waiting for my toast. So engrossed was I that I failed to notice Cloey sitting next to the toaster, taking more than a passing interest in what was going on inside it. Then it was done and we watched with amusement her bemusement as the slice popped up. I was less amused seconds later when she took a good mouthful off the corner of the still-warm toast. Never again was I able to leave the toaster unattended when she was in the kitchen!

12 Jolly Green Giant

As November approached, Mel and I recalled the many bonfire nights we had enjoyed, not just when the boys were small but in more recent years too. It seemed Andrew had the same thought at the same time. 'Are there any firework displays organised near you?' he asked on the phone one evening.

'No idea,' I replied honestly.

'I was thinking of coming down if there was,' he added. Knowing how much Mel and I would enjoy that I said I'd investigate. The most promising-sounding one was to be at Polperro, just twenty-five minutes drive from us. What I had no idea of was how good it would be. An e-mail to a website for nearby Looe elicited the opinion of one local that it was the best around.

I discovered that entry was not by ticket but by simply turning up and paying at the harbour entrance!

I thought I had got past the stage of picking up signals of broodiness from Mel, and then having to handle them, but there was no mistaking that look in her eye one evening as she sat with Chan curled up on her lap.

'I've been thinking...' she began. That was always a warning sign that the gauntlet of some new initiative or idea was about to be thrown down in front of me. I knew better than to rise to the bait so I just raised an eyebrow in her direction and left her to push on with it if she dared. She always did! 'Chan is the only one in the house where there's only one,' she continued brightly. Scenting the whiff of a barmy idea being tossed over in her mind so as to enable her to present it to me in the best light, I continued to act dumb.

'Only one what?' was my retort.

'Basenji,' she replied all too predictably, if a little sheepishly.

'Isn't that more than enough?' I asked, tongue slightly, but not altogether, in cheek. After all, the wayward ways of this unusual breed had taken a while to get used to. Not only had we struggled to come to terms with his propensity to do pretty well the opposite of what we wanted but he had proved intransigent in his continued insistence on dominating Zen, several times his size. What on earth would it be like with more than one, I found myself wondering involuntarily.

'No. I don't think it's fair, is it Chan?' she asked, knowing no response, let alone an audible one, was likely. She cuddled him a little more closely as she continued, as if to him but actually to me. 'Max has got Smartie. Zen's got Marma. Moss, Dandy and Cloey have got each other and...'

'...and I've got you,' I found myself saying.

'Exactly!' she replied triumphantly.

'But two Basenjis would be chaos,' I went on, knowing deep down that even discussing the proposition was giving it life.

'No, they'd be lovely together,' she said returning Chan's loving look. Whatever else he is, I thought, he's not stupid. 'He'd have someone to play with and she would keep him out of trouble,' she continued. 'And don't forget he's had two puppies come into the house that were smaller than him but both of which now tower over him.' I knew I was on a slippery slope so played for time.

'Let's think about it and not rush into it,' I suggested.

'We don't need to, do we Chan?'

'We'll talk about it after Christmas,' I said in my rush for the mental exit.

Justin, having discovered that the demand in the market place for his very special skills was lower than any of us had expected because of the fall-off in marketing and advertising expenditure, had come to terms with having a longer than expected stay in Cornwall. He was not the sort to allow his natural enthusiasm to diminish but he was running out of ideas. He had already proved he was more than capable of designing letterheads and other office stationery as well as getting the occasional commission to produce brochures. While his heart was increasingly in moving graphics, he decided to do whatever it took to bring in some money, keep his creative eye in and build up a track record.

It was as I was gently trying to help him to adjust to a longer timescale for the inevitable, I knew, lift-off in his prospects that I came out with it.

'Why not set up on your own?'

'Oh, I'd hate to be working entirely on my own,' he replied dismissively while, I detected, filing the thought away somewhere in his mind.

'What's everyone else doing?' I asked, referring to his colleagues from college. He reeled off the answer from which it was apparent that they too had found difficulty in matching their ideal career aspirations. One or two were working in graphic design but at a lower level than their skills merited. One or two had already accepted unrelated work while waiting for the market to improve.

Then Justin mentioned that he and one particular friend had chatted idly about going into business together. I explained the huge challenge involved in such a step but also the opportunity it presented in the longer term. I had no need to do so as he was ahead of me. He then quoted from a book I had given him the previous Christmas on setting up a design business. It was a short step from there for me to decide to swing my full support behind the idea.

'Why don't you talk to a business manager at your bank to see what help he can give you?'

With the war in Afghanistan just four weeks old, the Polperro pyrotechnics were to be an altogether more poignantly peaceful and happy affair. As well as finding the car parking easy and stress-free we also discovered that the entrance to the harbour didn't even stretch to the formality of requiring a fixed entrance fee let alone a ticket! We were merely invited to drop a contribution into the white plastic bucket waved under our noses.

James and Andrew had arrived the evening before and there was something of the excitement of earlier fireworks nights in the banter as we strolled down from the car park and then took up our positions on the harbour wall. Not having had any idea of what to expect, my donation on the way in had been £10 for all of us.

We stood in the damp, chilly, but thankfully clear air looking out on the black water reflecting the lights dotted around the village and the huge bonfire to our right. Music blared from some strategically placed speakers in a garden high above us. It was the most unusual backdrop for a fireworks display any of us could remember. Without warning, the first mortar shot up into the sky and exploded above the sea. The next hour or so was to be the most memorable of all the displays we had seen which included the nightly one we had seen at Disneyland in California some thirteen years before.

The atmosphere was perfect. A high quality performance in the most congenial setting imaginable and all for a good cause. The donations had been for charity and it was Andrew who, on returning past the harbour entrance afterwards, topped up my earlier contribution.

The following evening we went to the Sharksfin Restaurant at Mevagissey: we had discovered yet another good restaurant to add to our list. Then Andrew and James were on their way again.

Marma had managed to stay out of season for six weeks, just long enough to allow us to have her spayed safely. It was to mark the beginning of a new phase in her young life. She suddenly seemed calmer and more grown up: at last she became a real pleasure to have around. Even the Jag was able to breathe easier!

In the absence of a firm offer on the house, we had taken it off the market, as we felt we must, just seven months after first putting it on. It was a full three weeks later that we had a tentative approach from our agent on behalf of the couple who had previously been very interested. They were about to exchange contracts on their house at last and, while they knew we had taken the house off the market, wondered if we would still consider selling to them. Mel and I had felt we had been messed about by them before and were slightly reticent to entertain the idea lest they did so again.

'But we still want to sell it don't we?' asked Mel who had not quite given up on an early move.

'Yes, but we took the decision to take it off because we knew the house needed a break from being on the market as did we, particularly you as all the work fell on you really.'

'Yes, I know but if they're genuinely interested then we ought at least to discuss it with them,' she replied.

'Alright but I'll make it clear to the agent that we're happy to see them only if they are serious about making an offer in the region of the figure he had told us to expect.'

The agent assured me that the couple were, if anything, getting desperate to clinch a deal as their contracts were due to be exchanged and were aware of the minimum figure they would need to offer. With a degree of reluctance I agreed that they could come and see us on the Friday afternoon. Mel put on one of her little teas with a choice of Earl Grey and Lapsang as well as a selection of rather nice biscuits. The discussion went well and as they left an hour or so later they told us to expect an offer in the region of what they knew we required sometime on Monday if, as expected, their exchange took place that day.

Monday came and went without any contact from them as did Tuesday and Wednesday.

'Maybe their exchange has been delayed,' suggested Mel.

'Maybe,' I agreed, unconvinced. 'But surely they would have told us,' I added, 'especially if they were that keen to secure the house.'

The following day, Thursday, I decided to phone the agent.

'Oh, didn't we tell you? Sorry. They made an offer on a house they went to view straight after leaving you on Friday. Someone should have told you.'

'Yes, they should,' I agreed, unable to hide my irritation. Mel was naturally disappointed but I told her that I had had reservations about the people from the beginning. 'If people mess you about at the viewing stage you know you're going to have problems later, probably all the way through,' I told her.

'Yes, you're probably right,' she sighed. 'Makes old Colonel Masterson look like the perfect buyer,' she added wistfully, referring to the punctilious man who bought our previous house.

'Well, he might have been a bit scratchy at times but you knew where you were with him and I think he'd say the same about me,' I said in agreement.

'What do we do now?' asked Mel wearily.

'Have a rest and leave it for a year,' I said without hesitation. She gave me a mock scowl of disapproval.

We entered December, glad to have Christmas as a distraction from our house-selling exertions.

Mel came in from mucking out the stables sooner than I had expected. Somewhere in my mind, which was focused on something completely different, I had a vague idea she had not been gone long. Then the reason became apparent as she produced from behind her back a piece of bent tubing. She grinned as recognition dawned on me and I returned my glance from the wheelbarrow handle to her face.

'How did that happen?' I asked, knowing she couldn't have wrenched it off. By way of explanation she held the jagged end under my nose, still holding the rubber grip. I could see it had rusted through. Realising there was no way I could repair it, I simply said, 'we'll have to get another one then.'

'What do you suggest I do today?' she asked brightly.

'Can't you...' I began.

'...use a one-handled wheelbarrow?' she said, finishing my question for me. 'No I can't,' she replied firmly, without waiting for me to answer.

'Well it's a two-wheeled job so it should balance and be almost as easy...' I explained before tailing off in the face of her unspoken refusal to even consider the proposition I was in the process of unfolding.

'Then *you* do it,' she said, smiling as she gently placed the handle on my desk.

Knowing I had to prove my point, if only to save face, I agreed: 'no problem. I'll do it later.' Mel gave me a disbelieving look. 'No, I will. Just not right now.'

When I eventually went out to the barn, I saw the one-armed barrow still sitting forlornly in the middle of it, where Mel had left it, half full with its less-than-precious cargo. I quickly revisited the logic in my head with brief recollections of the theory of leverage and concluded that it really was a simple matter of just lifting the barrow with the remaining good arm which appeared to be quite unaffected by rust. The barrow had, I mused, plenty of life left in it and I would soon be able to convince Mel of this when I had successfully accomplished my mission.

I was, it has to be admitted, feeling quite pleased with myself when I returned to the house twenty minutes later. The whole process had been much easier than even I had thought.

'Well?' Mel couldn't resist asking with an inquisitive smile as soon as she saw me, no doubt convinced I would have to eat my words and agree the task had been difficult.

'It was even better than I thought,' I began. 'It just proves the power of positive thinking,' I continued mischievously.

'It didn't work did it?' she asked, now quite certain I was playing for time before having to admit defeat.

'Yes, of course it did,' I retorted. 'For a start it frees up one hand, for opening the stable doors and the gate. Secondly it makes it easier to turn left,' I explained, referring to the fact that it was the left arm which had snapped off. 'And thirdly,' I said, trying to ignore the laughter I knew Mel was having difficulty in suppressing, 'a one-armed man would find it a joy to use.' Her laughter finally escaped as she recognised my vain attempt to put the most positive gloss on things.

'But,' she said.

'But what?' I replied.

'But you are going to buy me a new barrow, aren't you?' she asked, more as a demand than a question I thought.

I had my first conversation, via e-mail, with a Basenji breeder and shower, Sally Wallis who, with her husband Marvin and their Zande Basenjis, lives near Hailsham in East Sussex. My initial contact came about as a result of my idly surfing the internet looking for information on Basenji puppies during a lull in the stock market one afternoon. Her website was full of useful information, not the least of which was contained in a lengthy piece in which she set out to put off potential buyers by describing what they would be letting themselves in for. I couldn't avoid laughing out loud at the accuracy of the warnings which closely matched our own experience. Far from putting us off, however, it served simply to crystallise in my mind what I already knew was in Mel's: we should get a companion for Chan.

Perhaps the most useful snippet of information went some way to explain the heightened animosity between Chan and Zen. Chan, quite irrationally to our minds, continued to push his luck in bossing the much bigger Zen until he would be pushed no more: Zen was becoming quite aggressive towards Chan.

Sally explained to me that November and December were the months for what she described as the Basenji rutting season! Wherever a male Basenji was, regardless of whether there were any bitches in the vicinity, in season or not, he would experience a heightened sexual drive. This went some way to explaining his overt aggression towards Zen or, indeed, practically anyone who took him on at that time.

Armed with this new insight and recognising Zen's own position as the largest of our dogs, we were able to change tack in our managing of the pack. We had to let Zen exert his new-felt authority, even if it did sometimes wilt in the face of the onslaught of snarled insults from the small dog. Gradually we were able to change the pack order so that Zen was very definitely second only to his sister. To this day Chan has, we feel sure, only ever paid lip service to this new order in the cause of self-preservation. Deep down he still feels he ought to reign supreme!

Before we realised the extent to which we were departing from what was left of our senses we found ourselves booking a bitch puppy from Sally's next litter, due in January.

It was on Christmas Eve when we had the three boys with us that we were conscious that a more than usually seasonal peace had descended on us. The appearance of a few nicks in Chan's coat told us he and Zen had had their high noon. At last Chan's increasingly constant, sometimes quite ferocious growls had ceased. The eery but welcome quiet was accompanied by what I could only describe as mild depression on Chan's part.

It was as late as the afternoon that day that Andrew and Justin cheerfully went off to Plymouth with James to help him finish his Christmas shopping!

We had our usual enjoyable Christmas and Justin had produced a remarkable surprise present for Mel. It brought a lump to my throat when he first showed it to me a few days before the big day and asked if I thought she'd like it. The moist eyes it produced from her when she opened it on Christmas morning was exactly as I had envisaged. Using his new-found graphic design skills he had produced a calendar of the highest glossy quality in which the days of each month were presented superimposed on a photograph of one or more of our animals. All were current except for those showing Jake, Sukie and Daisy. I knew there was no way that calendar was going to be discarded at the end of the year.

We had noticed that, increasingly, all three boys were giving us more imaginative and generous gifts, reminding us of how much they had grown up.

It was, however, on New Year's Eve that our levels of anxiety were driven up quite unexpectedly. I was rounding up the dogs, who were wandering around in the garden, for their usual morning walk round the field.

'Has anyone seen Marma?' I yelled into the hallway through the open front door as, unusually for her, she was not in evidence. Normally she would have exercised her right as head of the pack to rush up to the gate in front of me and the others.

'She's out there with the others,' Mel replied.

'I can't see her anywhere,' I answered, almost implying against my better judgement that Mel was wrong: about such things she never was. Justin came out to help me look for her. As she was nowhere to be seen, a pang of panic shot through me as I contemplated the possibility that after many months she had once more escaped.

Thankfully the yell that went up from Justin behind one of the bushes next to the cottage told me she hadn't. 'I've got her.' Then, after the other dogs had shot through the gate as I opened it, I looked round expecting her to rush after them to reassert her position. She waddled slowly towards me looking distinctly unhappy. 'She must have eaten some grass or something,' Justin called after me. 'She was drooling a bit when I found her.'

I could see she wasn't drooling but when I realised she just didn't want to walk any distance at all I knew there was something wrong. As I looked her over trying to work out what it was, the huge swollen stomach I suddenly saw when looking down on her back from above stirred something in my mind. All I knew at first was that it disturbed me deeply. In a split second I was back with our lovely bitch Jo-jo. Many years before we had lost her from distension or bloat as it is often known.

Panic was instantly transformed into action. 'Quick, go and tell Mum that Marma's got bloat and get her to phone the vet's to tell them I'm bringing her in.' Justin sprinted in the direction of the house while I gently guided Marma back towards it. It was less than half-an-hour later that Simon Draper called us into the consulting room. Our relief at discovering that he was there to take charge of events was huge.

'No doubt about that. It's bloat alright. Don't worry,' he said calmly and more reassuringly than he knew, 'we have a pretty good success rate with this condition these days.' All three of us were well aware, however, that time was not on our side. 'Let's get her straight into theatre and see what's what,' he smiled confidently. 'Why don't you go off home now and I'll phone you as soon as there's any news.'

'Why is it always the special ones,' sobbed Mel when we closed the car doors.

'They're all special,' I said softly.

'Yes, I know,' she replied, 'but she's such a loving dog. And so young. I couldn't bear it...' Her words tailed off as we both sat grimly for a few seconds before driving home more slowly than we had come, silently contemplating what the next hour or so would bring and each of us with damp cheeks.

The sight of Max waiting by the field gate to greet us when we drove up the drive gave us a brief respite from our gloom. Mel had finally replaced the old New Zealand rugs he and Smartie had with spanking new lightweight ones. Both were bright green and still very new-looking. 'He looks like a jolly green giant,' said Mel as we went up to fuss him.

'Green, undeniably and a giant without doubt. But jolly?' I replied. The moment had passed and neither of us was in the least jolly. It was good to feel the warmth of his neck as he stretched his head down to us.

13 Surprise, Surprise

I had firmly committed myself to the idea that Mel was to have a complete surprise on the night of her fiftieth birthday dinner. In the run up to Christmas Justin and I had therefore worked secretly on the preparations for Mel's big day. He designed all the stationery I used to keep friends up to date as well as place cards for the dinner I had booked at the Carlyon Bay. I was already planning well ahead and beginning to think about the logistics of the night itself. Quite apart from preparing directions for everyone, I somehow had to ensure a total surprise right up to the moment the penny eventually dropped.

Gradually this little project had climbed to the top of my agenda as there seemed to be some little detail to think about most days. How would I ensure Mel wore something appropriate on the night? She would naturally never forgive me if every woman turned up in her finery while she arrived wearing something suitable for, say, a meal out with me. How could I even be sure she had something to wear? Most men will know this was not something to be taken for granted: I would have to find a way of letting her know in sufficiently good time to buy that new dress or those new shoes I instinctively knew she would need! And what about her hair? I could hardly let her turn up under-groomed compared with all the others who would have had plenty of time to prepare!

What about the actual day itself? I knew it would be something of an anti-climax to follow what I hoped would be an evening to remember at the Carlyon Bay with an evening to forget at home or even one at any of the nearby restaurants we frequented. While I had to put that on the back burner for a while I knew something would come to me.

Then again, the boys could hardly appear out of the blue at the hotel. For one thing Andrew and James would have to stay overnight with us as Mel would be disappointed to find at the end of the evening that they were staying somewhere else.

In parallel with these conundrums ran that of Justin's future. I had been most impressed with the plans that he and his college friend had pulled together for a graphic design partnership. Following the principles outlined in the book I had given him, Justin produced, single-handedly and often working into the early hours, a three-year business plan that would have shamed many an established self-employed person. Acting as devil's advocate, there was little I could suggest by way of improvement.

They received a friendly reception from the first bank they approached who also suggested it would help their application if they applied to the Prince's Trust, set up by Prince Charles to support such initiatives by young people, for financial backing. They too were helpful and constructive and soon offered financial support which was dependent on a certain level of bank finance also being made available.

The two of them had had to attend a meeting with the Trust to be grilled on the detail of their plan and, in effect, this did part of the bank's work for them so they too soon agreed in principle. It was Justin's student loans which later blew the whole idea out of the water. I had taken the view that if the project was to succeed they should go through the discipline involved in getting the necessary finance. After all, if they succeeded as I expected they would then they would soon need much larger sums for expansion.

It was, however, not the lack of finance that finished off the embryo business but rather the late realisation by his friend that there were risks involved in borrowing relatively large sums of money. What if they failed? As soon as he started asking Justin this I knew the end of the road had already arrived.

Even the usually ebullient Justin had his enthusiasm dented by this disappointing reaction from his friend - for all of twenty-four hours. That's how long it took him to react positively to my instant suggestion to set up on his own. The turn-round was remarkable as he started to rework his business plan to reflect the income, costs and profit generated by a one-man business. I encouraged him to build on the faith he had already developed in his own ability.

While disappointed at having to abandon plans to move to Bristol on cost grounds and tentative about the prospects for such a business operating from home in Cornwall, he pressed on. The small printing tasks I gave him kept him constructively occupied while covering his petrol and leisure costs!

❧❧❧

While Simon Draper had been relatively upbeat about Marma's chances of survival, we knew from re-reading the sections of our dog books on bloat that these were usually put at no more than one in three. As I rushed to the phone ringing in my study about an hour-and-a-half after getting home, I was hit by a powerful feeling of déjà vu. It was barely sixteen months since I had taken a similarly poignant phone call from Simon about our previous brindle, Jake. On that occasion I had had to take on board bad news and agree to let him go.

How frighteningly quickly the emotions of that day returned. On that dreadful evening I had been so distraught that I did what I often did when overwhelmed by something: I poured my feelings out onto paper. Of Jake I had written the following, word for word, in my diary:-

Here was a good friend.

I shall remember you, Jake, for escaping through the fences at our last house. For being trodden on by a horse as a puppy and never going too near one again. For being happy regardless of the circumstances. For always being pleased to see me. For being so happy when we moved - it helped a lot.

You shared our distress when Mima died but were happy to come into the house at last.

You wagged your tail off...

You fought back when you were ill and we fought for you. I'm glad.

You kept wandering off up the lane and down the lane and I had to keep you on a lead for which I'm sorry.

You still came for your walk when you were really unwell for which, thank you.

You were a good friend to Sukie.

You were kind to Chan.

I will never forget you picking up Chan's toy when I led you out for what was to be the last time. I wish I'd let you keep it.

For everything, but especially your unconditional love and friendship, thank you. You will not have so long as the others to wait for us to join you, wherever you are. At peace. God speed.

PS I miss your great, warm, soft, stripey, loving head..........

I settled myself uneasily behind my desk. In the seconds it took to lift the receiver to my ear, my mind flicked back and forth contemplating first bad news and then good. The tension was unbearable.

Simon's voice began, 'she's doing alright...' He must have heard the surge of relief expelling the air from my lungs. '...the operation was successful,' he continued. 'She's got a ten inch wound from the middle of her tummy to about three-quarters of the way up her left side. I've stapled her stomach to the stomach wall to prevent it from twisting again.'

That strangest of New Years was seen in with a semi-comatose stripey dog laid out at my feet. Already we had initiated the rapid healing of her wound by using our aloe vera spray.

On New Year's Day Marma was clearly in pain: her most expressive, sad eyes kept looking at us imploring us to help. All we could do was to keep her warm and quiet. When she was settled we left her in the boys' care while we drove up to Minions to see the East Cornwall hunt depart. While keen equestrians, we had never been interested in or supporters of hunting and so it was purely in the interests of witnessing a traditional spectacle that we parked the car near the Cheesewring Hotel that freezing cold morning. Because of the iron-hard ground there were no more than three horses in attendance with around a hundred spectators and some thirty hounds.

But the freezing temperature was accompanied by bright sunshine: the Moor was looking at its crisp best. The gay temperament and obedience of the dogs was a delight to see. Most impressive was the fact that over fifty sheep were grazing on open common land within sixty feet of the loose hounds not one of which was tempted!

Whether it was our near-loss of Marma or simply the fact that we had had three Danes for most of the twenty-eight years we had owned dogs I wasn't sure. But when Jeanette Callan, who had bred Zen and Marma invited us to go and see her latest litter we knew we would have to banish from our minds the thought of having one. All the way there the conversation would come back to some variation of: 'we're definitely not in the market for another Dane.' This, we knew, was especially true when we had our names down for one of Sally Wallis' Basenji pups.

The first to greet us at the Callans' house, after Jeanette, was Paddy the brindle. Jeanette showed us the new additions to her home before taking us out to see the new additions to her family, and, standing in her hallway, I found myself stroking his huge, soft head as he leant more and more heavily against me.

Whenever we had gone on holiday in the past, within a day or two we were missing our dogs so much that we found ourselves making a fuss of any we met. This was even harder to resist on the rare occasions we actually saw a Dane. In fact on one such occasion in the south of France when the boys were small I had seen a superb harlequin dog looking out of the back of a small horse trailer. So convinced was I of the friendliness of this beautiful black and white dog that his ferocious reaction totally took me aback, to the embarrassment of Mel and amusement of the boys. 'He didn't understand English,' was all I could offer by way of explanation as I backed away from the trailer as it rocked on its suspension in time with his great woofs!

So, just half-an-hour after leaving home, it was Paddy who was ministering to my withdrawal symptoms! He was certainly a superb ambassador for the breed and, no doubt, played a small part in softening us up before going out to the kennel to meet his offspring. In the event, he deserved a commission because we were so taken with the conformation and, above all, temperament of the litter that we became a three Dane family once more. We had discussed in the kennel with Jeanette the way our minds were going and so weighed up the pros and cons of having a bitch or a dog.

Our past experience of bitches fighting was putting us off having two bitches but her view was two dogs with one bitch could lead to even greater problems. After due consideration, we agreed so narrowed our choice down to one of two fawn bitches. Jeanette's day-to-day knowledge of them clinched it.

'This pretty one's just a little bit smaller and quieter and would probably slot in better with Marma,' she reasoned. I tussled with my own normal preference for size and the sense of what she had said. Mel was in no doubt at all.

'Yes, she's beautiful,' she murmured, cradling her in her arms.

For some reason, James, who was still with us at home, was entirely unsurprised when we walked in and announced our prospective purchase.

'That was a foregone conclusion,' he said.

'No it wasn't,' I protested. 'We had no intention of buying one when we left home,' I said.

'No,' he said, 'but I knew you would.'

❧

The countdown to Mel's birthday continued relentlessly. The boys had surprised me on my fiftieth by putting a photograph of me in the local paper. Somehow, no doubt with Mel's connivance, they had dredged up one of me sitting in a pram which I hadn't seen for many years. Mel it was, I recalled, who had undertaken the painstaking, and what would for me have been the painful job of sorting through the many photographs in my parents' house after my mother had died suddenly just two-and-a-half years after my father.

It hit me suddenly about two weeks before Mel's big day while sitting in my study that I must do something similar for her. No sooner had the idea struck me than so did the photograph - right between the eyes. There on one of my bookshelves was one taken by her father at the age of about ten or eleven on horseback: it was perfect.

Next came a visit to the hotel to finalise the arrangements. Not only had I to check out the room they had allocated us but I also had to select wines and the type of menu required, the final version being down to the chef on the day. They really entered into the spirit of things when I explained the totality of the surprise and even allocated us the main bar for guests to collect in on arrival. As I had decided we would stay for the night I was also able to see for myself that the requisite sea view was to my liking!

Two days elapsed before I remembered the cake. 'No problem, Mr Cameron. Did you have any kind of theme in mind?'

I hadn't given that any thought but my mind instantly returned to horses again. 'Yes, horses,' I replied giving no further details on the basis that it was best to leave them to come up with something they felt comfortable about tackling. There was no point, for example, asking for a horse jumping a fence in the middle of the cake with no knowledge of the sculpting expertise available in the kitchen!

It was time to pin down the detailed arrangements for the evening and the subterfuges I needed to deploy to get everything to happen without Mel smelling a rat. It needed almost military precision combined with a criminal ability to cover one's tracks!

Twelfth Night 2002 was not just the day, as dictated by tradition, for taking down all Christmas decorations but the day to totally clear the decks as dictated by the arrival of Ellie. Ellie short for Ellen, perhaps? No: Ellie short for elegant which we knew our baby Dane girl would one day become! She had very dark eyes and a black mask with subtle dark shading round the eyes that any make-up artist would be proud to have applied.

Did this mean we were gooey-eyed over the arrival of a sweet feminine retiring little person? Not at all: she was as naughty as any other seven-week puppy. It was true that in the first hours she was a little reticent about the new dogs she had met but, of course, was soon at home with the Danes, so similar to those she had just left, allowing them to adopt her just as a human couple might adopt a waif in need of care and protection.

She found it more difficult to fathom the welcome she got from Chan. It was indeed a welcome as enthusiastic as we could have wished for. But it was an enthusiasm founded on a desire to have someone nearer his own size to play with and, not least, someone who, being smaller and less worldly, might go some way to restoring his esteem, diminished as it had been by the giants that had mushroomed in his midst.

'I feel rotten,' confided Mel after watching the two small dogs romping happily on the rug in the sitting room the next day.

'Why?' I asked, suspecting the reason.

'Well, they're having a lovely time but poor little Chan's going to have his nose put out when Ellie outgrows him,' she said, making exactly the point that had just gone through my mind. 'And it'll be the second time it's happened. He'll probably end up with a complex,' she added sadly.

'Ah, but aren't you forgetting something?' I asked. Her puzzled look told me she had. 'He's got a permanently little friend coming soon,' I reminded her. Her face brightened.

'That's true. But it's going to be bedlam,' she mused. 'Do you think everything will be alright, having two new puppies so close together and with Chan, Marma and Zen still quite immature really.'

'It'll be different,' I conceded, 'but it will operate even more like a pack. We'll just need to be very clear about the pecking order.'

'Which is?' Mel asked.

'Well right now it's Marma followed by Zen, Chan and then Ellie. But Ellie will soon be third and the new Basenji last,' I reasoned.

'I suppose so,' Mel agreed. 'But how do we manage the change with Ellie and Chan?'

'I think we just play it by ear. It's all down to size so as soon as she's bigger than Chan she'll move up.'

'Supposing the Basenji bitch puppy doesn't quite see it that way and bosses Chan like Marma does Zen?' I had no answer so shrugged.

'It will all sort itself out,' I said.

'I hope so, because I love them all,' she smiled.

'But you haven't even seen the new Basenji,' I pointed out, not unreasonably I thought.

Mel's face lit up with a huge smile: 'she's going to be lovely,' she said, her eyes focusing dreamily on some distant point across the room. I simply sighed in mock horror at the thought of two Basenjis!

❧

Having decided to leave it as late as possible to tell Mel that I was planning anything at all, the day finally came in mid-January that I had earmarked to start the ball rolling while still giving away no more information than she really needed to know.

'I'm thinking of taking you somewhere nice for dinner on the Saturday before your birthday,' I said in as casual a manner as I could muster while sharing a bottle wine with her one evening. Her initial reaction was to smile, in the sure knowledge that I was bound to be planning something. Her second reaction was to let her face cloud as she contemplated the implication that it was to be a celebration limited to the two of us. Aha! The confusion forming in her mind was exactly what I had intended so I built on it.

'Of course, I expect Andrew and James will want to come down but I haven't fixed anything. It may be that weekend or the following one,' I said, warming to my mission.

She then asked precisely what I thought she would. 'Why can't we all go out together?'

'Well, we can but I just want the two of us to have a special evening together.' She seemed to accept this. 'Just leave it to me. This way you'll have two celebrations.' She definitely bought that idea before moving on to what I knew she would have to ask, if only to fish about where I was taking her.

'I'm not fishing,' she fibbed, 'but I need to have some idea what to wear.'

'Darling,' I said, as seductively as was possible for a fifty-seven-year-old, 'I really want you to look your best for me that night.' I brushed her shoulder with the back of my fingers.

'Yes, but,' still fishing, 'do I wear smart casual, a smart dress or what?' Oh dear. I had to give away a little more.

'Dress as though you were going for an evening out in a smart place and then dinner.' It was hard to avoid being enigmatic.

'Hmm. I'll try a few things on and you can tell me what you think,' she replied, giving up for the time being. 'Will I need to get my hair done?' she asked, thinking my guard had dropped. I was ready for her.

'Of course. Where I'm taking you, you'll really want to look your best.' A small grin preceded her next question.

'Which is where exactly?'

'I think I've given away enough already,' I replied, smug in the knowledge I had done no such thing.

My own birthday was ticking round, to pass almost unnoticed I hoped. Mel bought me a very nice top quality radio for listening to in the utility room during the ten minutes or so it took me to feed the dogs each night and morning. 'I'm glad you're pleased with your present,' she said when I emerged one morning after feeding them.

'Yes, of course. Why wouldn't I be pleased?' I replied. She grinned.

'It's just that I've noticed it seems to take you longer to feed the dogs now.' I smiled, recognising the truth of her comment. I did tend to get immersed in the Today programme but I also had the constant buzzing around in my mind of the details of her birthday evening. I had obviously had to tell the invitees the venue, time of arrival and broad arrangements as well as communicating, as delicately as I could, the fact that I was paying. There was nothing worse than being asked out to dinner and being unsure on this point unless it was to be embarrassed about it. On the confirmation I sent out I merely added the words in the appropriate place 'as our guests.'

One small hurdle to be vaulted was the Jaguar Enthusiasts' Club Christmas dinner held, as usual, in January. This year it happened to coincide with my birthday and those friends who had already been invited to Mel's played a blinder in managing to avoid any reference to it, though one or two later apologised for actually having to avoid us to achieve this!

That weekend I received a phone call out of the blue from Tim Bruton, our long-standing friend from Wiltshire. While we had kept in touch via phone and Christmas cards we had not seen him and Georgie since that chance meeting with them outside Tesco's in Salisbury.

'Our girls have got a special birthday coming up, haven't they?' he asked. He had reminded me that Georgie was a near 'twin' of Mel's: they were born just days apart in the same year, Mel being marginally the elder.

'Yes,' I replied a little cagily as I had not at that point invited them to Mel's.

'Well, I'm putting on a little surprise party for Georgie on the 26th and wondered whether you and Mel would be able to come. We'd love to see you though, of course, Georgie knows absolutely nothing about it at this stage.' I tried unsuccessfully to keep a straight face and, sensing this had communicated itself to Tim, immediately returned the compliment.

'We'd love to Tim. I'm sure we can get Justin to look after the animals for one night. Tim, I'm doing the same for Mel and we'd love you both to come. That too is a secret as far as Mel is concerned.'

'Oh, that's marvellous Dex. We'd love to come. I just need to check with Georgie who's out at the moment.'

There began a peculiar double-sided deception for the next two weeks with Mel knowing about Georgie's party but not her own and Georgie keeping Mel's a secret while not suspecting Tim's plans. I was beginning, along with everyone else involved, to know just a little of what it must be like to conspire in the making of 'This is Your Life'!

It was exactly one week before her birthday, and just four days before the dinner that Mel first complained of a severe pain in her left knee which kept giving way. She could not put a finger on the likely cause but had trouble walking. She increased her intake of aloe vera in the hope of reducing the swelling which had become evident. She decided she would give it a couple of days before going to the doctor.

Ellie was growing fast, prompting me to snatch a beautiful photograph of her reclining on the small step down into the sitting room one evening. Like children, puppies and kittens - and foals for that matter - grew up quickly and it

146

was important to make a point of recording their progress because, before you knew it, they had completed an important phase which, of course, would never return. For that reason I tended to leave a loaded camera around to catch such moments for posterity.

Some moments I seemed never to be around to catch were the ones when she chewed through the other dogs' collars! Ever since Chan's little foray into neighbouring fields as a puppy, Mel had decided all the dogs were to wear collars with address tags whenever they were outside. Gradually we got out of the habit of removing them when they came in so they became a permanent fixture; until, that is, Ellie single-handedly (or should that be single-mouthedly?) started to run up a weekly bill for cheap collars at Trago!

In the last week before Mel's do, I had finalised the last details. Everyone was to meet in the Green bar at the hotel between 7.00 and 7.30 where the boys would greet and look after them. At 7.45 on the dot we would leave our room. I had gone over and over the sequence of events in my mind to ensure there was no chance of the surprise being spoiled. I had even been relieved when our friends the Carters and Wellings had told me they had booked into a neighbouring hotel as the Carlyon Bay was full that night.

It had also enabled me to tell Tim that the hotel was full and to offer to find him accommodation somewhere to his liking. It was no surprise when he declined my offer and said he'd find somewhere. It therefore gave me something of a jolt when Tim phoned me just two days beforehand to announce triumphantly that not only had he got a cancelled booking at our hotel but was even on our floor!

'That's great, Tim but...'

'... but you're worried Mel might bump into us...'

'Yes,' I replied.

'Don't worry, we'll make sure we're shut in our room when you arrive.' We went on to arrange precisely when it would be safe for them to emerge.

I still had the final story to concoct and rehearse with the boys, which I couldn't do until the Saturday morning after they arrived, while Mel was out getting the papers as usual.

'I've told Mum you all wanted to see her around her birthday and this was the only weekend you could all be here together,' I told them when she was safely out of the house.

'Did she believe you?' asked Andrew with a grin.

'Not sure. Think so,' I replied. 'She was a bit disappointed you weren't joining us tonight but I told her as she and I were away for the night, you'd agreed to look after the cats and dogs. I told her we were all having lunch together tomorrow instead. She seemed quite happy with that.'

'Are we?' asked James.

'Are we what?'

'Having lunch together tomorrow.'

'Oh yes. In fact the Carters and Wellings are joining us. I've booked a table at The Crow's Nest,' I replied. 'And just to convince her, I'm going to give you some money as we leave tonight,' I added. Three pairs of eyes swivelled in my direction. 'For a takeaway,' I explained.

'We thought we'd better get a taxi there later,' said Andrew. 'So we can drink,' he added superfluously.

'OK,' I said, 'you can use the money for that!' Dad still had a soft side, I thought.

'I want you there at seven on the dot to greet everyone and to make sure they've got a drink. It's no good being late,' I continued, shooting an involuntary glance in James' direction. I thought I detected a suppressed groan from around the room. 'Well not everyone knows everyone else and it will help get everyone chatting to each other.'

I went on to explain it was as important not to be early as not to be late.

'When everyone's arrived I want you, Andrew, to go to reception and ask one of the staff to phone up to our room to tell us our taxi's arrived.'

'What taxi?' asked Justin.

'Well there won't be one really. It's just a way of keeping your mother's mind off the possibility I've organised something. I've told her I'm taking her out somewhere special and then we're going for a meal after that.'

'Do you think it'll work?' asked James.

'Got a better idea?' I asked. The lack of response gave me my answer.

'What if someone's late?' asked Andrew.

'Good point,' I answered thoughtfully. 'In that case we'll just have to go ahead without them. I've told everyone why it's important to be there on time so I don't think that'll happen.'

Mel said goodbye to the boys just after six, the time I worked out we'd need to leave to avoid Tim and Georgie as agreed with Tim. It was difficult to get Mel to leave without letting on there was any strict timetable for the evening. Once safely in the car and nosing down the drive the next little challenge was how to avoid Mel guessing our destination, as I hadn't told her which hotel we were headed for. Knowing she would guess it was the Nare as soon as I turned the car in that general direction, I said, 'you can probably guess where we're going.'

'No,' she replied wide-eyed but unconvincingly.

'Well it's difficult to keep that secret as we get nearer,' I added mischievously. As we got close to the back way into the Carlyon Bay I took a chance on the fact that Mel hadn't been down that road before.

'Do you know where we're going yet?' I grinned after we turned unexpectedly left.

'Not a clue,' she replied honestly.

'I just felt I'd like to take you on a little detour to confuse you,' I went on dishonestly. 'It's just a bit more picturesque than the usual route,' I said, relieved that daylight at the end of the first tunnel of subterfuge was at last in view. As we crossed the beach road into the Hotel entrance drive I knew Mel's reaction was about to become apparent.

'Are we staying here?' I had no idea whether her question hinted at disappointment or... 'Oh good! I've always wanted to try it,' she said to my amazement and relief.

14 All Aboard

'What's the relative speed of a fly sitting on the front of a train?' I remember the question, posed by the head of our maths department with a smile which seemed to say, 'I know something you don't,' as if it was yesterday. It was actually over forty years earlier and I remember dreading it leading on to a question about how long it would take the fly to fly to an oncoming train and back again and so on until the two trains passed each other. But that was to come later.

The point he was actually getting at was that the fly, being smaller, would feel it was travelling faster than a human would on the same train because both fly and human would be judging how quickly objects their own size passed by. The speed would therefore appear much greater to the fly. Despite the detailed diagrams he drew on the blackboard showing the angle of vision of each and how objects their own size took up different proportions of them, to this day I'm not completely convinced!

What I am more sure of, however, is the comparable proposition that the older one gets the quicker time seems to slip through one's fingers. Was it, I wondered, simply because each day that passed represented a smaller and smaller proportion of the time that had been lived through so far? Einstein's theory of relativity had it that the passage of time could speed up and slow down so that one year could appear to pass at a different rate than another.

I wasn't sure whether I was caught out more by the realisation that sixty was bearing down on me at an alarmingly accelerating rate or that Mel, whom I had first known at the age of eighteen, was not so far behind me! It was she who had told me many times over the years that in her head she never felt any older. The more I pondered this the more it appeared to be true. When I shaved, the bespectacled eyes peering out of the mirror at me, beneath grey hair and from a face etched with lines were surely those of a much older man!

I was definitely a young man as I strode up into the Carlyon Bay Hotel, behind the porter carrying our bags, holding Mel's hand. A night away was always something to be relished. I found, however, that I couldn't help flicking my eyes to and fro, dreading them coming into contact with a familiar face. That would have given the game away right at the end of many weeks of careful concealment. I had already briefed the delightful young lady who had been responsible for the evening's arrangements on the taxi story but I knew I had to check with the receptionist on duty that night to ensure everything went smoothly.

'Wait here a moment, Darling. I need to check in and make sure the taxi's booked for later,' I said to Mel. For once she did as she was told without questioning it! The receptionist nodded conspiratorially that everything was in hand and pushed the checking-in form in front of me to fill in. As soon as the key was handed to the waiting porter, he led the way to the lift. We disposed of the usual question about whether we were on holiday by explaining we lived about fifteen minutes away and were there for just one night. My eyes were skinned as I slunk along the corridor, petrified at the thought of Tim's large ebullient form appearing suddenly in front of us. It didn't.

'What a lovely room,' said Mel as she looked out of the window as if taking in the magnificent sea view which was quite invisible in the dark.

'It's a lovely view as you'll see in the morning,' I assured her.

'Provided it's not foggy,' she chuckled, reminding me of the time we had spent a whole weekend in solid fog at the Polurrian Hotel at Mullion just after it had been refurbished. Despite being able to hear the sea we had not caught a single glimpse of it!

At last I could relax, knowing nothing more needed thinking about until Andrew prompted the receptionist to phone in just under an hour. We had a drink, watched something mindless on TV and then started to get ready. At least Mel did. In the end I had encouraged her to take the safe option of wearing a 'little black dress', if only because it seemed to satisfy her. I was just grateful that for once she was happily going along with whatever unfolded.

I had had to think about how to explain when we later went down to the lobby why we were turning left in the direction of the Green Bar rather than right, as she would be expecting, towards the entrance where the cab would be waiting.

I had told Mel to be ready by 7.30 as the cab was booked for then: one thing we could not be that evening was late. As was our custom we were both ready by 7.35! The ten minutes we had to wait for the phone call was, with the exception of waiting in church for Mel to arrive for our wedding, the longest ten minutes of my life as she got restless and I tried to calm her down.

'Why's he late?' she asked. Then, a few minutes later: 'aren't you going to phone up and see what's happened?'

'No, plenty of time,' I soothed.

'Are you sure you booked it for 7.30? It's nearly 7.45,' she said as the time ticked by.

'He'll be here soon,' I asserted. When it got to 7.47 I was beginning to wonder what had gone wrong but dared not show it.

'Why don't we go downstairs to wait?' she wanted to know at 7.48.

'Because it's not our place to wait for him,' I said, struggling somewhat by that time. 'He's late so he can wait for us,' I added, almost inspirationally, I thought.

'This is ridic...' she began before cutting herself off as she remembered the evening was something I had organised for her benefit. I had never before seen her decide to go with the flow unprompted and had to strangle at birth the smile that threatened to erupt at just the wrong moment.

The phone rang. The receptionist's voice said simply, 'your taxi's here sir.'

'OK. Thank you.' I smiled and nodded towards the door. 'Let's go. He's going to be another ten minutes. Some sort of mix up by the hotel. They've said to wait in the bar and have a drink on the house while we wait,' I lied rather convincingly as she swallowed, I guessed, yet another complaint about the way things weren't going according to plan.

We walked down the stairs: 'I hope you're not going to be disappointed,' I added, now back in my stride and lowering her expectations at a stroke.

'I'm sure I won't,' she assured me, almost bravely, I thought. 'It'll be wonderful whatever it is,' she added, her deadpan face confirming that I had succeeded!

'Where's the bar?' she asked, peering around the lobby area as I hoped that the next few seconds would not see us confronting the familiar faces of friends.

There were just feet to go. The door to the bar, usually open, was closed and curtained giving nothing away about its occupants. I took a breath, pushed open the door and held it for Mel. Her eyes fell upon Terry Chapman of the Jaguar Enthusiasts' Club. Later she told me her immediate reaction was surprise at seeing him but her assumption was he was there for a golfing function. Then she spotted Tricia Carter, her long-time friend from Wiltshire. Almost idiotically she asked, 'what are you doing here?' before collecting herself and saying, 'it's so wonderful to see you.' Then, next to Tricia and husband Jim, were Carl and Barbara Wellings. Swivelling her now wet eyes back to Terry she could see him and wife Margaret deep in conversation with Tim and Georgie whom they had never met before. The penny finally dropped and I could see Mel beginning to get into the swing of things.

Her final reaction was of utter delight at spotting the grinning faces of her three boys, dressed in suits and ties, looking smarter than we had ever seen them collectively before. I, too, felt my throat constrict with pride. They were beaming with reflected pleasure.

Andrew then gave me the explanation for the last minute delay in our 'taxi'. Unfortunately Mike and Jeanette Callan had a recently whelped bitch who was suffering from mastitis, an inflammation of the mammary glands. It is a highly dangerous, potentially fatal condition and she could not fairly be left with their son who had been deputed to look after their dogs for the evening. This was a disappointment but utterly understandable.

I had given careful thought to the seating plan as many friends had not previously met. I was staggered to discover that no less than four couples had or were in the process of restoring houses. Five bred or had bred dogs. Four couples were keen horse people and two of the men restored classic motorbikes. Two couples had cattle or goats. In addition, of course, were the Jaguar enthusiasts who had to be split up or they would have shown their enthusiasm all evening!

The net result was that I managed to sit people not only opposite their other halves but also next to someone they didn't know but with whom they had something in common.

After checking the room and seating I returned to the bar to find a throng of people, who had already mixed with those they didn't know, humming away in conversation. On a long table lay the presents they had bought for Mel, including a small one from me, pending her getting her proper one on her actual birthday.

The evening flowed just as freely as the wine. I started it off by walking round the table and, standing behind everyone in turn, giving a potted and humorous version of their life history. Whatever ice had remained unbroken was then shattered or, more accurately, melted for good.

It was some time after the three courses had vanished that a waitress reminded me about the cake. I hoped the kitchen had done justice to my request for a horsey theme. It was over coffee that Chris Roberts and I had planned for her to fulfil her kind offer to say a few words about Mel. In the few seconds available to me before I introduced Chris, I had to slink to the far end of the table, where Mel was seated, to pre-warn her and to 'suggest' to her she should give some sort of reply.

She clasped her left hand to her mouth. 'But whatever should I say?' she asked in a slight panic. Knowing she would have reacted in this way, even without the element of total surprise she had already had to take in her stride, I had taken the precaution of jotting down a few key points on a small card.

'Something I prepared earlier,' I grinned. 'I've just put down a few prompts but just say what you feel like saying in your own words,' I added before slipping back to my seat.

Chris finished her very polished and aptly worded little speech of thanks for the evening and sat down. I nodded to Mel who stood and gave a brief response which was exactly right, thanking everyone for going to the lengths they had to ensure the evening was a total surprise. None of us was in any doubt that we had succeeded.

The cake arrived. Mel's face lit up in spontaneous delight. When I finally got to see it close up, I knew the hotel had done a perfect job. With no clues from me they had put two horses on the cake, standing in stables with hay, broom, wheelbarrow and rake outside.

'How wonderful!' Mel exclaimed. 'Did you tell them to put two horses on it?'

'No. It was just coincidence,' I said. It was the perfect way of rounding off what had been an excellent meal. What had also been a brilliant evening was also drawing to a close. I had one more suggestion to make to Mel. 'Wouldn't you like to open your presents?'

'But it's not my birthday yet,' she replied.

'No but I'm sure everyone would be very happy for you to open them so they can see,' I explained, knowing how the pleasure from giving was always enhanced by the witnessing of the receiving. She readily agreed and when I let everyone know this was going to happen, it was someone much younger than fifty who opened them with such excitement. It reminded me instantly of the childlike joy with which Mel had first introduced me to Rinsey, 'our' rugged little cove in West Cornwall, all those years ago.

My own small gift was a simply-framed photograph of Ellie, at just ten weeks, lying lion-like on the step down into the sitting room. 'My baby!' was all Mel said, eyes moistening. It was all the thanks I needed. Of course, that wasn't the end of the evening and it was after everyone, old friends and new, had spent the next few hours chatting over a few drinks in the lounge that we finally fell into bed at around three. I had been tickled to overhear several of our new friends from Cornwall exchanging phone numbers with some of our old ones from Wiltshire as they were leaving.

'What a beautiful view,' Mel exclaimed on drawing back the curtains just after 8.30 the next morning.

We bumped into Tim and Georgie, already halfway through their breakfast, when we went down to the restaurant.

'Great night,' said Tim. 'Thank you very much for inviting us.'

'Yes, it was lovely to see you both,' added Georgie. Mel and I, almost simultaneously, had to restrain ourselves in our reply.

'Yes,' I replied, 'it was great to see you both.'

'Thank you so much for coming,' added Mel. 'We mustn't leave it so long. Perhaps you can come and see us in the spring, or summer maybe.'

Tim's relief that, in the hazy aftermath of the night before, we had not inadvertently let the cat out of the bag regarding his surprise for Georgie the following Saturday was palpable. In fact, I swear he dabbed his forehead with his handkerchief! They had to leave early to collect their younger son from boarding school en route but not before I contrived to slip alongside Tim as he was paying their bill to make the final arrangements.

'Get there before twelve because the boys are taking Georgie into town in the morning to give everyone the chance to arrive and surprise her on her return.'

I said we would and asked whether his earlier offer of a bed for that night was still open.

'Yes, of course,' he said with his own unique enthusiasm. 'But Georgie doesn't know of course so it'll be a bit chaotic...'

'Are you sure you want to spring that on her?' I asked.

'Yes, it'll be fine Dex.' Somehow I had my doubts that he would have total recall of the conversation in six days' time!

We both joined Mel and Georgie who were chatting animatedly in the lobby, as if battling to complete the three-and-a-half years' catching up they had only managed to make a start on the night before.

'At least we can leave without fear of bumping into you,' boomed Tim with a laugh as he kissed Mel goodbye on her cheek. 'Do you know,' he confided, as if still sensitive about the little deceit we had all perpetrated, 'I came quite close to letting the cat out of the bag last night around the time you were due to arrive.' He had my attention though, of course, I could let go the tension he had just created in my mind as it no longer mattered.

'I realised I had left my jacket in the car and had to come down to get it. I had to hide behind pillars in the hotel and bushes in the car park in case you turned up while I was there,' he added earnestly but twinkling with amusement. It enabled us all to say our goodbyes with our laughter echoing round the lobby.

On the slow drive home Mel looked at me, planted the lightest of kisses on my cheek, causing the Jag to momentarily forget its way, and said, 'thank you darling. It was, I think, the nicest night of my life.'

I settled for that, recalling that our wedding night had been spent surviving gales in the Bay of Biscay!

❧

I had, of course, one final surprise for Mel. The day before her birthday she still had no idea we were going away for the night, so whatever I sprang on her was bound to be well received. I finally gave her exactly twenty-four hours warning that we would be going somewhere, but not where.

At the appointed time we got into the car and I pointed it up the lane knowing it would instantly narrow the choices for her to guess at. I knew these would narrow further when I got to the top of the lane. Instead of turning right, in the correct direction, I turned left.

'Know where you're going yet?' I asked, anticipating the enjoyment of one final ploy to confuse her.

'Not a clue,' she sighed sinking back into her seat as if resigning herself to her fate, whatever it was.

We soon found ourselves heading towards Looe.

'Any ideas now?' I asked, beginning to wonder myself where I would take us next.

'No,' she replied. 'That hotel way above the river?' she guessed, looking at me quizzically. I merely smiled through closed lips.

At the next 'T' junction I turned away from Looe. I glanced at her and saw the resignation had turned once more to curiosity. 'Now I definitely don't know where we're going,' she said, leaning a little further forward in her seat.

I knew we soon had to head straight for our destination or we wouldn't make dinner for the time I had booked our table. I deliberately said nothing more about where we might or might not be headed. When we got to the back road to the Carlyon Bay Hotel I glanced briefly at Mel. She seemed to be anticipating an action replay of her party. I had to turn left and retrace our earlier journey. As we came up to the approach road to the hotel I could see she was relaxed knowing at last where we were going. Instead of crossing the beach road, however, I turned right and returned to the main road where I resumed our westward direction.

It was not long before we had to finally turn off left again. This time I could see the broadest of grins spread across her face indicating that she had made her final guess.

'I know where we're going now,' she said.

'Really?' I asked, trying to work out how to string it out a bit further. 'You can't. There are several places I can turn back onto the main road again,' I responded, obviously less convincingly than I had thought.

'But you're not going to,' she said.

'Might do.'

'No you won't.'

'You seem fairly sure about that.'

'Yep.'

'Go on then, where?'

'We're going to the Nare, aren't we?' I said nothing. 'Aren't we?' she continued, just a little less sure now. I still said nothing, struggling to keep a straight face. It was her tickling me as I wound the Jag round the twists of the lane that brought the last surprise into the open.

'Might be,' was all I said with a give-away smile.

Our room was high up with three external walls and a large round window like an oversized porthole, giving the impression of being on board ship. After an excellent, relaxed meal and copious amounts of wine, including a bottle of champagne while making our choice from the menu, when Mel got her proper present, we returned to our room. Our climb up the last narrow staircase, with its rope hand-rail, to our room, rather like ascending a gangplank, added to the impression of boarding ship.

The illusion was completed when we were awoken in the early hours of the morning by the crashing storm which enveloped us on three sides.

'I feel like I did on our wedding night,' Mel said sleepily.

'Oh no, you're not going to throw up are you?'

'No, of course not. It's just that it feels like we're on board a ship,' she explained. I got out of bed to go and look out of the porthole. The wind was right up and driving the heavy rain hard against the glass.

'You're right,' I said returning to the comfort of the bunk, er, bed. 'And the floor seemed to move a bit just then,' I said.

'It must be the champagne,' Mel muttered through a stifled yawn.

We had to go through yet another surprise the following Saturday when we arrived at Tim and Georgie's new home near Salisbury. It was a lovely barn conversion carried out in the grounds of their old home. They had retained most of the land and so, apart from exchanging a very old house for a very new one, the only real change was a much improved view across their fields towards their lake.

We all huddled together in the sitting room, out of sight, when Georgie arrived back from Salisbury. We then had to shuffle into an adjoining room so she couldn't catch a glimpse of us until Tim was ready to spring us on her.

Once more the surprise was total. Georgie was convulsed when telling us how, having no inkling of what was about to hit her, she had said almost idly on passing Tesco's, 'I must just pop in and buy a few things we're out of,' to the utter consternation of her two sons. The older of the two had had the presence of mind to warn his father in just about the only subtle way open to him.

'Yes,' laughed Georgie, 'he phoned his father on the mobile, told him that I was popping into Tesco's and asked whether there was anything he wanted. Apparently Tim then asked how long we'd be. All I know was I was frog-marched round that shop by the two of them. All they said by way of explanation was they were hungry and wanted to get back for lunch!'

We had a good night meeting up with old acquaintances and making new ones. I had no idea that I was still able to keep going until 4.00am and still less of one that I could consume the number of beers and glasses of wine that I did, together with the odd brandy, and still make sense! It came as no surprise to me that it was gone 4.00 before Tim finally told Georgie that we and one other couple who had travelled from Wales were staying the night. Nor that she took it all in her stride, completely reorganising the household's sleeping arrangements and making up beds, with help, enabling us all to tumble into bed around 4.30.

Our parting comment the next day was that we really mustn't let another year go by before meeting up again and that we'd love them to come and stay with us in Cornwall. But we have!

On our return home the next day, having called in on Andrew for lunch, I opened an e-mail from Sally Wallis telling us that, while her Basenji bitch had whelped, there had been just one puppy in the litter, a male. Such was her disappointment after such enthusiastic interest in us as new Basenji owners that she most kindly contacted a number of other Basenji breeders on our behalf. We too got busy on the phone and within a few hours had tracked down Frank and Barbara Williams up in Leigh, Lancashire, who had recently had a litter of their Custos Basenjis and had one or two puppies for sale, including bitches.

Barbara sent us numerous photographs by e-mail over the following few days enabling us to say 'yes'! Our red and white puppy would be able to join us around the middle of February.

'You'll soon have a friend just like you to play with,' Mel said to Chan after I put the phone down to Barbara. 'And she won't get bigger than you this time,' she said as if sensing his need for reassurance on this tricky matter.

'Yes, but it'll be some time before he realises that,' I said.

'What're we going to call her?' asked Mel. 'We've got a couple of weeks to think of a name,' she added quickly as if to forestall any quips on my part.

'Something to sum her up, I suppose. Something feminine but mischievous,' was all I could contribute.

15 Filofadds

Aubiose was put down at the beginning of February. No, it wasn't euthanasia of a geriatric animal with an obscure name so much as a matter of pandering to two not-quite-geriatric horse owners! It had been recommended to us by fellow Morgan horse owners over the border in Devon. It was a horse bedding made from the dried chopped stems of the hemp plant. Its main benefit was that, being extremely absorbent, it cut down the effort in mucking out stables. Instead of having to fork over the entire stable every day, all we had to do was remove the solids each morning and replace the sodden bedding once a week.

The main drawback was that it was considerably more expensive than the chopped paper we had been using. Within a few days, however, Mel and I were noticing how much more energy we had and, as far as it was remotely possible, even became enthusiastic about mucking out.

This came at a most welcome time as Mel's knee was becoming even more troublesome and painful. While it had improved over a period of weeks, it now seemed to be worsening again, a sure sign she should seek a medical opinion. It transpired that she had strained a tendon in her knee for which the cure was a course of physiotherapy. While this brought a rapid improvement, the physiotherapist's comments got us thinking about the possible cause: it was no good repairing the damage only to repeat the injury.

Of course, physical exercise, from housework to riding was out of the question and that particularly included mucking out which became my personal monopoly for a while. It was on the third or fourth day of doing it that I began to suffer the early twinges of what I slowly recognised were sympathy pains. It was the combination of these and the frustrations of opening and closing the metal field gate into the barn and Smartie's stable door that led to the dull clunk of a penny dropping. My annoyance with the gate and door yielded the conclusion that they had both dropped a little so that each bolt no longer slid home without lifting them a little. How did I lift them when I had got into my new daily routine? By sliding my toes under them and lifting them of course - from the knee!

My first task was to make the necessary adjustments to realign the bolts. The instant, rewarding result was total ease of operation. My second was to give Mel the good news that I believed I had identified the cause of her discomfort and had rectified it. Her initial pleasure was dented by the realisation that her normal duties could be resumed without further ado. We both learned a useful lesson about not unduly straining any part of our anatomy in future!

Mike and Jeanette Callan used the excuse of wanting to see how Ellie was developing to visit us and, totally unexpectedly, to present Mel with the gift they had bought to take along to her birthday celebration. The kindness of their gesture was heightened by the fact that it was a wall plaque of a puppy Dane head, hand-painted by its creator Ronnie Jones, from Summercourt, to match the colouring of Ellie. This she had seen in Jeanette and Mike's copy of the photograph of Ellie which I had given to Mel which Mel had wanted them to have.

The next birthday, Andrew's, was celebrated with his brothers at the Black Horse at Sawton near Honiton which we had chosen for being about halfway between our homes. I was able to point out to him that he was now a cube: he was twenty-seven! How aged must I then be, when he was rapidly approaching thirty, the age at which I first became conscious of the rapid passing of time? It was the longest we had left the dogs during the day and we were extremely relieved to find all dogs and fittings unharmed on our return.

This was not the case a few days later when Chan pushed his luck once too often with Zen. Given that Zen could have killed him instantly, Chan got off lightly with the odd nick and bruise to his left front leg but milked our sympathy for all it was worth by limping ostentatiously when we were watching him. After a cuddle from Mel the limp had gone some minutes later! But Zen, too, was in need of comforting. His face had looked quite downcast afterwards, as though he expected to be in trouble for something which had not been started by him.

Ellie, meanwhile, was getting into her own scrapes. She taunted and occasionally played too roughly with both Marma and Zen. They tolerated her with enormous patience, realising it was just youthful exuberance. One morning when she had pushed their patience to the limit, they both chased her into the shrubs in the raised bed between the house and the barn. My heart leaped into my mouth as I peered out of the hall window and saw her only means of escape was over the four-foot high dry stone retaining wall. A drop like that could damage the growth of her front legs. Zen had survived a similar drop at about the same age but luck might not be with us a second time.

Ellie's solution, however, was as elegant as it was unexpected. She launched herself onto her chest and tummy and slid gently down to the ground, courtesy of the dense rosemary cascading down the wall. Zen and Marma screeched to a halt, uncertain of the wisdom of following her. It was a tactic she was to successfully employ again and again in the days ahead!

Rosemary was also in evidence at the Nare on Valentine's night. We were unable to stay but could think of nowhere better for a romantic evening. Mel had lamb for her main course while I had three courses of fish: what bliss, especially the salmon in a delicate curry sauce!

The excitement of that evening soon paled against the looming expectation of the imminent arrival of our Basenji bitch puppy. The daunting logistics of collecting her from Leigh were soon resolved by Barbara and Frank, her breeders, offering to meet up with us somewhere in between. Barbara was due to judge in Wales and her suggestion was to kill two birds: we arranged to meet somewhere easy for both of us to find, a service station on the M5!

I checked with her in advance whether she wanted cash or whether a cheque would be acceptable. She said she was happy with a cheque. Such trust was truly heartening considering how misplaced it can be these days.

'What if you don't like Betsy?' I asked Mel tentatively on the way up the A30, for Betsy was her chosen name. It seemed to us to sum up the bustling nature we could expect from a Basenji bitch: always busy, in a feminine, fidgety sort of way!

'She'll be lovely,' Mel cooed.

'How do you know?' I asked.

'I just do. She looked beautiful in the photographs Barbara sent.'

'Yes, she did but photos can be deceptive and they did come via the internet so they were difficult to see clearly.' I was talking to myself.

On arrival at the service station we positioned ourselves near the entrance to the car park so Frank and Barbara could find us. We had already been in contact on our mobiles so knew we were ahead of them. In fact we had around half-an-hour in hand so grabbed a bite to eat as it would be our last chance until we got home. Just as we were finishing we got a call to say they would be with us in a few minutes.

Frank had a description of our car and found us instantly, parking nearby. It was a chilly, blustery February day and so our hellos were brief as we decided to go into the cafeteria for a coffee and to exchange the relevant pieces of paper. But not so brief that we did not first have the opportunity to meet the tiny puppy who curled up tightly against Mel for warmth in the cold wind. Barbara told me months later that it was at that precise moment that she knew it was love at first sight and her natural anxieties about Betsy's potential new owners subsided. Reluctantly Mel handed her back to Barbara as she would be safer in her travelling cage until our return than if loose in the Jag: or, rather, the Jag would be safer !

It was soon time for Barbara to say her tearful goodbyes to Betsy, give her one last cuddle and kiss and hand her over to Mel. In time I was to discover for myself just how involuntary was such affection for these delightful if challenging little dogs.

Just how tiny she was became apparent when we saw her with Chan, now fully grown. Each of her meals was just one tablespoonful of complete food with a little goat's milk with which we had been thoughtfully provided by Barbara. Needless to say, her introduction to the other dogs was careful and unrushed. But introduced she was that first night, when she took her place amongst them but protected by the small cage that Chan had used.

First thing in the morning I was greeted by a series of shrieks from the kitchen. Betsy was very much up and doing and demanding to be let out to get on with her day in her new home. The only precaution necessary was to ensure the Danes did not accidentally tread on her. This was short-lived, however, as she proved adept at dodging out of the way of their feet, each being bigger than her head, or of letting out a high-pitched scream if contact was made.

By the end of the first morning she had added to her defensive repertoire the typical Basenji growl! In short she had made her presence felt and seemed unimpressed with the underdog, bottom of the pack role we had prepared for her. Even Chan, still attempting to dominate Zen, was put in his place though, we knew, he did not mind so much.

The cats were less impressed by the newcomer, miaowing to be let out of the kitchen at frequent intervals until we relented. Like many PC users I had a number of yellow 'post-it' notes stuck to my computer monitor reminding me of various things. Moss got to the point of feeling the need to demonstrate his discomfiture at the new arrival by constantly seeking my attention. He would jump onto my desk scattering loose papers. Then he would leap to the top of my bookshelf, tuck his paws under him and watch me, blinking benignly for a minute or two before jumping down and then onto my lap, peering at the cursor arrow as it moved about the screen as if plotting the kill. Then he decided to investigate the screen more closely: on hearing my protest he started rubbing his whiskers on the edge of the monitor, winding his body round its corners. Then, as if bored by the whole business, he flicked his tail and hopped down to go for a wander round the house.

'What's Moss got stuck to his tail?' Mel called from the hallway. 'Yours, I believe,' she grinned as she came in and deposited a 'post-it' note on my desk.

I looked blankly at it and then recognised the message to myself. 'He's just stolen that,' I laughed. Taking the hint, I got on with making the phone call it was telling me to make.

By the end of February not only was Betsy settled and no trouble whatsoever but so was Mel's knee and she was signed off by the physio.

The Jaguar Enthusiasts' Club was responsible for us doing something we had never done before: they had us hunting treasure! We started in West Cornwall, taking in the area south west of Camborne and like any treasure hunt we were required to follow some esoteric directions, get answers to certain obscure questions and collect one or two unusual items on the way.

It was a lovely sunny, early spring day and the Cornish friendliness enhanced by the lack of any serious competitive edge made for a most relaxing and enjoyable morning. We were due to finish at the lovely farm house of Henry and Jane Marks. Jane had devised and organised the day and had also arranged lunch for everyone at her house. As we wound our way round the narrow twisting lanes, Mel and I focused on the place-specific questions first, reasoning that by leaving the objects until last we would maintain a good pace, not that time was a factor.

Others used their own approach and some amusement was to be had when one member and his wife overtook us only to pass us going in the opposite direction minutes later because they forgot to look for a name over a pub door! All went well until we started to search for a requisite piece of slate. Anyone familiar with Cornwall knows it is full of slate. Slate from Delabole adorns many an entrance hall floor and, of course, slate roof tiles are everywhere. On that day, however, short of stealing a fragment from someone's roof, there was none to be found.

Then I saw it. A gateway to a field had black material scattered in front of it to give grip to any vehicle needing to go through it. Most of the material was dark grey gravel but I found just one tiny shard of slate which was, of course, all we needed. We had no trouble finding a sprig of flowering gorse which was brightening up many of the Cornish hedges. But the final item had us utterly defeated simply because we had never heard of it. We were required to collect some filofadds. Mel and I delved into our memory banks but nothing was unearthed. We, or rather I, as it was my traditional function, tried logic but nothing obvious sprang to mind.

'It must be Cornish for something,' I concluded with disappointment. Henry and Jane were certainly Cornish and not beyond a little joke and the word did look faintly Welsh at the end.

'But that would be unfair,' reasoned Mel with impeccable logic and challenging my traditional role.

'Mmm, I think you're right. But what can it be then?'

'No idea,' said Mel, 'but it would a pity not to get the last item.'

'I know,' I replied with a minor burst of inspiration, 'let's phone Justin and get him to look it up on the internet.'

'That's a good idea,' said Mel, rummaging in her handbag for her mobile phone. 'The signal's very weak. You'll have to stop when I get a decent one,' she added after failing to make contact. 'Here!' I stopped in a wider part of the lane away from a bend so she could make the call.

I gazed idly at the bank to my right in the bright sunlight, dreaming of the summer days to come. I started lazily identifying the different flowers I could see. Apart from gorse there were fading primroses. I looked for pink campion but realised it was too early. Then to my delight I saw the tiny, exquisite yellow bloom of ...'

'Why is it taking you so long?' Mel asked Justin. 'He says your computer's a bit slow,' she mouthed in my direction by way of explanation. 'F-i-l-o-f-a-d-d,' she spelled out to Justin slowly. I had a mental picture of him keying in the letters as she spoke.

'Got it!' I exclaimed, feeling pleased with myself.

'What? Hold on a minute Justin,' she said, turning her face towards me. 'Got what, darling?'

'Filofadd,' I replied triumphantly. 'It's an anagram.'

'What of?' she asked, frowning uncomprehendingly.

'I'm looking at one,' I smirked, returning my gaze to the bank. 'Isn't it beautiful?'

Mel's smile lit up her face as she explained to Justin, 'it's alright, your father's just worked it out. It's an anagram of daffodil...' I didn't hear the response at the other end but I guess it was as amused as Jane was when I told her later about our attempted use of technology.

'But that would be cheating, Dex,' she laughed as I went through our little story in her kitchen.

❧

March came in with a benign roar. Mel's knee was fully recovered, enabling her to start riding again. For Mothers' Day Justin gave her a montage of numerous photographs of her with her beloved Basenjis.

I went to London for a board meeting and in the restaurant car on the way back found myself in close proximity to two characters. One was a local Liberal democrat MP who appeared to be working for ninety per cent of the time when he wasn't eating. That was a slight eye-opener but then it was Thursday evening which was another. I was sure MPs didn't actually work a four day week!

The other was a larger than life bald Cornishman, in a cream suit with red braces, whom I have subsequently seen on television in his business capacity but over dinner he treated us to a hilarious description of the punishment meted out to a member of his local football team and a visiting side for fighting on the pitch. For reasons of delicacy I will omit the details but it had our section of the carriage rocking not just over the tracks but with laughter. I was getting used to the camaraderie which so spontaneously erupted between long distance travellers on the First Great Western Golden Hind express each time I returned from London.

I am reminded here of the remark of Sir Andrew Lloyd-Webber during the bleakest period I can remember on the railways, following the go-slows in the wake of various accidents and weather damage to the track. After being heavily delayed he was finally forced to break his train journey to Plymouth, where he was attending the opening of 'Cats', by taking a bus. 'It isn't first, certainly not great and on occasion even has trouble being western,' was the gist of what he said. Things have improved since then.

Soon upon me was an annual event which I had never managed to attend: a dinner for the ex-senior management of the company I had been with before I retired. My reasons for not attending in the past were neither disinterest nor disinclination but rather displacement: I was no longer working full time in business as some still were nor was I living in the same part of the country. But there was something about the special invitation - almost a challenge - from my old boss which stirred my curiosity. Some of those present I had not seen for ten years or more as they had retired before me. Most of the others I had not seen for eight or nine years.

It was a weird sensation, somehow simultaneously travelling back in time to pick up where we had left off and forward as the realisation sank in of the years that had passed, with their attendant ravages of our appearances. I knew that each reaction in my head to 'old so-and-so' looking older, fatter, greyer or iller was matched by at least one of those descriptions being applied as each looked at me!

I was glad I went, as I explained to one of the women, to say goodbye. Not, as she evidently guessed, because I was on my last legs but rather because I wasn't. My earlier instincts had been correct all along. I had moved on as, I'm sure, some of them had too. 'Will you go again?' Mel asked when I got back to Andrew's house where I had left her earlier in the evening and where we were staying overnight.

'Probably not,' was all I could answer. But I knew nothing was for ever.

Another round of minor improvements to life at Upper Penwithiel followed. The two small Basenjis seemed increasingly likely to egg each other on to thread their way through the more penetrable fence running along the bottom of the main field and adjacent to the lane. Once they initiated such a game, three larger Great Danes would inevitably follow. I had observed all of them rushing along the (impenetrable) fence in the garden in pursuit of passing cars and I needed no more warning of potential disaster to take avoiding action.

Our neighbours the Trevithick brothers, Luke and Simon, had a lot of experience in erecting cattle-proof stock-fencing and so I tentatively enquired whether they would be interested in putting some up for me. They readily agreed: my normal instinct at this point would be to agree a price or at least some basis for one.

'Oh, don't worry Dex, we're not expensive. You just get on and order the wire and posts and we'll do the rest,' was Simon's final word on the subject. He specified the type of stock-fence, calibre of wire - 'make sure it's high tensile, mind' - and size of posts. He offered to supply the staples on the basis that they always had lots lying around.

'It'll have to wait until we can fit it in and the weather's OK,' Simon added superfluously.

It was just a week or so before work began. In fact I decided to fence the eastern boundary alongside the lane, the southern boundary adjoining our neighbours' field, which Max and Smartie had previously infiltrated, and along the top of the steep bank just to the south of the barn. This was to stop Smartie charging down it at supper time. Despite her natural athleticism and agility, a broken leg was something we certainly didn't want to risk. Max, needless to say, was not so tempted after one clumsy descent which nearly took him through the fence into the back garden below!

The work took a number of days. Usually the two of them worked for half a day after tending their cattle which were the main source of their income though sometimes they were interrupted by prolonged rain. I spent a little time in conversation with them each day because I usually learned something interesting, often about the immediate locality, sometimes a historical tit-bit. It was Simon who related the story, with obvious affection and natural humour, about their late father's exploits in the Home Guard in the war.

'They had a small wooden hut at the top of the lane with a little brazier outside to keep them warm,' he explained.

Bearing in mind that the lane was all of a mile-and-a-half long with just six farmhouses and cottages in those days, I was intrigued as to the Home Guard's duties in such a small remote community.

'Oh, they had to guard the viaduct,' Simon continued, referring to the railway viaduct at the bottom of the lane, some mile-and-a-half from their little 'base' at the top.

'Guard it? How? Who from?' I asked.

'Well, it was thought the viaduct was at risk of being sabotaged by the enemy,' Simon expounded with a grin, 'so they had orders to make sure if ever a train was to stop on it no one was allowed to get out in case they were enemy agents.' It would never have occurred to me that this little backwater could have been so directly impacted by the events in Europe but nowhere, I guessed, would have been totally unaffected. 'Then one day a train did stop,' said Simon, warming to his story. 'And a naval officer opened a door to get down onto the track.'

'British, presumably?' I needed to know.

'Oh yes. You see it was full of forces people on their way from Plymouth and the train broke down on the viaduct.' Nothing new there, I thought to myself! Simon went on excitedly, 'and this naval officer needed to get out to go to the toilet, see, so father, armed only with a pitch fork, which was all they had in they days, wouldn't let'n! "You just get back on that train and stay on'n," Father said!' Simon mimed the prodding action already being played out in my mind. Simon and Luke were laughing with me at this amusing and touching anecdote of so many years ago.

I was intrigued by the irregular spacing between the posts, especially as they had carefully paced out each run of fencing to quantify the requirements for materials. In the first run along the lane boundary the spacing appeared to reduce in a geometric progression, ie each gap was a fixed proportion of the previous gap. If even spacing was most pleasing to the eye, such proportionally reducing spacing was the next most attractive! I suppose this was because of my automatic viewing of most things from a mathematical perspective.

The last thing I was going to do was in any way criticise the work because I knew it would be very strong and fit for the purpose (as well as retaining large dogs it would have to withstand the lazy leanings and sub-conscious scratchings of two horses) and because I knew they would be very cost-competitive. They were also good neighbours. Eventually my curiosity was strong enough to enable me to formulate a sufficiently subtle question.

'How do you work out where to put the posts?' I asked Simon on their second day. I needn't have been so sensitive.

'Oh, I hoped you weren't going to notice, Dex,' replied Simon grinning. 'I said to Luke, "I hope Dex doesn't think we can't measure properly". No, Dex, there's no more to it than this,' he explained.

'Ah, is it because of the roots of the trees?' I interjected, suddenly seizing on the obvious reason.

'Well there is that, Dex, but no, the real reason is so as we can bang in the posts without cutting our hands on the gorse and brambles.' This had not occurred to me. Both of them looked at me, waiting for my reaction. I was unable to stifle a smile.

'Oh, I see,' I said. 'Amazingly the size of the gaps fits a pattern,' I added, deciding not to go into the mathematical relationship between them. They both stood back and peered at the completed run of fencing.

'Oh, no, Dex,' said Simon, ''tis completely random.' Luke nodded in agreement. 'It's not a problem, I hope,' said Simon earnestly.

'Oh no, of course not,' I replied honestly. Not only could I already see the strength of the fence but I knew the strained plain wire would withstand the attentions of the horses without risking the dreadful damage of barbed wire. More to the point it was all the better for being the honest work of two who had lived their whole lives in and loved this small private corner of Cornwall. Somehow there was a harmony with the natural rhythm of nature that would have been missing with boringly equal spacing. I still look at the completed work with an interest that would otherwise have long since diminished!

The other little improvement was courtesy of Mark, the carpenter and joiner who did so much work for us when we first arrived at Upper Penwithiel three-and-a-half years before, including the largest and most robust stables in Cornwall. We had decided to construct two runs for the dogs. The larger, in front of the barn and opposite the cottage, needed to be Basenji-proof (both in penetration terms and destructibility terms) and horse-proof because it would, we had concluded, be very useful to have a holding area. This proved to be prescient as will become apparent later.

The smaller one, outside the external door to the utility room, needed to be dog-proof but also, because of its proximity to the house, attractive. More specifically, to be dog-proof it had to be both Basenji-proof and Dane-proof. This awkward combination meant there could be no small gaps at the bottom and it had to be high enough to prevent the larger dogs jumping over it. This was not a combination likely to lead to the most stylish of additions to our house, I thought, but Mark found the ideal solution. The bottom three feet or so was a strong wicket fence with the palings close enough to allow no more than the first inch or two of an enquiring Basenji nose to poke through it while at the top was a single narrow bar four inches deep, just high enough to deter even the most athletic Dane from vaulting it while permitting one to peer nosily through the gap without feeling the need to stand on its hind legs. The result was something which was both functional and pleasing to the eye, confirming yet again that such tasks were best left by me to those who knew what they were doing!

The end of the month was marked by Andrew and James descending on us. As Justin missed no opportunity to remind us, he was the only member of the family so far not to have been to Rick Stein's restaurant. I compromised and we all tried his bistro, altogether better value for money though still at the upper end of local prices for comparable meals. He was undoubtedly benefiting from the value of his franchise, enhanced as it was by his TV fame, and I, for one, couldn't blame him. It was Andrew, I believe, who broke the impasse about whether we would have a pudding.

'I just want an ice cream,' he announced replacing his menu on the table.

'Same here,' agreed Justin.

'Good idea,' echoed James.

'Are you sure?' I asked, giving Mel a quick glance.

'I don't want anything really,' she said.

'OK.'

So, minutes later we topped off our sophisticated Rick Stein two course lunch with ice creams from a small shop window, eaten on the hoof by the harbour in Padstow!

The following afternoon we decided to walk along the coastal path which joins West Looe to Polperro. It was a beautiful sunny spring day and the views as we climbed were glorious, reminding us just how uplifting the sea could be. The task of lifting ourselves many feet above the rocks below took its toll of Mel and me and to mock groans of disapproval from the boys we retraced our steps when we had got about half way. Of passing interest were the few minutes we spent observing the site of the recent running aground of a timber-carrying cargo ship. There below us, despite the best efforts of local 'wreckers', were dozens of planks of wood which had been washed ashore where days ago there had been hundreds.

After a welcome cream tea with the largest scones in the world we learned the news on turning on the radio when we got back in the car that the Queen Mother had died.

Andrew returned home the next day leaving Justin and James to accompany Mel and me to Port Isaac for lunch two days later. We had told them that was the place where you parked your car on the small beach, tide permitting. They clearly didn't believe us until we got there and did just that. The calculation of how much time we could take over lunch without returning to find the cars submerged proved tricky but we had an uneventful hour or so in the delightful fishing village since made famous by the very amusing film 'Saving Grace', part of which was shot there.

As they had not been to Tintagel we completed our visit to the north Cornwall coast by taking them to King Arthur's Castle. There was little castle left to see but one could only wonder at the feat of construction involved in building at the top of such a steep climb from sea level. The view of the churning, white-capped sea below wrought its usual magic: I will never take for granted, nor tire of, the proximity of so many such stimulating places. Whatever the truth behind the legend of King Arthur, magic is an apt adjective for this small corner of Cornwall.

16 Bumps in the Night

One of the challenges of getting older is to maintain a fresh outlook and to always be open to change. Change abounded in our lives. Zen and Marma were maturing fast though Justin gave me disbelieving looks when I told him that the giant Zen still had further room to grow. Ellie was growing faster upwards than outwards, taking her through a gangly phase though mentally she was still very much a puppy, taking over from Marma as the chief mischief-maker.

Chan was slowly learning to keep out of Zen's space rather than challenging him at every turn, thus increasing his life expectancy markedly! Betsy had been reluctant to go outside after each meal as all our dogs had been required to from a young age. We had put it down to wariness of the much larger Danes, unsurprising perhaps, despite their amazing gentleness towards her. Marma certainly seemed to think she had been lumbered with a Dane puppy who was never going to grow! But even Betsy was moving on and celebrated the arrival of spring by boldly taking the first steps out with the others with no encouragement needed from us.

The cats themselves were fully mature of course but their relationship with the various dogs had continued to develop. There was a delicate balance of power in place with the cats being chased across the garden by one or more of the dogs but always escaping by an agile leap onto a fence or by deftly darting through a tiny gap. Indoors it was slightly different. There was still the excitement of the chase and last second escape but there were also moments when the cats were happy to play with the dogs, albeit with the cats apparently mesmerised to the point of stupidity on occasions. The Basenjis started by gently nuzzling them all over with their small pointed noses but could never resist giving them a quick last-minute nip, leading to an angry yeowl and leap to a higher level.

The horses, too, had continued to strengthen their bond, with Max continuing to play a responsible role when we were out riding. When Smartie decided she really didn't like the idea of going past the huge black plastic-wrapped hay bales up on the farm track, Max always showed her the way, pretending to take no notice of them while casting a suspicious glance out of the corner of his eye as we went past, just in case...

Justin, too, was going from strength to strength. No longer was he dependent on Dad to keep him occupied with little design tasks, though his help continued to be required. He had, to his credit, continued to develop his knowledge of design software, focusing more and more on motion graphics. He soon produced a showreel which contained examples of his design commissions, static and moving, which he burned onto CDs. An old college friend transferred these onto video tapes so that he could begin the process of telling the world via e-mail, ordinary mail and advertisements what he was able to offer. It was not long before the world, the design world that is, began to respond.

Very quickly he made some valuable contacts, discovered there were other honest, hard-working and creative designers like himself and the work slowly began to flow his way. When the flow eventually turned into a flood my own modest requirements took longer to fulfil! But it was all in a cause I was happy, no, relieved, to take second place to!

The Queen Mother's procession on 5th April to Westminster Hall started outside St James' Palace, not far from where I used to go to board meetings before they were switched to the City. Whether Royalist or not, who could fail to be moved by the band of pipers accompanied by those muffled drums?

But for the rest of us, life went on. Little Betsy for example decided that she *would* sit for her Bonio as the others had long done! Young Ellie decided to go lame on the day of the Queen Mother's funeral. She was clearly in some pain though we knew not the cause but suspected it was an over-robust response from Marma to Ellie's continuing pushing of her luck in playing rough with her. That evening she ate only half her normal food and seemed sleepy. Late as usual, our instincts kicked in and the aloe vera came out. Within days Ellie was dramatically better.

It was around 4.30am a day or so later that I emerged hazily from the deepest of sleeps. I seemed to have been dreaming of banging sounds: as I awoke they were coming from the loft above us. It was a bit loud for bats, which we knew had been present in the past, but suddenly my mind jerked into stark reality. There were loud banging sounds but they were coming from beneath our window.

'What the...?' I muttered, not quite under my breath.

'What is it?' asked Mel, coming round quicker than she usually did.

'Notshure,' I slurred as I shook off the last remnants of sleep, crawled out of bed and went to a window to investigate. I immediately felt relief that the house was not after all under artillery bombardment or even being broken into.

'It's the horses,' I exclaimed, then fully awake.

'What?' shrieked Mel, joining me to see what was happening. 'Quick, check the front gates,' she instructed. I started to wonder why because they were usually kept closed but then so was the field gate. They had been out at night for a week or so and I couldn't believe I had not properly secured the gate after walking the dogs. None of that mattered right now so I donned my dressing-gown and slippers, shot downstairs, turned off the alarm and went out to do I knew not what.

First I checked the gates to the lane and, in the glare of the security lights, could see they were shut, to my instant relief. But where were the horses? Grazing the back lawn, I rapidly discovered. Calmness at all times was a useful quality to cultivate in oneself when around horses but never more so when danger was at hand or panic would ensue, first on the part of the horses and then oneself. I was ever so quiet and reassuring as I approached the munching Smartie.

'That's a good girl,' I said as soothingly as I could, sinking my annoyance at this unwelcome disturbance of my slumbers. Instead of turning and galloping back round to the front of the house as she had the last time they got out, she seemed willing to go along with whatever I had in mind. I knew too that Max would soon follow so I guided Smartie gently by the nose back towards the drive. Max did indeed follow, more slowly and quietly than could have been imagined. Once up in the vicinity of the field gate, still ajar, I walked carefully past them and opened the gate very slowly.

'Walk on Smartie,' I urged, slapping her rump lightly with the flat of my hand. It was just enough for her to take that reluctant first step back to the more boring field she had left not half-an-hour before. Then, when she was in the field, I slapped her harder, making her leap forward and then trot away from me. Max, of course, had no option but to follow to ensure his friend was coming to no harm. I slammed the gate shut, checked the catch was firmly in place and wandered back to the house and, I hoped, a couple of hours' more sleep.

As I approached the front door it swung open to reveal Mel standing in her dressing-gown.

'What's happened?' she asked, sensing that all was not well and wondering whether she should come out and help.

'They're both back in the field and without so much as a lead rope in sight,' I announced with some pride.

'How on earth did you manage that?' she asked incredulously. I smiled.

'I have a way with horses,' I said before slapping her on the backside as she turned to climb the stairs. She shot forward and up the first few steps, having no more idea why than Smartie had just minutes before. I turned the alarm back on and followed, allowing myself, for the first time since I had left my bed, the luxury of a yawn. I never did work out how the horses escaped. It was not a problem with the catch I discovered the next morning, so I really must have failed to close it properly. That worried me! As did the appearance of a few wisps of hay on my dressing-gown. I had no idea how they got there as the horses hadn't been near the stuff for weeks.

The horses were not the only ones to attempt to do a runner that week. Mel and I had decided to have a meal at a restaurant we had often walked past in Looe. We were always on the look out for new restaurants and she had been told she should try it by someone. Half way through our meal, the young man who had been wining and dining his girlfriend on a nearby table started to complain loudly about the quality of their food. After the girl got up to leave, he told the owner that she had to get some air because the food had made her ill. When he made to follow his girlfriend the waiter intervened, requesting payment for the meal, which had included a bottle of wine.

'I'm not paying for that. It was disgusting. You should be ashamed selling disgraceful food like that,' he said loudly enough to make the other few people scattered at tables round the room interrupt their conversations and look in the direction of the rumpus. We knew our food was very good and so couldn't understand the reason for complaint. Then the penny dropped.

'You seemed to enjoy the wine,' the owner said, firmly placing himself between the man and the door through which his girlfriend had just passed. 'I think you should pay for that.' Eventually the man did and left muttering.

I was furious, not least because I felt indignant at the fact, as I saw it at that instant, that I had subsidised what could only be described as a couple of thieves. That feeling subsided into sympathy for the owner who had actually incurred the loss. He came over to apologise for what had happened.

'They were obviously intent on not paying,' he said.

'Why didn't you call the police?' I asked, naively it turned out.

'Well for one thing it would take them too long to get here. I could hardly hold onto to him until they arrived. Then he would most likely get off anyway and, for good measure I'd probably find a brick through the window in the morning. Sadly it's easier just to get what money you can from someone like that.'

I concluded that in practical terms he was right but it was a sad reflection on modern life that even in safe, quiet, out-of-season Looe such inner-city behaviour was not unknown.

Things often go in threes, they say. The third escape of the month was quite unexpected. Mel had been driving home up the lane when she had to stand on the brakes as a small white, black-faced lamb wandered out of the field next to us and across in front of her. She got out and shooed it back in. She told me she thought the lamb had got through the barbed-wire fence so I went to investigate. Too late! About a dozen sheep and lambs were milling about aimlessly in the lane, leaving woolly clues on the barbed-wire showing where they had got through. I made a few phone calls only to discover the Trevithicks had agreed to keep an eye on them and so it was Luke and Simon who came down within minutes to get them back in and make the necessary repairs.

When Harry 'the Hedge' Perkin arrived to trim the, well, hedges, I discovered he played in a small local group rejoicing in the name 'Rum and Shrub'. They specialised in singing shanties and not only toured in France each year but had also brought out a CD or two. The name, it transpired, was taken from a drink of the same name. What a sheltered fifty-seven years I had lived, having tried most drinks in my time but having never come across that one. The band also played in local pubs, unsurprisingly I now thought, including our old favourite the Blisland Inn. It was there that I eventually lost my virginity, so to speak, and had my first - rum and shrub that is!

The next day, 26th April, saw another first: Mel spotted the first swallow. The next first, of course, was May Day. It was marked by protests in London, purportedly about globalisation. Whatever the real reason for them I couldn't help making a comparison with the May Day celebrations in Padstow. Was my mind deceiving me or was one essentially an expression of positivity and the other of negativity? I was sure I knew which made the participants feel happier and in tune with life.

It was also the day that the Queen kicked off her Golden Jubilee tour of the country. She was in Falmouth for part of the day and later, after visiting Truro, left by train. I was gardening at the time the train passed us, the main line being some half a mile away. What told me it was the royal train? The relative silence of the engine compared with the usual diesels!

The day was memorable, too, for a totally unconnected reason. Betsy managed to squeeze herself under the field gate when I was taking the others for a walk. I thought about recapturing her and putting her back on the right side of the gate, less because of her being flattened by the Danes than because of the risk of obliteration by the heavy feet of the horses. I abandoned the idea, first because I couldn't catch her and secondly because I knew she would now do everything she could to gain re-entry to the new heaven that had just revealed itself to her. So it was by default that all the dogs had their first walk together round the field.

Predictably she took all her cues from Chan. Not for her the cautious-ness of the Danes who were happy enough near the horses as long as they didn't walk towards them, when they all tried to hide behind me. Chan, of course, was quite adept at running round and round the horses and dodging their feet instinc-tively. My heart was in my mouth as Betsy followed him like a shadow. I needn't have worried. If anything she was even quicker at putting herself in the right place at the right time.

This became, then, our new daily routine. The next day the horses, possibly irritated by the Basenjis or frustrated at their inability to deter them from their annoying little habit of running round and round in circles, decided to ignore them and focus their interest on the Danes. Both were used to them and had the confidence to deal with them: the Danes too knew what was good for them so no problems arose, except one. Smartie had never forgotten Sukie, whom she had once cornered and licked from head to tail. She managed to corner Marma on this occasion and Marma obligingly froze to the spot, allowing Smartie to refresh her taste buds! I managed to persuade Smartie to let her go only for Marma to escape into our small side paddock. When both horses followed her amiably up to the top she panicked and shot through a hole she had found in the dense hedge and into the field next door.

Certainly it was too dense for me to follow so I had to go to the bottom of the garden and clamber over the barbed-wire fence. It was, of course, full of sheep including those who had recently escaped into the lane. My prime consideration, naturally, was to ensure Marma didn't chase the sheep or worse. My heart was therefore in my mouth as I scanned the field for signs of the well-camouflaged dog. The sheep appeared calm enough, grazing quietly on the far side of the field. I could see them gazing inquisitively towards the hedge up to my left. There she was! Marma was lazily ambling along the hedge enjoying the slightly different scents she had found. She knew the sheep were there because she occasionally flicked her eyes in their direction. But her clear intent was to keep the maximum distance between them and herself. Of course! She was as wary of them as she was of the horses. What if sheep liked licking dogs too?

She was far too heavy for me to lift her over the four foot fence so I had to find the gap she had escaped through and send her back through it. It was with something akin to grateful relief that she dived back through the brambles when I found the place for her.

It was precisely two days later that I had two surprises. Moss arrived proudly in the conservatory to present me with a half-constructed birds' nest. That at least meant no harm had come to its owners or their offspring. On close examination I could see it was perfectly round and tightly constructed of black horse-hair from the manes and tails of Smartie or Max.

The second surprise was less welcome and consisted of something relatively shapeless, loosely constructed and white from the wool of sheep. It was half the ovine contents of the neighbouring field, Marma's new acquaintances, but in our small paddock! Clearly they had been attracted to the gap she had found and had decided to visit. I eventually persuaded them that even if our grass was greener, theirs was safer. A little Basenji on a lead seemed keen to round them up and they took the hint. The Trevithicks were soon doing their best to effectively 'darn' the hole with fencing and, the farmer's best friend on such occasions, baler twine!

The following day took us to a part of Cornwall which was totally unknown to us, not least because it was in the 'wrong' direction, ie towards Plymouth. The reason for our visit was simply that a delivery driver who had stopped for a chat, as they always did, had recommended that we visit it. He was Cornish born and bred and had never been there until a recent delivery had taken him there. For no other reason than that, natural curiosity and a determination to keep an open mind, Mel, Justin and I sought out Cawsand for lunch on a lovely warm Sunday in early May.

Our informant was correct in that it was a far more picturesque and relatively unspoilt area than we would have guessed though Mel and I knew we would probably never return. But two things stood out that day: the glorious coastal views along one stretch of the journey, between Crafthole and Knatterbury, and what I still maintain are the best chips in the world! These were served up by the Cawsand Hotel, situated right at the water's edge, and, despite my asking the secret of their crunchiness, was no wiser when the answer I was given was, 'it's all down to seasoning'. But it wasn't: it was down to finely ground bread crumbs I think!

Cawsand runs right into Kingsand with no obvious point of separation and they share a tiny beach. I could only guess that the throng of visitors that day had come across the Tamar from Plymouth.

Mel and I were pleased to have had Justin with us that day: he is always good company though a few years earlier he would have understandably felt uneasy coming out on his own with his parents for the day. But he was now grown up and, as we all three knew, was unlikely to be living with us for very much longer...

Helston's Flora Day was something we had always wanted to go and see, ever since Mel and I first went there together in 1970. She, of course, had known it since the mid-fifties when she had stayed at the Seven Stars with her parents. 2002 was the year we finally made it!

All was obviously well organised as we had no trouble parking, in the cricket ground as it happened. A stroll down towards the town centre enabled us to gauge the atmosphere on what was thankfully a warm and sunny spring day. We knew we were too late for the early dances which started at 7.00am, long before we even left home. We just missed the children's dance, unfortunately, but passed many of them as they skipped, ran or ambled home or to wherever something of interest awaited them. Both boys and girls were dressed in white, an eloquent reminder of the innocence of youth and of days gone by. The girls were also wearing flowers in their hair.

We were in place before noon, in time for the next adult dance, a much more elegant and sophisticated affair than I had imagined. This was no raw, raucous Cornish folk dance but one where the ladies wore their smartest dresses, more like ball gowns, and the men their dapper morning suits. They were led and followed up the main street by the two halves of the Helston Town Band playing the famous Furry Dance. They continued dancing, circling slowly up to the very top of the town before returning.

On the way back down they threaded their way, still dancing, into and out of the open shops, including those of some of the national chains which, I idly mused, would have had to flex their no doubt uniform national policies to accommodate this very localised tradition. Most of the shops themselves were decorated with branches of yellow flowering gorse and spring flowers, mainly bluebells. All the men, including those in the band and the accompanying police (needed to clear the way so as to avoid collisions between dancers and onlookers) wore sprigs of lily of the valley.

What a wonderful tradition! I just hoped that all the folk of Helston appreciated just how lucky they were to have grown up with it. I was sure they valued it because only a Helston-born couple were allowed to lead the dance and being selected to play in the band was a highly regarded honour for which children were groomed from a young age. We, of course, were mere grockles or trippers that day and fulfilled the role by having pasties for lunch and then eating an ice cream as we strolled to the bottom of the town before returning to our car, if only we could remember the way!

⌾∼∞∕∽⌾

James joined us for a few days and didn't seem to object in the least, as once he might, to accompanying us, with Justin, to the Lanhydrock horse trials. He probably saw it as an opportunity to be with us as we did something we always enjoyed: watching horses. There was the usual humorous banter but coupled for once with a genuine desire to understand what was going on and to see things through our eyes. Seeing the legendary Mary King put her horse through its paces at close quarters was reward enough on its own.

The following day saw us calling in on Perranporth for the first time in thirty-two years to see how it had changed. While it undoubtedly had, it hadn't in terms of our recalled perceptions of it! We were sure it would follow the uptrend so clearly visible in the rest of Cornwall in time to come.

177

On the day James was due to return to his new temporary home in Bath,he suggested we all went somewhere that morning. Concluding that it shouldn't be too far away because of his long drive home later, we started to rack our brains. In the end he came up with the idea of visiting a local visitor attraction which we had not been to before. It was the Carnglaze Cavern just a couple of miles from home.

While it was not impressive as natural phenomena go, I, in my usual romanticised way, was impressed by the descriptions of the conditions that had to be endured by the men who had worked the mine for slate over so many years. There was no electricity for one thing and the effect on their ears of exploding gunpowder, courtesy of Trago powder Mills in the days long before the Robertsons ran the big shop, could only be imagined. No unions or health service, let alone sick or unemployment pay, in those days meant they had to keep working to live...

As we drove back down towards the A38 in Justin's car we noticed the huge bright blue smear of bluebells from the lane up through the woods to the top of the steep escarpment, easily the greatest profusion of them I had ever seen.

Unfortunately when I got out in the drive at home I didn't notice that I had left my seat belt dangling outside the door when I closed it. Two hours later Justin noticed it but, too late, Zen had made a hole in it: he hadn't chewed it but just put one of his huge canine teeth clean through it. This later caused Justin to fail his MoT. Naturally I felt morally obliged to foot the bill for a new one. As yet his freelance earnings were scant and it was important not to demoralise him at so early a stage in the proceedings!

As always, these little interludes, enjoyed at a sensible pace of life, contrasted starkly with my periodic visits to London. This time it was to attend the biennial dinner of the Institute of Actuaries, accompanied by Mel, at the invitation of my professional colleagues at the company of which I was a director.

I knew Mel would enjoy the whole trip, right from lunch on the train to the view from our room on the fifteenth floor of the Hilton as well, naturally, as the social discourse in the evening. She had been involved in many similar events over the years during my full-time employment at my last company. It was not until we awoke to the early morning traffic in Park Lane far below us that she said, 'I can't wait to get out of London again.'

I smiled. 'I've thought that for years. I always got a kick out of boarding the train for Salisbury at Waterloo. I never got over the feeling that I was going home to an area that many people only ever visited on holiday. Now when I get on a train headed for Penzance the feeling's even greater.'

A day or two later we were awoken, not by the noise of traffic in the lane - there wasn't any - but by Angus barking, followed by a flash and a tremendous crack of thunder, very close to us. A quite violent storm unleashed itself upon our little valley, prompting Mel to say blearily, 'I do hope the horses are alright. I hate them being out in this but it's better than being in their stables.'

'Why?' I asked, forgetting what she had told me a number of times before.

'It's better for them to be able to run if they're frightened...' Ah, yes, I thought to myself. It allows the adrenaline to work its way out of the system and the fear to dissipate, much in the same way as deep breathing to get rid of panic when flying.

After an even louder roll of thunder, more reminiscent of heavy gunfire, my own pulsing adrenaline found an outlet: I leapt out of bed to see if I could see the horses in the next flash. 'Can you see them?' asked Mel, less blearily now.

'No. Yes,' I said, suddenly spotting them at the top of the field next to the hedge.

'What are they doing?'

'Grazing,' I replied, 'what else?' I had never seen them looking any less fazed than they were at that moment. As I watched and the next flash lit up the valley, Max shuffled forward slowly to the next luscious patch of grass. Smartie followed, as if needing to keep close to her older friend who had, of course, seen it all before. That didn't stop me muttering a few words of hope to myself that they come to no harm. They didn't.

As I walked the dogs back along the top of the field the next morning, I was, as usual, lost in thought. Despite the natural drainage supplied by the steep slope which ran for most of its length, that part of the field was fairly saturated from the overnight deluge. I was only vaguely aware of the Danes romping along behind me, followed by the sound of a flock of low-flying birds. But there were no birds, I realised, as I slowly re-emerged from my thoughts. It was the humming putter of eight Basenji feet on the sopping wet grass as they shot past in hot pursuit of I knew not what, though, as I well knew, pursuit in their case never resulted in catching. It was the thought that counted, along much the same lines as travelling being better than arriving. As I watched the two of them swirling and changing direction on a sixpence, as if connected, they indeed reminded me of two birds on the wing diving and darting after each other in the air.

When it started raining again, both Chan and Betsy ran from tree to tree to benefit as much as possible from the brief shelter they provided. Betsy, it transpired however, was not averse to paddling and also soon discovered the joys of drinking the freshest of water from the puddles. As I cast my eyes in the direction of the woods to the north-east I could see the smoke of drifting rain as it swirled up from the bottom of the lane.

It was raining even more heavily again at 10.00pm that night when Carl and Barbara Wellings arrived for a weekend with us. We suggested a visit to

Pencarrow House the next day, Saturday. It was closed when we got there so we went on to Padstow for lunch outside a pub. We discovered, however, that Pencarrow House was open on the Sunday so we returned for an interesting little tour of a totally unspoiled house still lived in by the family. The Cornish history lesson alone made our return worthwhile. The simple lunch in the red brick-vaulted restaurant rounded off a pleasant respite from our usual routine and their short break.

That evening Mel and I were to be treated to a gourmet meal by Justin. As he was the chef, the welcome meal we got as a small recompense for keeping him fed and watered while he built up his business made less of a dent in his cash pile than a meal out or a takeaway but Mel and I enjoyed it as much or more. It was to become a regular feature in our lives.

It was 5.50am the next day that I was awoken by something unknown. Then, as my senses made themselves known, it was quite apparent. The digits on my radio alarm were blank, telling me that there had been a power cut. Why a light disappearing should have stirred me I do not know. I waited for the usual culprit to own up with a crash but there was no thunder storm. The cause was to remain a mystery. All I knew was that a trip switch had tripped indicating a problem inside the house.

Betsy at that time was really settled with us and beginning to show her real character. Any thought in our minds that we needed to keep her in place at the lower pecking order of our little pack was obviously not shared by her. She was the smallest in stature but demanded more than her fair share of attention and respect but we did not have to support her in this: all the other dogs seemed only too willing to accommodate her so we took our lead from them. If she wanted a chew or Bonio no one was going to object, with the sole exception of Marma whose authority was absolute.

Chan deferred to Betsy at every turn, hoping, naturally, that one day the favour would be returned. Ellie, still a puppy herself, was only too pleased to co-operate with her partner in crime and remain detached from the, now boring, adult dogs. And dear Zen, whose battle for supremacy over Chan had undoubtedly wearied and exasperated him at times, clearly had no stomach for beginning the process all over again with this new upstart. Besides, he was besotted with her, frequently lying on his side with a protective paw across her tiny sleeping form. Alternatively she would drape herself across his front legs and snuggle up under his chin, her body still smaller than his head.

That still left one even larger challenge for her: the horses! It was towards the end of May that I first noticed Betsy's interest in Smartie. After bringing the dogs back in from a walk round the field, I realised she wasn't with us. That was not, of course, unusual because she was, after all, a Basenji. What was usual was for the two of them to disappear together, either to sneak in under the gate at the far end of the barn for a romp in the horse bedding or to take themselves off for another circuit of the field unsupervised.

But Chan had, for once, shown signs of growing up and had come in with the big dogs. So where was Betsy? I eventually found her in the middle of the field. She was sitting, closely observing Smartie as she grazed in front of her. Even my approach was not enough to distract her, two erect ears focused firmly on the chewing horse, and she continued to sit there, mesmerised, allowing me the rare luxury of catching her without a chase. I already knew that she had learned from Chan the art of dodging horses' flying hooves so it was with amused rather than anxious relief that I scooped her up and took her in.

Over the coming days, her fascination with Smartie, though not for some reason Max, continued. One evening after a walk I decided to rescue her when I saw her following behind Smartie as she moved to a new area of grazing, with the end of Smartie's ground-length tail clenched between her teeth, much as a bridesmaid would follow a bride holding her train. I rushed the last few yards when, against all odds, Betsy decided she had mustered enough knowledge of the situation to try to drag Smartie backwards. Elementary physics suggested otherwise and after Smartie turned to give Betsy the kindest of puzzled glances she continued to edge gently forwards, nibbling grass and pulling the little dog, against its mighty will, behind her. I doubt that she would have abandoned the attempt without my timely intervention!

Ellie, meanwhile, continued to confound us. This quiet bitch, according to her breeder, was in fact quite jumpy. If she was told off too abruptly, however reasonably, she went and hid behind something. But she was certainly mixing it with the older Danes, despite being considerably smaller. Once again she came off worse after playing too roughly and started to limp. I was certain she had hurt her back and so, after a day or two of no improvement, we whisked her off to Rosalind Boisseau, an animal physiotherapist at St Issey, near Wadebridge. We had used similar services for Max in the past, it being not uncommon for a horse to have a misaligned vertebra on occasion, so we saw no reason not to apply the same principles for a young dog clearly in discomfort.

Ros also treated horses and, even more reassuringly, people, so we knew Ellie was in good hands. The manipulation she performed was both firm and gentle and half-an-hour or so later Ellie emerged into the bright sunshine walking more easily than she had walked in. It was apparent within a day or two that the discomfort had gone and her 'pinched' appearance had been replaced by her more usual bouncy, well-rounded self. The challenge was going to be to prevent a recurrence of the injury so I decided she would not accompany us on our daily walks for the time being. This would at least avoid the boisterous play the dogs indulged in when they found themselves in the free space offered by a five-acre field!

Ray, our farrier, however, was going through a more difficult time as one of the little dogs he sometimes brought with him - a Westie - was seriously ill with lung cancer. It was not a disease I had ever associated with dogs but it was a real enough worry for him.

17 A Ton of Nails

'How about Zennor for lunch?' I asked Mel on the first Monday in June. We were not about to dine on our beloved Great Dane but Andrew and James had descended on us for a few days in the week of the Queen's Golden Jubilee and ideas were canvassed about where we could go for a day out. Mel and I had wanted to visit the Tinners Arms since our first foray into Zennor a couple of years or so earlier. Andrew wanted to go for a walk near the sea and James and Justin were happy to do anything so long as a meal was involved somewhere along the way.

We arrived to discover the village fete was under way with flowers everywhere and children wandering around in fancy dress. Over a simple lunch and a few drinks in the totally unspoiled surroundings of the old pub, we caught up with each others' news.

We had chosen another gloriously sunny day so I was intrigued to know whether my earlier recollections of the turquoise sea, reminiscent of many a Greek beach, were accurate or merely romantic imaginings. As the five of us ambled along the path from Zennor village to the coastal path we passed the small paddock where we looked in vain for the donkeys we had seen on our previous trip and for the magnificent black Dane at the house on the right. As the sea came into view I was elated: not only was the sight of it uplifting in its own right but it was precisely as I had described it. The turquoise water was as inviting as before and if only it had been warmer I would have had to go in for a swim.

As it was, I left that to the basking sharks which a visiting family from the Midlands assured us they had just seen. We found a rocky outcrop to sit on and spent the next half hour looking out for them without success. We then strolled eastwards in the direction of St Ives before taking a path inwards and upwards to get back to the car park.

Mel and I then decided to visit the Wayside Museum, small as museums go, which housed a collection of household items and agricultural and other tools typical of such a Cornish rural area over the years. I was amused at the realisation that many of the items were around in my own childhood, underlining my own antiquity! It was a strange feeling, as if I, too, should be a museum piece. The boys, needless to say, preferred to go off and make the most of what remained of the day somewhere more interesting, namely St Ives.

I had asked Andrew who, after all, had a National Diploma in photography, reflecting his one-time interest in photography as a career, to take some photographs of the animals. The fine weather the following morning gave us an excellent opportunity. It was always going to require patience to persuade them to stand or sit still while ensuring their photogenic qualities were adequately brought out.

The Danes were the most amenable though awkward to pose properly. We settled on less-than-show standards of presentation provided they looked attentive and happy. On paper the Basenjis were always going to be difficult if only because of their aversion to being still for more than fractions of a second. In practice they were brilliant, sitting or standing exactly where we asked and giving off their natural air of intelligent inquisitiveness.

Max was less than co-operative, initially refusing to be caught - until tempted by an apple which Andrew got from the house - and then lunging at him as if defending us from whatever dubious intentions he was so obviously harbouring. Smartie on the other hand was an absolute sweetheart: she stood still, head and ears erect and almost smiled! Then she pursued Andrew back to the gate insisting on being given the other apple which she knew in all fairness he must have secreted about his person: he didn't.

Even I had not contemplated the difficulty or, rather, impossibility of getting the three cats into the same picture let alone to pose. I tried holding all of them together but the two females fell out, neither being prepared to be upstaged. In the end I settled for individual shots.

It was the day of the Queen's procession in her gold coach to the Guildhall in London. After watching that, which evoked my memories of her travelling to her Coronation in the same coach when I was just eight, we had a relaxed barbeque.

After lunch when Andrew had asked whether I needed my old computer printer, as I had just got a new one, we started to bargain light-heartedly. Just as we were close to a deal Mel pronounced that I was being mean and as Andrew had just taken some lovely photographs (how could she know until they were developed?) she thought I should give it to him. My meanness of course was no more than a desire to be fair as I had nothing of similar value to give to James and Justin.

My explanation along these lines fell on very deaf ears as far as Mel was concerned, not least because Andrew would be returning home later in the day and it would be a while before we saw him again.

James picked up on this and said that he, for one, was not bothered at my making this one off gesture though he suggested that I hid an envelope somewhere in the field which Andrew would have to find before he could take his prize, 'just like you did once when you gave him a bike for Christmas.' Andrew was then about ten and he had had to follow a series of clues around the field at our last house before he was led to a key which unlocked the shed where his shiny new bike awaited him.

I settled for simply detaching the printer from the computer and handing it over with the spare cartridges I still had. When I eventually got the photographs printed I knew I had got a bargain. The result was a superb record of all our beloved animals, with me keeping them under some sort of control, and which we will always treasure.

❧

It was just after I had got up and gone to make the morning tea that the power tripped off again. It was not so easy as resetting the trip switch because it just tripped straight off again. This time I had to get to the bottom of it. I called Mel to come and help. We had to turn off each appliance in the kitchen and utility room one at a time and try to reset the trip switch in order to isolate the problem. We narrowed it down to the toaster which was then despatched to the appliance resting place in the sky.

Mel and I finally managed to sufficiently organise ourselves to visit the Royal Cornwall Show, thankfully restored to its usual month of June after the previous year's foot and mouth disruption, on the right day for the Dane classes at the dog show. The previous year we were given the wrong day and one year we missed it because the Queen was opening the show that day and we wanted to miss the crowds. We received a very warm welcome from our old friend Paddy, the Callans' brindle, and later Jeanette asked me if I minded holding him and two other dogs of hers when she went into the ring. I didn't, of course, already suffering from my old complaint of Dane withdrawal symptoms if ever I was away from ours and saw someone else's. Paddy completely relaxed when he found I didn't object to his leaning on me for moral support!

We also bumped into Chris Roberts, recent chairman of the Jaguar Enthusiasts' Club, as we emerged from the horticultural tent. She chaired the committee that organised the horticultural display and we were delighted to compliment her on it.

Another momentous event was the discovery that in the Trago Mills tent the well-known local discount store was actually piloting credit cards! The firm had always resisted the idea on the basis that it added to costs, threatening their trademark lowest of the low prices, so this was as noteworthy as a teetotaller taking to drink, unthinkable but understandable in certain circumstances!

On returning home later, fences were on the agenda again. While giving the dogs their evening constitutional I noticed three or four hoof-sized gaps in the stock fencing between us and next door. While stock fencing has sizeable mesh anyway, the wire had been snapped, clearly as a result of a kick. It had to have been Smartie as Max just didn't lower himself to such behaviour, especially towards a female as the neighbour's sole remaining pony was. After being left in the garden with the other dogs following our walk, Zen was nowhere to be found when I went to get them in for the night.

Instinctively I checked all the gates as well as the other places that one or other of them had escaped through in the past but all was secure. I checked behind all the shrubs and bushes, recalling only too vividly the time that Marma disappeared when she had bloat. He was simply too large to overlook so I consulted Mel, as she often came up with suggestions that hadn't occurred to me.

'Have you checked the field?' she asked.

'No, darling. There's no way he could get through under the gate or through the fence.' She ignored the logic of this and went up through the gate into the small paddock. 'Where are you going?' I asked, genuinely bemused.

'Well the sheep got in didn't they? So he could have got out. Maybe he's gone through into the next field.' I knew he had to be somewhere, so why not there, I reasoned to myself. I joined her in the hunt. It was on our slow thoughtful walk back down the drive, having drawn a blank, that we spotted him.

'Oh, Zen. How did you get there?' Mel asked. There he was, staring at us pleadingly through the topmost bars of the double gates into the lane from the wrong side. 'He must have found a hole in the fence,' Mel concluded.

'No, he couldn't, I checked it all,' was my open-mouthed, dumbfounded response. As keen as ever to show up any deficiency in my defence, Mel went hole hunting.

After several minutes she called over to me, 'found it!'

'Found what?' I replied dejectedly, beginning to doubt the thoroughness of my own check.

'Where he got out. Look.' I went over to the stretch of stock fence between the bottom of the large lawn down from the cottage and the lane. Mel pointed. There, quite clearly, the top of the fence dipped in a shallow arc between the posts.

'How do you know that's where he got out?' I asked blandly, knowing she would have the answer ready.

'You can see where the nettles have been flattened the other side.'

'Hmmm. I think you may be right,' I conceded while concealing a sigh as I contemplated the inescapable requirement of my having to immediately go off in search of hammer and staples with which to restore tautness to the top wire.

'I know I am,' Mel replied with a certain inevitability.

'Trust us to own the only Great Dane in history to have mastered the Fosbury flop,' I muttered as we strolled back to the house, referring to the revolutionary 'back first' high-jumping technique pioneered by Dick Fosbury for the 1968 Olympics. Mel gave me one of her knowing smiles: knowing my silly joke was a weak attempt to cover my admission to myself that what had been a potential near-disaster was of my own making. Why a potential near-disaster? Because while I was working on the fence around thirty cars drove past, those further back being emboldened by the convoy ahead to travel faster than they otherwise might. What brought this extremely rare incursion into our quiet lane? A police diversion down on the main road because of a serious accident. Zen had been lucky indeed.

'You don't think he could do it again, do you?' were the comforting words from Mel after I had completed my task in the failing light.

'Not unless he gets very athletic. I've raised the height of the mesh by two inches all along that section and added an additional wire. It's now about four-foot-six high.' I hoped it was enough.

The next day showed it wasn't. Although he didn't get out in the same place, he found another section, buried deep in the brambles and holly lining the entrance to the drive just beyond the gates. I spent the next half-an-hour fighting off the prickliest of assaults on all parts of my person as I struggled manfully to re-establish the impenetrability which had existed before Zen's brave challenge. As before, thankfully, having made good his escape, he immediately let us know he wished to return but without even attempting to retrace his exit route! It was to be many months before he got out again.

While not the most ardent football fan, having spent my formative years playing with a differently shaped ball which you carried, I couldn't resist the big matches. So why did I choose the day of the key World Cup match between England and Denmark to upgrade my version of Microsoft Windows? Because, I reasoned, if I started at 9.30 in the morning it would be completed by kick-off. How wrong I was! It was finally completed at 8.00pm. While I had seen most of the match between flitting into and out of my study to check progress, I had managed to miss each of the three England goals. A sacrifice too far, I felt.

The next day, being Fathers' Day, had Mel releasing various gifts from their hiding places. Not from her, of course, but from the two boys in absentia, Andrew and James, who had had the forethought to plan things in advance of their recent visit. Justin of course handed his over personally. They ranged from something to eat, something to drink and finally to something to watch, possibly all at the same time!

The man from SWEB, or Western Power as it now is, arrived early on the Monday morning, as previously arranged, to discuss the cutting back of trees and hedging so as to preclude their interfering with the overhead power line.

'We need to avoid having to return for at least five years, so we need to get a three metre clearance.' I instantly translated this into ten feet and gulped at the thought.

'I'd be very unhappy for you to take that much from the two oak trees. It would ruin them,' I said, pointing to the majestic guardian of the drive entrance and to the gentle giant providing early morning shade to the back garden.

Fortunately he required my signature on a form to that effect, opening the way to a degree of negotiation. I took him up to the top of the field on the western boundary from where we could see the rough wooded area lining our side of the lane.

'If you cut back to ten feet below the power line you'll turn a wooded area, which is a bit wild perhaps, into no more than a hedge. It would also reduce our privacy and security.'

'I can see that,' he replied. 'I can assure you that as a countryman born and bred myself, I am very keen to preserve what I can of your natural surroundings but as a contractor of SWEB I have to look after their interests too.' I was beginning to be suspicious. Even if I agreed to a certain amount of cutback what would stop them taking even more than that. It would be easy for the man in charge on the day to turn a blind eye if his men were a little over-enthusiastic.

'And there's the horses,' I added. He looked blankly at me. 'At the moment they're screened from the road and there's a natural barrier. If you remove it they could be frightened by traffic, or worse, escape onto the road more easily.'

'But you've got a good fence,' he replied, indicating the excellent work of the Trevithick brothers.

'Yes, I know, but I'm just explaining why I'm unhappy for you to take so much away.'

'How much would you agree to?' he asked, taking the wind out of my now billowing sails. I stopped and pondered in case it was a trap.

'No more than a metre,' I eventually replied honestly and objectively after mentally removing that much from the trees below us. I was not in negotiating mode but he evidently was.

'What would you say to two?' he asked quickly.

'Too much,' I instantly retorted, realising my mistake.

'One and a half?'

'No. One,' I repeated hopefully.

'Well, I'll take a note of that, Mr Cameron and I'll ask you to sign your agreement to that on the form but I can't promise that SWEB will find it acceptable.'

I heard no more until just before the day of the cut some weeks later.

That evening Mel and I went to the Hall of Cornwall for a concert by the Manfreds. Manfred Mann himself, who I had first seen performing live at the Green Man on Blackheath many years before, was not in evidence but Paul Jones and Mike D'Arbo very much were.

Mel had taken to persuading me to go to such concerts in recent years, knowing I would not even consider anything more recent than 70's music. But even I was sceptical about this particular evening. However much the band evoked fond memories of the sixties they had never been of special interest to me so my expectations were low. But I knew how much she enjoyed such concerts even if they were not her particular brand either. So we went. As with our earlier experience there of a Pete Townsend concert I had to eat my words. The music was of course familiar but the quality of the instrumentation, as well as the vocals, was excellent.

I even had to grudgingly concede that one of the supporting acts, Chris Farlowe, was far better than I had remembered though it suddenly dawned on me that he, too, had experienced forty years of life in the interim, adding to the grittiness of his performance. As far as the other act, Long John Baldry, was concerned I was regrettably able to concede nothing. I never understood the reason for his popularity all those years ago and it was still passing me by!

My failure to properly organise a card and flowers for our thirty-first wedding anniversary had more to do with a faulty memory of the computer variety than the merely human version installed in my head! I had experienced a severe increase in crashes since upgrading my windows system rather than the reduction I had hoped for. As that had coincided with the installation of a much more complex charting system for stock prices, I had no idea of the cause, just the effect. It was chaotic and so it was the hours spent correcting the results of the crashes that took my focus off the romantic aspects of life.

It was therefore at 7.45am of the special day that plan B began to take shape. I went round the garden in my dressing gown rounding up a posse or, more accurately, posy of flowers, including a few wild foxgloves which Mel loves. In a rather poor substitute for the real thing, I had composed the following rhyme for the card:

Roses are blue
Violets are red
I'm in love with you
So nuff said!

For reasons which escaped me, these two gestures seemed to get me off the hook. My real salvation came, though, as a result of my having had the foresight to book a room for the night at the Carlyon Bay Hotel in the week before my computer became deranged.

Just before we left home, Mel went out to the front of the house to get the Danes in and there was no sign of them. She then spotted Ellie lying on the lawn opposite. She jumped up and barked at Mel before recognising her. This had the instant effect of galvanising Zen and Marma who rocketed round from the back of the house, barking ferociously. 'Ahhh,' said Mel, 'they're protecting their baby.'

We arrived at the hotel in time for lunch and afterwards had a stroll along the cliffs in front of it and down onto the beach, just to impress on our minds that we had had an enjoyable, if brief, break. The magnificent view of the Bay from our room the next morning slowly started us thinking how wonderful it would be to have a house with a view of the sea.

✐✐✐

We decided to take the horses out the following Sunday. I was up at around 6.30am as was increasingly usual because of the early light. Having let the dogs out, I could not get Betsy and Ellie to respond to my call when it was time for them to come in for their breakfast. When I went out in search of them I heard Max's heavy feet clatter into the barn so I went up to shut him in so I didn't have to chase him round the field later. He resisted my attempt to guide him into his stable but seemed to prefer wandering into Smartie's. That was good enough for me so I closed and bolted the door behind him. I was even more pleased with myself when Smartie appeared two minutes later and, naturally enough, she sauntered into Max's stable enabling me to spring the trap on her too.

The clouds that morning were very high up and thin with fine streaks like icing roughed with delicate brushstrokes. The overall impression in the early morning sun was of pink-tinged ostrich feathers. That early promise was to be slightly disappointed later when we found all our usual fields recently ploughed, freshly re-sown or under maturing crops. It was to be walk and trot but no canter that day.

When Mel found the horses waiting in the stables she couldn't resist asking, 'why did you put them in the wrong stables?' I did manage to resist giving the answer that first sprang to mind.

Days later, Ellie was walking awkwardly again after playing roughly with Marma and coming off worse so it was another trip to see Ros Boisseau. Before going I decided that Ellie's nails needed trimming. It was never my favourite job though all the dogs had had to get used to having it done regularly. It was just that she objected more than any dog we had owned in nearly thirty years. I had to coax, cajole and finally wrestle with her to get the job done.

Having made a start I decided to do all the dogs' nails. The Basenjis were only marginally easier, with my technique for containing the squirming antics of the ever-difficult Chan being akin to holding a set of very vigorous bagpipes under my left arm as I struggled to hold each paw still for long enough to snip off the end without hurting him. If I had done this, by cutting the quick, I felt certain he would never let me do them again. So he had to be held in a vice-like grip.

The other two Danes were easier but permanently suspicious that I was going to do something they didn't like. Only Angus submitted completely and with absolute trust. Afterwards, dripping with sweat, I was passed by Mel on the stairs who said, 'you look as though you've just had ten rounds with Mike Tyson.'

'It feels like it, too,' I replied. 'Do you know,' I continued, 'I've just counted and I've cut a hundred nails.'

'A hundred?' she asked, mentally adding up six dogs times four feet per dog times four nails per foot. I knew she would take time to arrive at ninety-six so I did the arithmetic out loud for her.

'So that's ninety-six plus two dew claws each for Chan and Ellie,' I explained, referring to the extra claws on the front legs which never touched the ground. 'That's a ton altogether!'

18 Summer Blazes

Early July brought the welcome sound of a fluttering of wings. Justin's rapid progress in his new freelance graphic design existence signalled his impending take-off. This was not just in terms of financial independence, as witnessed by his readily taking over responsibility for his car insurance from its renewal date. It also told Mel and me that the day our nest was finally to be emptied for good could not be far off!

Naturally our feelings were mixed. It was nearly twenty seven years since we had last been truly alone. We were therefore not quite sure how it would feel. There was, of course, a sadness that an important time in our lives was drawing to a close. On the other hand there was the small matter of total release from the financial obligation of supporting our little brood and the reduction in the day-to-day involvement in their lives. While this certainly had a large positive element, for example our observation of Justin's amazing progress in his work, there was also the small matter of being sucked into all the inevitable little frustrations and problems that arose.

Mel and I determined that we would enjoy the last weeks or months of our old existence before throwing ourselves wholeheartedly into the new.

We never seemed to be prepared for the sadnesses that life seemed to throw up on a routine basis. It therefore struck us surprisingly hard when Jeanette Callan phoned us to tell us their beloved Paddy had died of a heart attack. This gentle brindle giant of a dog had, like all Danes we had known, wormed his way into our affections. We realised, of course, that we were not on his people radar, so to speak, simply because we had only seen him on half-a-dozen occasions but he was on our screen without a doubt. He would have been just four in the coming month. Mike and Jeanette were understandably devastated.

It was at that time that Ellie began to experience problems with Betsy. She, Betsy, was adopting the same aggressiveness towards her larger companion that Chan had with Zen. Not wanting any repetition of that situation, Mel consulted one of her Basenji books which had a section on psychology. This gave us the answer. Whenever the offending dog (and attacking another of the same pack was undoubtedly an offence!) needed putting in place the way to do it was to quickly flip him or her onto his or her back and hold them there until they calmed down and peace could be expected to reign. This tactic worked perfectly with little Betsy.

So well in fact that a week or so later, when I had to impose my will on her again while feeding them in the utility room, she was upturned on Sukie's old bed and slid down, on her back with my hand holding her in place, into a four-inch gap between the soft, PVC-covered foam and the wooden surround. When I thought she had got the message I removed my hand and continued mixing up the feeds. Minutes later, when I went to put the bowls in front of them, I saw she was still lying there on her back, squeezed into the gap, gazing round the room, front legs folded floppily on her chest, patiently waiting to be told she could get up again!

This little trick, combined with the tactic of deliberately ignoring her when she was vying for attention, also helped to moderate her bossy behaviour. It was hard, however, to avoid being touched by the pathetically sad look she gave when this was being deployed. For a while she also seemed to be trying to compensate by attempting to keep up with, and in with, the pack when it went round the field for its daily constitutional rather than completely doing her own thing as usual!

On American Independence Day there was a palpable sigh of relief that there had been no further terrorist attack on America along the lines of 11th September the previous year. Our relief was compounded by the fact that Justin had gone off to London to undertake a special new project for the design company he had forged such a good relationship with.

We were of course delighted that his freelance business was taking off, apprehensive about the possibility of any terrorist attack on London and strangely comforted about the fact that he would be back in Cornwall in a few weeks, even though, in our heart of hearts, we knew each success was a stepping stone to his eventual freedom and leaving home for good.

Meanwhile, Mel and I were enjoying a modest amount of freedom ourselves. We did not have to consider anyone else when we wanted to go out for the day and thoroughly enjoyed our day at the Newnham Park Driving Trials near Plymouth. While a relatively small gathering of enthusiastic carriage drivers were there that day, the fact that the points earned by competitors went towards national competition awards meant that they came from other parts of the country. We were particularly delighted to see in action two of the most famous and capable drivers in the business. First there was Karen Bassett whom we had seen on two previous occasions, both when she was giving demonstrations in Hampshire when we lived in Wiltshire. We had seen her demonstrate in an indoor arena her amazing skill in driving through hazards no less than eight of her beautiful

Trakehner horses in hand, a truly magnificent sight. No less impressive was her performance at Newnham where we saw her skills tested in the reality of mud and water-filled ditches.

The second delight was to see in action a true legend in this field, George Bowman. We had not seen him before but had certainly read about him. He was, by then, so much older than Karen but no less competitive and courageous in the way he seemed to charge round the course.

All this gave some slight encouragement to Mel to learn to drive Smartie, something Morgans were particularly suited, and known for.

I had known virtually nothing about horses when I first had Max, though Mel more than made up for that deficiency. She had always drummed into me various dos and don'ts but after more than seven years in which I had got to know not just my own huge 17-hand horse but also Mel's various mounts, not the least of which was the feisty Smartie, I felt I knew my way around horses. This didn't stop my heart from leaping into my mouth when we saw at a distance one particular team of four try to go both sides of an obstacle, a wooden post. Not only did the horses jar themselves but they began to show signs of panic when they found they were unable to free themselves. Mel, too, frowned with anxiety as the horses seemed to be making matters worse.

Then a groom jumped down and went to the heads of the leaders. A nearby spectator who was rather less knowledgeable was beginning to express her concerns out loud to nobody in particular.

'Why doesn't somebody do something before they get hurt?'

'That's right,' I said to Mel. 'A quiet calm approach.' I could see the groom talking to the horses as he carefully disentangled their harness. Even from where we were it was obvious that in response to his words and manner the horses instantly relaxed and waited patiently for him to sort things out. 'There you are,' I went on, ignoring the glances from the nearby onlooker, 'a steady approach is all you need.'

'And they clearly know and trust him,' added Mel, pointing up yet another factor which our neighbour had overlooked. What we were really doing, of course, was indirectly countering her words of concern lest anyone else nearby should pick up on her implication that perhaps this was all a little unfair on the horses. Naturally, like all horses, they enjoyed doing what they had been trained for, provided, of course, that every now and then they were given their heads. This particular equestrian sport was a prime example of this principle in action. Come to think of it, however, none came to mind where this was not the case.

I was well into the rapid eye movement stage of a deep sleep when the door bell rang at around 12.30am. It was Justin returning late from a weekend at Andrew's where he had stayed on his way back from his stint in London. We knew he was coming, of course, but I absent-mindedly, out of habit, slipped the latch on the front door, locking him out. Normally he had some keys but being away for so long he had wisely decided to leave them at home.

The next morning he was in a very positive mood. His work was being truly appreciated by his ultimate clients which seemed to come as a surprise to him though not, of course, to us. This was a bit of a contradiction because he was always extremely confident about the quality of what he was doing. Perhaps it was simply the confirmation that this confidence was not, after all, misplaced which lifted him.

He buzzed around for days afterwards, tweaking his website, updating his showreel and e-mailing others who may have need of his services. We could see him stretching and flapping his wings before our eyes!

The following evening, when Max came in for the night, his feet beat out an irregular rhythm on the concrete floor of the barn. This was followed by the lighter, more even clip of Smartie's much daintier hooves.

'Oh, no!' I exclaimed as I lifted his feet one at a time to pick out any dirt or stones wedged between his frogs and his shoes.

'What's the matter?' called Mel from the other side of Smartie whose rug she was clipping up.

'He's lost two shoes,' I replied. In reality it made little difference whether it was one or more: either way he couldn't be ridden until they were refitted. It was just that, while the loss of one was inconvenient, two at once was unheard of. 'I wonder how he did it.'

'Ray's always saying it's the rough places in our field.' Ray was our farrier and he always had a theory about anything that happened to the horses. It was sometimes he who first noticed a small cut or graze when lifting a horse's foot during shoeing. On the rare occasions he had to refasten a shoe he could usually determine a cause from the way the clenches, or nails, were twisted.

'Can you see the way this shoe has somehow been twisted off?' he would say. Or, 'look at the way the shoe's bent. Must have caught it on a rock somewhere.' He was referring to the isolated surfaces of large lumps of rock buried beneath the field which showed themselves where the horses had eroded the soil with their feet. They were not, however, protruding far enough from the ground to even trip a horse let alone wrest a shoe from it!

When, a few days later, his van dieseled its way up the drive, it was relief that Max would soon be on an even keel again which dominated our thoughts.

'Come and look at this,' he said ten minutes later when he was inspecting Max's front hoof, prior to refitting the shoe which I had found lying in the middle of the field while out walking the dogs - the other being nowhere to be seen. In fact Ray had no trimming and very little filing to do because, of course, a few days of Max tramping round the field shoeless had taken the edge off both unmetalled feet.

As ever, Mel was the first to bend over the foot to peer at what Ray was pointing to, not least because I was at Max's head keeping him calm and still.

'What?' she asked, peering closer still.

'Can't you see it?' Ray grinned. 'It's a tiny pinprick but he's punctured his sole,' he explained.

'It's very difficult to see, isn't it?' Mel said, straightening herself up. 'Look, darling.' I did but could see nothing of consequence.

'Good job I spotted it before it went septic,' said Ray, scarcely containing his feeling of satisfaction. 'You'll need to poultice it and keep him in until it's healed,' he added with authority. 'Do you know how to do that?' he asked Mel, knowing I would be a lost cause in such matters. Seconds later she re-emerged from the shed we use as a tack-room brandishing the necessary equipment.

'I'm impressed,' he grinned.

'Well it's something I've always kept but in twenty years I've never had to use it,' she replied.

I groaned inwardly as I contemplated a further, uncertain, period of being unable to ride Max.

'How long will it take to heal?' I asked, addressing myself to Mel who was always good at knowing answers to things like that.

'I don't know, a week, maybe two if we're unlucky,' she answered. There was nothing else for Ray to do other than tidy up the two unshod feet. Certainly there was no question of re-shoeing the injured foot and no point replacing the other shoe so Max was left with two shoes on and two off!

The larger dog run which we had had constructed in front of the barn came into its own in the days that followed. Often a horse with such an injury would be confined to its stable for long periods of time to avoid any re-injury or reinfection. We both knew such a confinement would worry Max who had been used to being out every day for years.

The run, being about thirty feet or more square was the perfect size for a little perambulatory exercise for him. Being level concrete there was no chance of any further damage being done. To preserve our sanity and theirs we had to allow the horses to stay together. Apart from boredom their only problem would be that of eating. We gave them each a small mound of hay, plus one to minimise disagreements, in order to keep them going and, as an occasional treat, I led Max on his head-collar through the narrow gate into the small bank area where our three departed Danes and Daisy the Burmese were buried. The grass there, not being treated to a short back and sides so often as the rest of the lawn area, offered lush pickings which Max enthusiastically nibbled and tore at. I, meanwhile, took the opportunity to sit on the nearby mounting block and soak up the sun while keeping an eye on him.

Smartie, inevitably, was not at all impressed by this temporary enforced separation. Not so much, we suspected, because she was missing Max's large presence, which she undoubtedly was, but more because of what she thought she must be missing out on. For once the grass really was that little bit greener on Max's side of the fence!

The following day we noticed Max was stiff in his right hind leg, the other corner of him which was unshod. We decided to keep an eye on it in case he had injured it.

Mel worked hard on healing the foot over the coming days with regular changes of the poultice and frequent putting on and taking off of the special protective rubber boot she had spotted at nearby Mole Valley Farmers. Max, for his part, worked hard too. Worked hard, that is, at being a model patient and just putting up with the restrictions placed on him without getting het up in any way. Even Smartie who, having had her daily routine disrupted, had even more of an excuse to play up had shown how grown up she now was by accepting the new regime. We had eventually judged the right moment to let her alone into the field and, in the end, neither had objected but sweetly she had stayed grazing close to the fence next to the dog run.

Both Mel and Max were rewarded for their efforts when, just six days later, Ray agreed with our assessment that Max was fully recovered and could have his shoes back. The only sign that anything had been amiss was his slight loss of condition. But the summer grass soon rectified this and within a few days he was back to normal apart from the lingering stiffness in that hind leg.

Justin, however, was doing anything but lingering. He had been commissioned for another large project in London where he was to work for some four weeks as part of a team. He was tickled at the appearance of his name in publicity for the project, organised by the consultancy concerned. For Mel and me the nest-emptying was turning out to be a more gradual process than we had expected and for this we were grateful.

One afternoon, as Mel and I were enjoying a well-earned break with a cup of tea in the sitting room, we both heard a busy buzzing from the direction of the hearth. It was, of course, the prime time of the year for flying insects and we were used to the odd bee, moth, wasp or other unidentifiable bug buzzing inside the house. Closer examination, however, revealed that this particular busy-ness, or buzziness, was emanating from behind the closed doors of the woodburner.

Mel was allergic to bee stings so it fell to me to release the small prisoner which, I could see at close quarters, was in fact a wasp. We had had previous experience of wasps' nests - in the barn here and in the roof of our last house - so we were sub-consciously tuned into them. There was no question about it: any nest should be dealt with swiftly. But how could a wasp, detached from its comrades, have found its way into our woodburner?

Logic naturally suggested that the only way in was down the chimney but a near twenty-foot flight down a sooty flue with a bend in it seemed unlikely. At that moment we were joined by one of its friends, then another and another.

'Quick, shut the doors,' instructed Mel. I always did as I was told and complied. 'The nest's in the chimney,' she added. We made a quick exit to the garden and lifted our eyes, shielding them from the sun in the south west. A non-stop shuttle to and from the top of the chimney of small black dots confirmed Mel's conclusion. 'How do we get rid of them?' she asked with urgency in her voice. Then, answering her own question: 'we'll have to get someone out from the council.'

'That could take days,' I replied.

'Have you got a better idea?' she asked. I cupped my chin in my hand while I pondered.

'Smoke them out,' I finally said.

'Smoke them out? How?' I looked at her and communicated my thoughts. 'Not a fire. That's cruel,' she said as the penny dropped.

'Why not? The smoke will drive them out rather than kill them and the nest will then be useless,' I surmised.

'Hmmm,' said Mel doubtfully. 'If you're sure.'

'Well, what's the choice? A continuing influx of wasps into the sitting room one or two at a time - and we're bound to get them coming in the bedroom windows too...'

'I suppose you're right,' she sighed. 'We won't have honey running down the inside of the chimney, will we?' I looked at her to see if it was a serious question. Apparently it was!

'No, darling,' I assured her with some confidence.

Smoke emerging from our chimney as we enjoyed a blazing log fire on one of the hottest afternoons of the year must have given the neighbours something to think about.

The height of summer brings with it a reduction in our riding options because the fields we are so generously permitted to ride round tend to be host to various crops from cereals to potatoes or to cattle or sheep. It was not until late July that I spotted an opportunity to ride round a field we hadn't tried before. It had been - still was - full of potato plants but at last we were able to justify taking the horses into it for the first time.

It was no longer a totally virgin green field because tractors tending the plants over the weeks had etched out a number of broad tracks round the edge of and to and fro across the field.

'We can't ride in there,' said Mel, fresh-faced from the walking and trotting we, or more accurately the horses, had done up the mile-and-a-half of lane to get there. She was always understandably hesitant about not overstepping the mark in such matters but I knew we could be restricted to a less demanding and therefore less exciting ride along the main track if we didn't take such opportunities when they presented themselves.

'It'll be alright if we're careful to keep strictly to the tracks between the crops. We can't do any damage, can we?'

'I suppose not,' came the rather unconvinced reply. I led the way. Max, as ever, was brilliant, keeping to the dry, dusty pathways between the neatly spaced haulms. Smartie was less disciplined, seeking to investigate the unfamiliar-looking undergrowth!

'Don't get too far ahead of me,' pleaded Mel. 'Or she'll take off across the potatoes,' she yelled after me.

'No, she won't. It's all good practice for your leg-yielding,' I replied as we trotted, referring to the direction provided to the horse by pressing the appropriate leg on its side. As the tracks wandered back and forth we saw good stretches over which we could canter, then slow to a trot or walk, turn and then once more resume our canter. The clouds of dust thrown up by the horses' hooves only added to the sensation of riding the range! The sight of green Cornish potato leaves waving gently in the breeze reminded us that we weren't!

Another advantage in the dry weather was that, unlike fields laid to grass, the ground was soft, having been cultivated a relatively short time ago. This brought one disadvantage too: we had to take care to avoid any large stones or small lumps of rock so as not to injure the horses' feet.

'That was the best ride I've ever had on her,' declared Mel breathlessly when we started on the journey back down the lane half-an-hour later.

'Why's that?' I asked.

'Well, it's what you said. I had to work really hard to get her to follow the track as it weaved about and it did both of us good. She's just brilliant now. All my fear of riding her has gone. We just know and trust each other.'

'So our strategy of getting a foal and training her from scratch has finally paid off,' I grinned. Mel had not retained unswerving faith at all times that it would all work out. But she had stuck with it and the reward now that it had finally arrived had been well worth striving for. 'She's wonderful,' she said as she leant forward over Smartie's neck, threw her arms round it and planted a kiss on it just behind her ears.

'You wouldn't have done that a few months ago,' I commented, referring to the temporary relaxation of her grip on the reins.

'I wouldn't have done it a few hours ago,' she beamed. 'I just know I have finally turned the corner as far as riding's concerned,' she said. 'And Smartie's the one that's done it,' she announced triumphantly.

'And Lionel and Trudy and Kate,' I added, referring to the training she and Smartie had had.

'And you,' she grinned before blowing me a kiss. It was at that moment that I, too, finally accepted that it was so. I fought to restrain a tear as the anguish of the last few years streamed through my consciousness.

'Congratulations,' I finally replied. 'I know what a tough battle it's been but well done!'

'Don't, you'll make me cry,' she just managed to blurt out before succumbing to her self-fulfilling prophecy.

19 Space Invaders

'How would you and Mel like to come sailing?' was the question fired down the phone at me by Peter Hopkin, my erstwhile business colleague who, with wife Nicky, had a holiday home in Rock.

'Er, love to,' I replied. The hesitancy was not indicative of any lack of enthusiasm on my part but merely of surprise at this out-of-the-blue invitation. We had not heard from them for many months and had hesitated to phone too often, knowing they were both going through the trauma of fighting Nicky's cancer. As, even now, Peter had volunteered no information, I was reluctant to ask the question burning in my mind.

'Good. Why don't we go out for the day and then find somewhere for supper when we get back?' he asked.

'Great idea,' I replied, still unsure whether the 'we' included Nicky.

I finally summoned up the courage to ask. 'How's Nicky?'

'Oh, she's fine,' he replied. 'Pretty well recovered in fact. Of course we have to keep our fingers crossed and she'll continue to have routine check-ups but, no, she's doing very well.' I'm sure my relief travelled down the phone line ahead of my words.

'That's wonderful news, Peter.' We went on to fix a date a week later, the day before they were due to return home to Oxfordshire.

Perhaps that was so far ahead as to tempt fate. Sadly the weather intervened and we didn't get to go. 'It's a great shame, Dex, but neither you nor Mel would have thanked me for taking you out in this,' he explained, referring to the unseasonal, high winds, just about sub-gales.

'Er, no, Peter, you're probably right,' I agreed, hoping I sounded as though I was talking solely on Mel's behalf though, in truth, I, too, would have been less than keen!

'Let's make sure we do it another time,' Peter replied in his usual bright, enthusiastic way. 'Maybe next time we're down but that probably won't be before winter.'

We were by then well into our fifth year in Cornwall, defying the Jeremiahs who thought we wouldn't stick it out for more than a couple of years. The truth was we felt so at home in this wonderful place that we could only contemplate a move much later on when, perhaps, our age began to tell and we wanted to move closer to our sons. But that notion was to be revisited and severely questioned a few weeks later.

Of course the issue was not academic because we had merely put on the back burner the question of selling Upper Penwithiel and moving elsewhere in Cornwall. We knew the additional year we had decided to allow ourselves before pondering it once more was almost up. With Justin making more and more definite noises about leaving home we felt a natural window was about to open. The subject gradually seeped more and more into Mel's and my conversations and the idea of planning a move in the spring of 2003 began to firm up.

It was while walking the dogs in early August that my mind started to wander to the day when we would be leaving Upper Penwithiel. We had been truly happy in the years since we moved in so why move? We had always recognised that at that time the size of the house was important with two of the boys still based there and the third wanting to visit frequently. But within a matter of months it would be just the two of us for the first time in twenty-seven years.

Location had worked its way to the top of our list and second was manageability. We had to have a few acres for the horses and we would still need four good-sized bedrooms for when the boys, friends or family visited, or, rather, invaded us. One day that would probably include grandchildren so were not going to throw the baby out with the bath water.

It was at that moment of musing to myself that I saw them: we had suffered a different kind of invasion. Through the hedge between the big field and the small paddock I could make out one or two white patches. The sheep were back! Either they had been undaunted by their previous confrontation with three Great Danes and two Basenjis, they had short memories or they were different sheep. Whichever it was I did not want to find myself returning an injured or dead sheep to its owner so I had to make haste in a subtle enough way as to not draw the attention of the dogs who as yet had not noticed them. Max, of course, had and so I found myself rather ridiculously trying to obtain his collusion in keeping the whole thing quiet.

'You just stay there Maxie,' I said out loud, knowing that while horses were trained to do all sorts of marvellous things, 'staying' wasn't one of them! Yet he did. He stood watching me in his usual benign and amused way as I sidled down to the gate at the bottom of the field where it adjoined the little paddock. To my credit, and that of Max, I almost made it. The soft ploddering sound of twelve Dane feet, accompanied seconds later by the plittering of eight Basenji ones fortunately alerted me before the sheep. Deftly I swung open the five barred gate and waved the Danes down into the drive, followed most uncharacteristically by Chan who never did exactly what was asked of him.

That just left me and Betsy whose jungle hunting instincts diverted her at full tilt up into the little paddock where she delighted in the immediate response of the, now three, sheep grazing there. In a word, their reaction was to panic and back they went, no doubt via the same small opening through which they had come, to rejoin their flock in the adjacent field.

While Betsy's natural predilection was to follow, the rather nasty prickly things growing in the hedge made her rethink her plan.

Meanwhile Mel and I had been rethinking our own plan. When we were asked in future about where we wanted to move we knew the answer had to be, Cornwall, of course. Where in Cornwall? That was more difficult. We knew where it wasn't. It wasn't going to be too near a town - any town - too far west, too far east or on the north coast. Ideally it would be on the Roseland except for the lack of riding country. We later got out a map to mark up our target areas. We ended up placing on it a series of very small rings. We then knew it wasn't going to be easy. We would have to fall back on our usual cop-out and conclude that we'd know it when we saw it!

Further invasions were to follow in the coming days. Ellie had her first season, forcing us to break up the pack with Angus, Chan and Zen in the utility room and the bitches in the house. Mel got an unidentified bug, forcing her most unusually to take to her bed for the day. As ever, I was slow on the uptake, being flattened by it the following day. A major side-effect was the return of all the accumulated aches and pains usually kept at bay by aloe vera and my bioflow magnets!

I recovered just in time to repel a further, more determined invasion by the sheep. Clearly the earlier escapees had gone off in search of reinforcements, for this time there were more than a dozen sheep in the big field. Recalling the effectiveness of Betsy, I decided to take Chan, this time on an extending lead. His unrestrained enthusiasm, voiceless of course, was more than enough to put the wind up the ovine intruders. They may have seen dogs before but dogs that were silent? They didn't hang around for any kind of explanation. As one they shot down to the bottom of the field and up the little paddock, avidly seeking their exit route. Of course they had less time to navigate the way out than they had had when it was the way in and so it was something of a nervous and disorderly queue that presented its rump to us when we caught up. I slowly reeled in my secret weapon and waited for the last marauder to disappear, much like a patient police dog handler would oversee the last straggle of football fans leaving a stadium after a disappointing match.

Could I rely on this effective means of expulsion as a permanent deterrent? A few days later I got my answer. The sheep were back, apparently oblivious to any possible danger, leading me to wonder how their attention span compared with that of goldfish.

A more robust approach was clearly called for so I enlisted the aid of a length of stock fence. This was actually just a small stretch of about two or three feet in a hedge a hundred yards long, marked out by white strands of wool attached to those same prickly things!

Poor Max also suffered around that time: the cuts to his fetlocks, the joints above his front feet, had reappeared. Ray, the farrier, had thought it was fence wire that was responsible. After a thorough check of the fencing round the entire field I concluded there were just two places where he could have hurt himself, possibly by standing by a fence with his feet protruding beneath the bottom wire. Both were adjacent to two old gateways where he and Smartie sometimes stood 'chatting' to the pony next door. However, I was very doubtful that he had. I ensured that couldn't cause any further problems by half-burying huge six-inch deep planks along the two sections and stapling the bottom of the fence to them. He would never be able to stand there with his feet beneath the wire again.

A new invader arrived shortly afterwards in the form of Andrew at ten o'clock one Friday evening. The next day was very hot and sunny, ideal for a lazy day in the garden and a barbeque in the evening. Instead Mel and I were treated to a day out at Paignton Zoo! My initial resistance was soon discarded as we all three enjoyed a day together, sometimes reliving happy moments from the boys' childhoods.

But, very much back in the present day, he later delighted in taking us for a very enjoyable meal at the Food For Thought Restaurant in Fowey. I realised that evening just how good a job we had done in educating him in the finer points of life!

The next day saw Betsy follow Ellie precociously into season, some months before we were expecting her to. It also saw Moss advancing up the drive towards Mel and Andrew with the extremities of a bird just visible at either side of his mouth. Swiftly and silently Mel descended on him and grabbed him by the scruff of the neck, gently forcing him to open his mouth. As he did, a tiny wren flew out, up and away, confirming our long-held suspicion that he was no red-in-tooth-and-claw hunter: he was just a pussy cat!

James joined us the next day and after a day of recuperation, took Andrew off for a few hours canoeing from Fowey to Golant and back. It exhausted them!

We all took to the sea the following day, hiring a small motor boat in Falmouth and chugging across to St Mawes. I experienced a strange feeling of obsolescence as Andrew and James took turns to steer and navigate, leaving me to lean back in the stern and observe benignly.

As I closed my eyes and felt the sun and breeze on my face I was instantly back on any one of the boat trips we had taken the boys on as youngsters. Yet here were the two of them taking responsibility for me! I relished the hour or so of total relaxation, allowing myself only two admonishments as James seemed more interested in riding the washes from larger craft than in our comfort or taking the shortest route between two points. The second came as, between them, they took a rather confused approach to mooring which I thought for a second was going to put my deposit at risk!

The family completed itself when, late in the evening, Justin arrived on the train from London where he had been working. The motivation was that the following day was James' twenty-fifth birthday.

We spent his day on Carne beach, beneath the Nare Hotel, but contented ourselves with a picnic from the cool box. While the sea was not as warm as I had known it there in mid-August, it was warm enough even for Mel to be persuaded to come for a swim, the first time we had all done that together for a few years. The perfect end to the day was a superb meal in our favourite local fish restaurant, Trawlers in Looe.

I think we all experienced something of holidays gone by in that week.

Sunday morning brought another challenge to the puny barricade I had put in place in the little paddock. There were this time, however, just two woolly trespassers. They had abandoned their old entrance and pushed their way through a new weak place in the hedge. A brief scout around in the barn brought forth an old wicket gate left by our predecessors which was duly pressed into service.

When I had finished securing it with wire, deep in the heart of the hedge, I withdrew with less than total confidence that they would not open up yet another way in: to date they haven't. Max was sufficiently interested to spend some minutes investigating the new wooden addition to his boundary, presumably wondering whether there was a way he could open it with his nose, as he always did with all gates and doors, and discover pastures new.

Days later I spotted renewed cuts to his fetlocks, prompting me to check all fences all over again. I found no clues as to what was causing the injuries.

There was no doubt whatsoever about the cause of the injuries to James' knees the next day. After Andrew and Justin had left us once more, he stayed on. We returned to Carne Beach because our earlier visit had stirred his imagination. He had decided to mountain bike his way to the top of Nare Head, so Mel and I enjoyed an afternoon on the beach while he went on a circular tour, taking in the fringes of Portloe.

We had watched him gradually become a speck on the horizon and then disappear over it. The speed of his climb told us how fit he was, reminding us of the day he ran down onto Logan Rock. It was on the way back that he hit something buried in a track which punctured a tyre and threw him to the ground. Covered in blood, sweat and dust, he arrived back on the beach an hour or so after leaving us.

Into the sea he went, emerging exhausted but refreshed half-an-hour later. I cast my mind back to the distant days when I was that age, just before I met Mel, but had not even the dimmest recollection of ever being that fit

It was Ray who finally pinned down the riddle of Max's fetlocks when he next came to shoe the horses.

'He's doing it getting up,' he pronounced after puzzling over them for a few seconds. We must have looked blank because he went on to explain. 'Sometimes when a horse is getting older it can't lift itself back up using its feet so it uses its fetlocks a bit like a knuckle.' He demonstrated with the knuckles of his right hand in the palm of his left. Suddenly it became obvious. Max confirmed Ray's theory in the days ahead: we saw him rolling and rushed out to see how he got up. His fetlocks were badly grazed. If only we could take him into the sea: it would help to heal the wounds much as it had James'.

It took just minutes to locate an equestrian store on the internet which stocked a special boot which we decided he was going to have to wear when out in the field from then on. At night, his stable was inches deeper in Aubiose to prevent him scraping himself on the concrete beneath.

It was just before James was due to return to Wiltshire that I had yet another nostalgic reminder. I had got quite out of the old habit built up over the years of assisting one or other of the boys in finding a new car. James had been pondering the replacement of his old student car for some months and it was the day before he was due to leave that I found myself sitting alongside him as we drove up the A30 and M5 towards Taunton to look at a Golf GTI, a bright red one which he eventually bought.

I had gone along in the expectation that my negotiating skills, carefully honed over a working lifetime, would be of assistance to him. I was instead treated to a master class in how to buy a car. In a blistering approach he had, totally unaided by me, got a significant increase on the trade-in value of his old wreck, a substantial reduction in the price of the Golf as well as a useful increase in the free tax offered from six months to a year. In addition to that he threatened to walk away without a free tank of petrol! I almost felt sorry for the poor salesman when he finally had to cave in.

But I had learned something: I was not as tough as I had thought!

It was nearly midnight towards the middle of September when the phone rang. Mel was in bed asleep and I was reading so I went round to her side of the bed to answer the phone as, amazingly, it didn't wake her.

It was her father who asked to talk to her. When I told him she was asleep there was something in the way he asked me to wake her which put me on warning. He had to convey to her the devastating news that her mother had died earlier that evening. While she had not been fully fit for some years, we had not known of any serious threat to her life, so the shock was total. In the weeks ahead I found myself drawing on my own experience of losing both my own parents unexpectedly a few years earlier.

20 Many a Slip

There is nothing more therapeutic than going out on a horse. Mel has often said that, even when she was battling against her loss of riding confidence, perhaps even more so then. She maintained that you had no chance to think about anything other than the job in hand. Certainly I had come to agree with that which was why I suggested it several times in those weeks. It didn't, of course, remove her sadness but it gave her a chance to deal with it.

On one occasion Smartie proved uncharacteristically obstinate, first refusing to walk at all then refusing to canter and finally throwing in a succession of bucks when Mel finally got her to canter before stopping suddenly again.

'Whatever's the matter with her?' she asked as Smartie misbehaved on the way round one of our usual fields. Feeling a little fragile when we first decided to go out, she had been most insistent that I tighten Smartie's girth so that the saddle didn't slip. I guessed she had been more anxious than usual to avoid any mishaps at a time when she had so much on her mind, so I ensured it was truly tight. She soon answered her own question. She stopped and leaned down to check it. 'It's very tight,' she said.

'That's what you said it should be,' I replied, a little bemused.

'But not that tight.'

I turned Max back and stopped alongside. When I leaned over to slip my fingers beneath it, I couldn't.

'Hmmm. It is a bit tight,' I conceded. Mel then slackened the girth off one hole and we resumed our ride.

'That's better, Smartie,' she smiled as normal service resumed.

'Speak for yourself,' I said, out of breath, when I caught her up after a long fast canter back across the field towards the track home.

'Why?' she grinned with relief that some new problem had not, after all, materialised.

'It's catching. For the first time in the seven years I've had him, Max bucked,' I explained.

'Really?' She failed to hide her amusement.

'Yes. At first I couldn't understand what was happening. I thought he'd stumbled, started to slip sideways in the saddle and prepared myself for a flight through the air. Then I settled back in the saddle and had just worked out what had happened when he did it again - twice!'

'He's just happy,' she suggested. I wasn't so sure. He was too old for that sort of thing. More to the point, so was I!

It took a while for me to realise why Chan had started to make amorous overtures towards me when I went to feed him and the others one evening. Then I remembered. I had had Betsy sitting on my lap earlier and the smells caused by her 'interesting condition' had not escaped him.

It was in a phone call to Jeanette, the breeder of our Danes, that Mel got a tip from her. Applying a little eucalyptus oil to the haunches of a bitch in season would deter even the most persistent of interested dogs. I had my doubts: a Basenji, after all, was in a class of its own! Her idea did seem to work, however, though I remarked to Mel that the two of them, Betsy and Ellie, were going round reeking as if their backsides had a cold!

Because Ellie had stopped her season and then started it again after Betsy had decided to join in the fun, the dogs and the bitches were to be separated for no less than six weeks instead of the usual three.

When they were eventually reunited we decided to respect the pack order and let Marma and Zen out together first. As we had expected, that was a non-event except for the fact that Marma's instant response was to ensure poor Zen hadn't forgotten his place: she made aggressive faces and noises at him before finally playing with him, showing him how much she had missed him.

We knew that Ellie had to be next to be let out with them. Her only reaction was to show utter subservience to Zen who clearly didn't know how to handle it. She kept rolling on the ground in front of him. At first sight we concluded she was merely flirting, albeit a little late. But we finally decided she was frightened of what he might do to her but we knew he was too much of a softie to do anything to offend!

We then played safe and let Chan and Betsy out together without the Danes. Barbara Williams, Betsy's breeder, had warned us of the possibility of a skirmish between the two of them, another quirk of the breed we understood. However, to our surprise it was another non-event.

In fact the only real fun came when we finally put all five of them back together in the garden when various rumblings told us they were busy testing and retesting the old pecking order. In the end I decided to take them all for a walk round the large field and let them act like a pack once more. The result was total success as they again bonded together against whatever potential enemy might be out there!

Western Power, as the providers of our electricity, were responsible for the maintenance of the overhead lines which run the length of the lane. It was true that under more liberal regulations we could now buy our electricity from the gas company. Whether it was having no gas supply, some illogical loyalty to the local electricity supplier or sheer inertia, I had not been motivated to do so. That had given me, I felt, a slight moral edge when I had argued against no more than a metre of branches being removed beneath the power lines. It was probably more out of lazy sentiment than any well-considered ethical stance that I instinctively decided I was on the side of the trees concerned!

When the time finally arrived for the surgery to be carried out, I was already powering my computer from the generator I had had to hire for the day the work was due to take. Western Power had agreed to pay up to £50 for it. I checked with the foreman exactly what their instructions were and was relieved to hear it was just the one metre that was to be removed.

That, of course, didn't relieve me of the responsibility for continually checking up throughout the day - just in case some element of over-enthusiasm crept in. After all, once removed, the branches could not be put back!

They were, however, as good as their word and after they had gone I was hard put to tell from my vantage point at the top of the field just where they had been cutting. The natural line of the trees along the lane had been preserved and all the loppings had been removed. I even had the full bill for the generator paid despite the fact that it was slightly more than the £50 offered. Reason enough, I thought, for me to phone the area manager a day or two later and thank him. This was so rare, I believe, that he was quite taken aback, replying simply, and through, I detected, a wry smile, 'we do our best.' This time it was more than enough.

In fact the only problem we were presented with that day came as the result of natural Morgan curiosity. To avoid the men panicking the horses with their power lift and chainsaws we had consigned Max and Smartie to the little side paddock for the day. Just after the saws started up, however, Smartie vaulted five feet over a fence in a gap in the hedge to get a better view. They had to be confined to the barn for the day with a supply of hay and water, reminding us of that faraway first day at Upper Penwithiel. Once again it was removal men that took their idly munching attention: branch removal on this occasion.

Justin was soon able to celebrate his business success by taking delivery of the first car to be paid for by his own efforts. To me this was another important milestone: yet another accustomed expense was to cease to be my responsibility for good. Mel and I were also relieved that he was going to be driving round in something safer than his rusting student car.

In fact Mel and I had already booked a few days at the Nare for our customary though irregular break. Knowing that Justin might not be at home to look after the animals for very much longer we had booked four nights in September. The funeral of Mel's mother which of course we knew we would have to attend had not been finalised until just before we were due to go and was actually to take place on the second day. The Nare were extremely understanding and offered us what few alternatives were available.

Thus it was that we rearranged our short holiday for immediately after the funeral but split between two breaks of two nights away, returning home for one in the middle. Neither they nor we had experienced such an arrangement before but Mel and I knew we both needed those few days of breathing space more than ever, not least because we had had to travel from Cornwall to Surrey and back in a day: there had simply been no alternative as the three boys were with us and had been unable to look after the animals.

As it was, we had to leave the dogs for over twelve hours, the longest we had ever left them. We accepted that whatever mess they had contrived to make was the price we had to pay. When we eventually returned there was no mess. In fact no evidence at all that they had been left for such a time. Their reaction was just slightly more enthusiastic than if we had simply left them to go to the local shops!

Our brief stay at the Nare provided us with five days of total relaxation, despite the night at home in the middle. We were relieved to discover that, at last, steps had been taken to halt the erosion of the small cliff in front of the hotel. Perhaps no higher than forty feet, a huge bite had been taken out of it by the sea, threatening the long term security of the hotel itself.

The fixing, while we were there, of copious drapes of netting, held in place by giant screws driven into the cliff face and the piling up of some substantial granite boulders at the foot promised to arrest further slippage. We knew we would be back to check!

∽

Just over a week later I had a pleasant reminder that my responsibilities for the boys' cars had well and truly gone for good. Justin had been waiting in his car outside a shop for James when the driver of the van (yes, it was white!) parked in front of him, returned, jumped in, started up and then reversed straight into him. His excuse later turned out to be that his foot had slipped off the clutch.

I was well into my internal groan as I listened to Justin's account on the phone when, picking up what was behind my studied silence, he very brightly said, 'but at least it's not your problem now, is it?'

'No. No, I suppose it isn't,' I replied even more brightly. I knew then that he, in fact all three, were going to manage without the sort of involvement on my part which I had become used to over the years.

In a similar way I was reminded that Mel, too, was managing very well in one area of her life without my continuing involvement. It was as we were riding up the one-in-three section of the lane that Smartie slipped, almost going down on her knees. Despite heroic efforts by both of them, gravity dictated that there was only one place for Mel to go. She ended up sitting on the road, hanging onto the reins to ensure Smartie didn't take off. Just like Max, however, she merely stood looking down at Mel with a bemused and slightly worried expression. I turned Max and went alongside to take the reins from her.

My big concern was that this might yet be the event that finally dented the confidence that she had so carefully rebuilt with Smartie. Mel got to her feet rubbing her backside, grinning.

'That was my fault, I shouldn't have let her go forward so quickly.' She was soon back in the saddle and to my relief we continued as though nothing had happened.

Further on, after reaching the top of the lane, Mel noticed that one of Max's brushing boots, which protected his legs from accidental contact from his feet, was loose. I jumped down to refasten it. Mel, wise as ever, had warned me when I was buying my new jodhpur boots, of the pitfalls of steel toe-caps. If a horse did tread on them there was a chance of trapping your toes under the indented steel, prolonging the agony. I had decided that, on balance this was less likely to be a problem than bearing the full weight on them in the first place.

While I was about to remount him from my improvised mounting block - an old hay bale nearby, he managed to step back onto my foot, avoiding the toe-cap, however, merely crunching my instep!

As we were cantering round a field minutes later, both horses passed a silage cutting machine with absolute nonchalance. I was sure I saw them wink at each other!

21 Close Encounters

There was no doubt about it: Zen was in love. Not with Marma, of course, because he knew that wasn't right. Nor with the delectable Ellie. He was definitely besotted with Betsy. One evening he was lying on his stomach with his head resting across his front paws when Betsy settled next to his huge head. He rolled away from her onto his side and lifted one paw. She then rolled the same way, snuggled up closely under his chin and he gently lowered his paw onto her. They slept like that for some time that evening and on many more occasions.

Days later Mel had a close encounter of a different kind. She had been mucking out when she had to duck to avoid a sparrowhawk in close pursuit of a blackbird, in a similar way as she once had to at a birds of prey demonstration at a country show when a kestrel had whistled past her ears.

I was soon to have my own strange bird encounter in the barn the next time it was my turn to muck out. I had been talking to a robin which was rooting around beneath the food bucket in Max's stable, searching out crumbs Max had spilled over the sides, to reassure him I wasn't going to harm him. When I finished I took the food buckets to the tap outside the far end of the barn to wash them out. To my amazement I found him perched on the bracket fixing the tap to its post, head cocked to one side. Just seconds later when I went back to tackle Smartie's stable there he was again. A jet-propelled robin, I thought to myself.

When I got indoors later I related this to Mel. Rather than being impressed as I had expected, she laughed, which I hadn't.

'You idiot, there are two robins in the barn,' she explained rather harshly I thought.

'Two? I thought they were very territorial.'

'Well, yes, so did I but I've definitely seen two out there. They don't seem to mind each other.'

'Maybe they've reached a demarcation agreement. Or maybe that just teaches me not to believe everything I was told as a child!'

While we had always regarded our animals as being part of the family we had tried to avoid over-sentimentality. We had always treated the dogs as dogs, cats as cats and horses as horses. This not only extended to their diets which were strictly formulated according to their species - except for the occasional left over vegetables, meat or gravy for the dogs - but to the way they were dealt with. For example no animal had ever been allowed to sleep upstairs, let alone in our bedroom and never on the bed. This was less to do with hygiene and rather more to do with getting a good night's sleep. Besides, there were always too many of them and it would not be fair to allow any one of them special privileges!

This approach also meant that we had never bothered with Christmas or birthday presents for them because they simply wouldn't have understood. Thus it was as much a surprise to Ellie as to us when she received a card on her first birthday! She was to be the first of our animals ever to do so. Unsurprisingly it came from Jeanette, her breeder.

This served as a little reminder that she was indeed growing up, albeit slowly. One example of this occurred a few days later. One of the Basenjis had taken it upon themselves to remove Ellie's collar at every opportunity so Mel had got into the habit of only putting it on her when she was going out. This was a precaution against her escaping and getting lost: the Basenjis had theirs on twenty-four hours a day!

When Mel went to get them in she noticed that Ellie was without her collar. Ellie then went back to where she had been standing and, after a little difficulty, finally succeeded in picking up the collar from the cobbles and bringing it to Mel.

It was just one week later that Mel burst into my study after putting the horses out. 'Come quickly,' she demanded urgently. It was unusual for her to disturb me at that time of the morning when I was getting into the rhythm of the stock market's gyrations.

'What is it?' I asked as calmly as I could in an attempt to prepare myself to deal rationally with whatever it was.

'Just come, now,' she commanded. My mind ran rapidly over the possibilities. Perhaps one of the dogs had escaped again. Or maybe one of the horses had injured itself. It was that sort of emergency that I detected in her voice.

'Whatever is it, darling?' I asked, my rationality starting to give way to mild panic.

'It's Moss.' I hadn't considered a problem with one of the cats: we simply never had any worries about them. That suggested something serious. 'He's been run over and he's badly injured.' The words collided in my head. On the one hand I was relieved to know he was still alive but on the other I had to take on board that he was badly injured. What did that mean? I sprang from my chair and followed Mel out.

'Where...?'

'He's down the lane, halfway between Middle and Lower Penwithiel.'

'How do you....?'

'Malcolm next door told me. He was driving down and Moss just jumped out...'

'What sort of state is Moss in?'

'Don't know. Malcolm offered to put him down. He thinks he's too badly injured to save. Didn't want him to suffer.' The coldest of shivers ran up my neck as I contemplated our poor, beautiful, funny, floppy, cuddly, loveable Moss in pain.

On the way down the lane we passed a distressed-looking Malcolm.

'I'm so sorry, Dex. I wasn't going very fast. He just jumped out and I slammed on my brakes...'

'No, no, Malcolm, we can't blame you for it but where is he?'

'Just down there,' he said, pointing into the hedge running alongside the gully which was now a stream in full flow following the recent rain. My mind conjured up a picture of him lying comatose in the middle of the lane. But he was nowhere to be seen. Just beyond the fresh skid marks we heard him cry out.

'Where is he?' asked Mel in anguish.

'Here he is. He's running down the stream.' My heart leaped when I saw Moss not only conscious but walking or, rather, limping. I could see his left hind leg was badly damaged but there was hope that the rest of him had escaped any major impact. Mal, the only one of us with wellies on, splashed into the stream and scooped him up as gently as she could. Then I winced when I saw his front left leg was also broken.

Mel carefully wrapped him in one of the boys' old cot blankets which she had grabbed on her way out and passed him over to me. The tears started to well up as I walked back up to the house, his cries getting more desperate. By holding him loosely in the blanket I was able to avoid causing him any unnecessary discomfort.

I found myself gazing down into his deeply troubled eyes. Then it occurred to me to talk to him. As soon as I did, he seemed to calm down a little despite being in acute pain. We passed Malcolm once more who repeated his apologies. Again I told him we didn't blame him. He kindly offered to contribute to the vet's bill but I declined. To do otherwise would seem to imply we did.

Within minutes Mel had spoken to the surgery, got the car out of the garage and whisked us into them. It was no more than fifteen minutes later that Simon Draper looked at Moss, being very careful not to add to his discomfort by probing too closely, and said he would do everything he could.

'It's amazing how many animals do survive a nasty accident like this. Of course, I can't guarantee he'll be alright but he's a young healthy cat so his chances are good.' We agreed to go and wait at home for more news later.

'As soon as we put him under the anaesthetic then we can have a good look at the damage and assess what's best. I can't really do that now because it would be too painful for him.'

22 The End of the Rainbow

'We could have called her Lady,' I suppose. Mel was up to her usual trick of starting a conversation with me which she had apparently been having in her head before bringing me in on it.

'Called who Lady?' I asked, looking up from my crossword.

'Marma of course.' Of course. I waited for some elaboration but none came.

'Why Lady?' I asked in all innocence.

'Well we called her Marmalade because that was Jeanette's name for her.'

'Y-e-s,' I agreed cautiously.

'And we shortened it to Marma. Maybe we should have called her the second half of the name instead of the first.'

'Ah, Ladey. It would look silly with an 'e' in it,' I sighed.

'Yes but it would sound the same to her.' That was undeniable.

'I'm happy with Marma. Anyway to change it now would only confuse her.'

'I suppose so.' I went back to 10 across.

We had noticed over the months some idiosyncratic little habits developed by the dogs. Zen, for example, had convinced himself that water straight from the tap by the barn tasted infinitely better than that supplied by us in the nearby bucket. Each time we washed out or refilled the horses' water buckets we had to allow an extra minute for him to have his fill. Much of it went anywhere but in his mouth so we were surprised he was so persistent in drinking this way, which he still does. Needless to say, the Basenjis just had to try it but, disliking water as much as cats, it was only once! In Betsy's case she seemed to stalk the thin stream of water first, as if to show it she had the upper hand. The succession of snorts and spluttering, followed by a strategic withdrawal, cast doubt on this.

The Basenjis' own little peccadillo was one which had been permitted, no encouraged, by Mel. They would wait for her to settle in her armchair in the evening and then wheedle their way onto her lap. Naturally I looked down my nose at this. Dogs were dogs after all and in almost thirty years none had ever been allowed on chairs. True, it was a different proposition for Great Danes. If we wanted a seat they had to be banned!

The truth is, Mel enjoys cuddling her little dogs and as all Basenji owners know, Basenjis like nothing better than being tightly curled up and warm either on a lap or near some other heat source. It was only when Mel went out of the room that they looked around for an alternative. It happened to be my lap one evening and I was too weak-willed to say no. The wry smile on Mel's face when she returned showed that any authority I might have had on the matter (probably not much) had evaporated for good.

Chan himself had also developed an odd little fetish all of his own. He had become passionately fond of corks. Not just any old corks but specifically wine corks. Neither of us can pinpoint when this first happened but he now jumps down from Mel's lap and sits patiently in front of me whenever he hears the rattle of the levered corkscrew!

Another little habit all three Danes had was to play footsie with you. Whenever there was a Dane at your feet it would want to place a foot on yours. Even if you were just passing what you thought to be a sleeping Dane, a paw would stretch out to gently pat your leg. We had never experienced this with those who had gone before.

The horses, of course, had their own little ways. Max showed his affection by nudging you with his nose. Unfortunately the sheer weight of his head and power of his neck muscles made this a hazardous gesture of which to be on the receiving end. Smartie's own peculiarity was to paw the water in the trough if it wasn't to her liking. We could sometimes hear the fervent sploshing and occasional metallic clang, as shoe met trough, from inside the house, telling us to refresh the water!

The cats, having been on the scene longer than the dogs, with the exception of Angus, had already established their behaviours. The most endearing, perhaps, was Cloey's camouflage trick. When she came into the sitting room in the evening, when the dogs were with us, she tried to disguise her presence by tucking up her paws under her chest on top of the lower of the two bookcases alongside the various dog models, some almost her size, which resided there. If we couldn't locate her in the room Mel would suddenly spot her and say, 'she's being an ornament again!' Alongside the sand-cast buff American Cocker, almost exactly her colour, was her favourite resting place.

Perhaps the most spectacular ritual was one concocted by the dogs and horses between them. Its continuing viability is dependent on a cold war-type balance of fear. The horses had been used to dogs, of course, ever since they arrived but the current young dogs had had to grow up with the horses. This meant I had a reasonable understanding of the group dynamics involved. I had ensured the dogs had come face to face with the horses when they were still very young, with a gate between them. This meant the dogs had a healthy respect for the horses by the time they were introduced on the same side of the gate.

Being flight animals, the horses had a natural inclination to run away from anything which frightened them. This was less true of Smartie than Max simply because she was a Morgan! The dogs, being natural hunters, needed no encouragement to chase anything running away from them.

Marma, like Sukie, our oldest Dane so far, had attracted Smartie's attention and had been licked from head to foot by her more than once. This instilled in Marma an inclination to keep her distance. Zen, however, was bolder but not inclined to get too close to the heavy hooves he had felt vibrating through the ground. Ellie was outwardly timid though, probably, the most intelligent of them so her idea of fun was to join in anything exciting or mischievous without risking being identified as a miscreant.

The Basenjis were natural rounders up of anything that moved, regardless of how many times bigger than them it might be but never, ever slowed down enough to be caught by anything as lumbering as a horse. Or a Great Dane for that matter!

I can't remember who started the game that has become a ritual but I was suddenly aware of Max turning on his heels and sprinting to the top corner of the field one day, soon to be followed by Smartie and then one, two, three Great Danes and a pair of Basenjis. My heart was in my mouth, which in turn had dropped open, as the seven of them raced away from me. Naturally I followed though not, it has to be admitted, at anything like a sprint. As I neared the middle of the field the horses stopped by the hedge, having nowhere else to go, snorting and looking quite magnificent.

The Basenjis were next to arrive and they proceeded to circle the horses before going right up to them. Of course they had no intention of getting anywhere near those iron-clad feet. Indeed their game seemed to be to play chicken, knowing they had lightning-fast reflexes to get out of the way before the horse had realised its foot had even left the ground.

The Danes arrived so close together that they concertinaed into each other in their determination to keep a safe distance. Then they looked round at me as if seeking guidance as to what they should do next. Their answer came to them the instant that the two horses turned to face them. It was to put more distance between them! They began to backtrack in my direction, leaving the Basenjis to continue their little dance.

This surprise result appeared to embolden Max: never before had a tactic of his been so successful. There was only one thing he could do with such wimpish pursuers and that was to turn the tables. He, followed by Smartie, proceeded to chase the Danes which then scattered. The Basenjis were even more delighted by this new turn of events, whereby the desired outcome of driving the horses in my direction had been achieved with so little effort on their part.

My arrival on the scene, somewhat out of breath, seemed to calm matters with both horses and dogs looking to me for protection. The Danes, in particular shadowed me closely on the return to the bottom of the field while the horses, if anything, looked disappointed at being cheated out of their turn to be the chasers.

None of this is to be encouraged because any horse owner will be aware of the potential dangers. But knowing our animals as I do, I recognise every aspect of their behaviour and would soon be on hand if required. Suffice it to say that our daily walk is often accompanied by this ritual being played out, most frequently as a result of Max walking down towards us when he hears the gate catch and waiting until the dogs are close before charging off to the far end of the field with Smartie in tow. The result is always the same: a stalemate followed by a boring return to a normal amble once the fun is over.

The most spectacular display is after a prolonged dry spell when the seven of them put up a dust cloud that would rival any chase across the prairie in a western! The only danger to have presented itself so far has been of me falling over the Danes as they attempt to hide behind me after a chase when the horses start to turn round!

The fact is that all our animals have a place not only in our lives but in each other's. Perhaps the most benign one is between the horses and the cats. The horses accept them in the barn, for example, much as they do the robins and the swallows.

❦

We had a long wait for a phone call from Simon Draper. Like most animal owners in similar situations we had run the gamut of emotions while waiting. First we felt sure Moss would be alright and a comforting feeling that this was so settled round us. Then we feared the worst and braced ourselves for the pain and anguish that would bring.

The news when it came brought the deepest sensation of relief.

'The poor little chap's got two badly damaged legs,' said Simon Draper down the phone. 'So we've had to pin the back leg with an external metal splint and the fracture in his front leg is best left to heal so we've put it in plaster.'

'How is he otherwise?' I found myself asking inanely, as if to block out the seriousness of poor Moss' situation.

'Well, he's not out of the wood yet. He's had a nasty accident followed by a serious operation and we need to see how he responds in the next twenty-four hours. But if he recovers as quickly as he looks like doing then you may be able to have him home tomorrow or possibly the day after.'

'Right. Thank you Simon. When can we come and see him?'

'I don't think there's much point in you coming to see him tonight because he wouldn't really know you're there but why not phone in the morning. All being well you could come and see him then.'

Mel and I did not sleep well that night. When we weren't imagining our poor little Moss alone in his cage at the vets we were contemplating the fact that his very existence was on a knife edge.

We could hardly wait for 8.30 to come round the following morning. Once more we experienced relief that he had made it through the night.

'Can we come and see him?' was our sole response to the news given to us by the nurse.

'Yes, of course you can. He's still very poorly and not really with it but he has come through his ordeal surprising well.'

Our visit was short-lived simply because he was sleeping fitfully, his response to shock and to painkillers. But we were reassured to see him progressing and only too grateful to be able to gently stroke his head, the severe pain he had been in the last time we had seen him being significantly reduced. We arranged to phone after 2.00pm to see whether he was able to return home. Mel and I had planned carefully how we would nurse him back to health, being only too well aware it would be neither quick nor easy. We were just so pleased at the prospect of being able to help him, ably assisted, we knew, by aloe vera. It would be a challenge of the most rewarding sort.

We had even agreed that Moss would sleep in our bedroom in those first nights so that we could be at hand quickly if needed. He would have to be kept away from the dogs, too, not least his great friend Chan.

The phone rang at just after 1.30pm. The news from the duty vet that Saturday afternoon was unexpected and devastating. Moss had quietly slipped away a short while before. The effect of the shock on his system had been too great and we had been denied the opportunity and privilege of helping him beat the odds.

❧

The loss of Moss was to hit us harder in the coming days than any we had experienced for a while. It certainly gave the lie once and for all to the notion, once implied by a friend, that the more animals you had the less you felt the loss of any one of them. If anything the exact opposite was proving to be the case. Moss had his own very special place in our lives and in those of the others. It was as though a key brick in a wall had been brutally removed.

We found that we had been hit at a philosophical level too. We were reminded how swiftly life can turn on you. We should live more for today and enjoy each day to the full. Maybe we should ease some of the pressures we applied to ourselves. In short this saddest of events posed the question of what life was really all about.

We struggled, too, to fathom how it could have happened. We had long revelled in the fact that our lane was so quiet, not least because of the safety it afforded the cats. But we knew Moss was a very laid-back sort of a cat. From Malcolm's description of what had happened Moss had just flopped lazily down the bank on our side of the lane, about two hundred yards down, on his morning perambulation and was about to go for a wander in the woods on the other side. He was never a hunter and so was unlikely to have been causing any harm to anyone or anything. He had been simply unlucky.

Eventually we realised that the impact on us had really been down to this harmless innocence - despite his mischievous demeanour, to his young age - he had never had any previous illness or injury and to the fact that he represented all we had ever looked for in a cat. He was a rich character. We knew we would always miss him and for many days afterwards either Mel or I would think we had heard or seen him.

The first thing James said the next time he was home was, 'I'll never be able to push him across the floor on his back again.' This was one of the first things we had thought of in those miserable hours that Saturday afternoon in November.

Oh how we longed for him to return and clumsily disturb the ornaments in the sitting room, to hide over-conspicuously on the top shelf in my study, scattering everything in his path on the way up and then down again or try to steal a flake of kipper from my breakfast plate with a deft flick of his paw when I wasn't looking, all things for which he was regularly admonished.

Above all he had been a very happy cat and that had made us happy too.

It was the next day, at around the time that Moss had died, when the strangest thing happened. I had been moping rather aimlessly in my study on what had been a drizzly day, trying unsuccessfully to cheer myself up by catching up on some paperwork when Mel came in and gently led me out into the front garden by the hand. The sun was out.

'Moss has returned one last time to say goodbye.' I had no idea what she was referring to. 'Look,' she said, pointing north, down past the Littles' house.

'What?' I asked, still oblivious to whatever it was.

'There,' she said, looking up into the sky. Then I saw it. A full, richly coloured spectrum: a rainbow.

'Oh yes,' I replied, not being sure there was any direct connection.

Realising this, Mel explained: 'look where it finishes.'

I looked and slowly realised it appeared to line up with the exact spot in the lane where he received what turned out to be his fatal injuries. 'But it wouldn't appear to do so if you went down there,' I said, blankly.

'No,' she replied softly, 'but that's not the point.' And it wasn't. From that moment we slowly started to come to terms with what had happened, armed with the sure knowledge that there is only ever one thing to be found at the end of a rainbow.

23 Is Life Worth Living?

The punctuality of Paddington trains had slowly improved since the knock-on problems of the recent spate of accidents. The one-and three-quarter-hour hour delay in the journey one December evening to my board meeting in London was therefore unexpected. So was the cause. It was due to someone throwing themselves in front of a train ahead of us, the second time I had experienced this.

Naturally I felt for the driver concerned who would have had no warning and to whom no blame could be attached. No doubt it would take him some time to put the incident behind him.

But what of the poor soul whose mind had left him or her no alternative but to end his or her life? The clue to how someone could take such a drastic step was in those very words. They believed there was no alternative. I tried to understand how they might have reached such a conclusion.

I once worked for someone who used to say, 'every problem predicates its own solution.' I can still hear his clipped words in my head. I had failed to see what he meant the first time I heard it but he had been proved right. What he meant, of course, was simply that every obstacle had a way round it, you just had to find it. I found myself ruminating on what sort of predicaments one could find oneself in that led to a closing down of the mind in that way.

My guess was that the most likely possibilities were financial problems, terminal illness, guilt or a broken heart. Whatever it was, the person concerned could either see no way through the situation or could only see options which they dismissed as unacceptable. Perhaps they could see only bankruptcy and shame rather than facing facts and starting again. Or an end to pain and hopelessness rather than enduring and delaying family heartbreak. Or a lifting of self-loathing rather than exercising self-forgiveness. Or relieving the agony of loss rather than finding anew.

The true reasons could never be known to me but what I felt certain of was the fact that at the moment of disaster that person had been alone. It has long seemed to me that at the point of death, every living creature is totally alone: it is a step that they alone must take, no matter how much help and support is at hand. But suicide is, by definition, premature death and I couldn't avoid feeling convinced that the person ahead of us could have survived, and been glad of it, ifonly they could have shared their feeling of hopelessness in time.

It was our recent untimely loss of a young and healthy cat that had underlined for me the sheer frailty of the thread of life by which we all hang. And it was that realisation which, in those moments of delay waiting for the train to continue its journey, deepened my sorrow that someone who I would never know did not have the chance to pause and reflect before transferring to those who cared for them a burden of sorrow equivalent to whatever burden they had lifted from themselves.

I had seen an appearance on television soon afterwards by Richard Wiseman, a psychologist who had been fascinated by the part played in our lives by luck. He had eventually devised a means of getting people to define themselves as being generally lucky or unlucky in various aspects of their lives. These included work, money and love. He then set out to obtain an objective measurement of just how genuinely lucky or unlucky they actually were.

His amazing conclusion was that there was a large degree of self-fulfilling prophecy involved. Those people who, using his scale, felt themselves to be very unlucky generally were. They tended to find poor jobs, unsatisfactory partners and lead unhappy lives. Those who felt themselves to be lucky, on the other hand, usually were. They made better choices and enjoyed life more. He had found a scientific basis for the concept that you make your own luck. More intriguingly, his research, set out in his book 'The Luck Factor', had led him to formulate a method by which those who believed themselves unlucky could turn their lives around and become lucky. It apparently even helps those who are already lucky to get luckier! If only everyone who felt 'unlucky', or just down, could have access to such a strategy: perhaps their lives would be transformed.

Maybe those who live superficial lives or flat, uninspired lives could yet have a near-life experience!

❧

Dear little Betsy had not only picked up Chan's little cork habit but had developed a party piece all of her own. She started to turn head-over-heels in front of us in the sitting room while teasing the more sedate Danes one evening. At first we thought it was unintended but she has continued to perform them, whenever she has felt so inclined, ever since!

It was true that she did not feel so inclined in the days after she and Ellie were spayed but she was back in form within days. We reintegrated them with the rest of the pack soon afterwards and the others treated them amazingly carefully for a while. Not wishing to be outshone by Betsy in her acquisition of new attainments, Chan astonished us all by showing us he could bark. At first it was a solitary yap and then it was two in quick succession. It was, however, only in indignation that he had not been given a Bonio when the others had after his dinner one night. Thankfully it has rarely been repeated, avoiding the loss of the honest distinction that Basenjis don't bark!

The events of recent weeks, with the weather, had conspired against our riding. When we eventually did go out, Mel's relief was palpable. 'This horse is wonderful,' she said on the way back, grinning from ear to ear. 'It was just like putting on my favourite slippers. She was so relaxing and comfortable to ride.'

Max was, of course, always like that as far as I was concerned. But I had noticed he was quieter than usual: perhaps he was beginning to feel his age. He was, after all, rising nineteen which was a good age for such a large horse. I could only accept this sad fact and laugh it off by saying we were growing old together.

A curious phenomenon became apparent in the weeks after Moss' death. The fact that Cloey and Dandy, who was after all his litter sister, were a little subdued, even somewhat insecure, was not a surprise. They knew, of course, that there was a gap in their midst but their reaction to it caught us by surprise. Mel and I began to notice each of them taking on some little aspect of Moss' behaviour which had not been apparent before. Cloey appeared to take it upon herself to be feline spokesman in respect of the dogs. Where she had been brave but cautious she was now bold to the point of recklessness, stretching herself to her full height, such as it was, and striding up to Chan as if to say, 'it's me you'll have to deal with now.'

And Dandy, never one to hang around the stables, while not averse to passing through, suddenly took to Moss' role of prowling the tops of the stable partitions. He often did it, as if to get as close to the much larger horses as was sensible for a cat but, until then, she never had.

We were also grateful for the fact that, from then on, their excursions to the outside world were briefer. It was as though they were frequently checking in, just to let us know they were alright.

Christmas that year was notable for two things. Justin, no doubt having a little too much time on his hands, had produced his own labels for his presents to the rest of us on his computer. Each had a doctored photograph of us set in a superimposed image, for example wearing a clown's hat, precluding the need for the recipient's name to be written on it: and none of us needed telling who it was from, either!

Betsy, meanwhile, had been quite taken by the Christmas tree and no amount of admonishment seemed capable of deterring her attention. The lights were gradually shifted higher until they were like a ridiculous garland around its neck!

On the thirtieth, Mel and I decided to go west in an attempt to discover how far we might be willing to move. Upper Penwithiel was on the market once more and our minds were beginning to focus.

We drove through a few villages between Helston and Penzance before continuing beyond Penzance. We eventually found ourselves near St Buryan before stopping for tea at the Lamorna Pottery where we knew there was a small corner dedicated to the late Derek Tangye, the renowned Cornish writer and Jeannie, his wife, also a writer. But not before we had decided, on the spur of the moment, to attempt to walk the coastal path from Lamorna Cove to the boundary of their erstwhile home, the cottage called Dorminack.

It was a grey day with the weather descending on us as we started out around 2.00pm. The sea below, frothing and bubbling grey-green and white like a giant boiling cauldron, added to the dramatic, threatening backdrop. The path was lethal, climbing and then dropping between the rocks that held together the base of the steep slope as it fell away from the coastal meadows above us, now out of sight.

The effort of lifting ourselves up over the rocks and then steadying ourselves on the way down again was greater than we had expected and was certainly far from being effortless as had been our little expeditions along the base of the cliffs at Rinsey, a few miles to the east, some thirty-two years before. Time had, indeed, told! But we drove ourselves on in the sure knowledge it would be worth it, once more, to inhale the atmosphere of that place, created so magically in the Minack Chronicles.

Surely that was Carn Barges. And there, somewhere above us, must be the cottage. No. I estimated the distance we had come half-an-hour later and we could only have been about halfway. The light was dropping and so, more significantly, was an offshore drizzle. The already difficult rocks were becoming slippery and the path muddy. Any moment, thought Mel, one of us was going to slip. Here it might mean a loss of dignity brought by a fall to the ground or there, worse, a crashing onto the rocks below and, maybe, a watery end! Still we pressed on.

'It would be a pity to give up just as we were getting within sight of Dorminack,' I said.

'I know,' said Mel, 'but the weather really is closing in and I'm not sure this is the best place to be.'

'No, I suppose not,' I agreed. 'But let's push on for another ten minutes and then decide,' I said, willing our target to spring into view over the next outcrop. It didn't. I knew the decision was mine as Mel would do anything to avoid thwarting our objective that afternoon. My slip a few yards on confirmed that she was right. Reluctantly I suggested we turn on our heels and head back for the car park. We really didn't want to fall into the ridiculous trap being set for us and end up as yet another of the all too common cases reported in Cornwall each year. Young men half my age and twice as fit seemed regularly to end up as casualties at the bottom of a cliff.

On our way back along the path, I pondered the question of exactly why we had set out that afternoon. We were no star-struck teenagers hanging onto the coat-tails of some distant idol. Certainly, as the Tangyes were no longer there, there was no expectation of seeing them. The answer was simple. The books had woven into them the atmosphere of the reality of that special part of Cornwall as well as the hopes, the dreams and the ideals of a man and his wife to whom we could both relate. Like many others, we had simply wanted to sample a little of what they had experienced of that rugged coast.

'We can always return in the spring when the weather's better,' suggested Mel, reading my mind and trying to stave off any feeling of defeat.

'Yes,' I replied cheering up a little at the thought and of the reviving pot of tea that steamed into my imagination as the car wound its way back home and via the Pottery. Our consolation prize was to buy a copy of a video of Derek and Jeannie at home describing their life there. We watched it at home later and knew that, like Everest, the cliffs beyond Lamorna were there to be conquered!

❧

When grooming Max for our next ride out I was shocked to see he had lost condition. His coat was staring and his ribs were casting a slight shadow in the dim light of the barn. I stood back. I called Mel over.

'Yes, I thought he had lost a bit of weight when I put him out yesterday but he's even thinner today.' We puzzled over what the cause might be and concluded that, as he had been leaving half his hay in recent days, maybe it was not very appetising. However, he seemed his usual self so I decided to continue with the ride while keeping an eye on him.

Smartie, however, had no such problem, either of fussiness with the hay or of weight loss. Even so, we needed more hay and so asked our supplier to let us have the best quality he had.

A day or two later, after the new hay arrived, it was still strewn around his stable the next day so we focused on his teeth. Because, unlike ours, horses' teeth continue to grow they occasionally acquire a sharp edge which could make the mouth sore and eating uncomfortable. The vet came and rasped his teeth but there was no improvement. The weight continued to come off Max but we persevered, trying him out on haylage for the first time. Even I was tempted by the fermentation smell, reminiscent of a rather good beer! But he was only luke-

227

warm. He was to continue to lose weight slowly.

～✶～

It was not long afterwards that Andrew confirmed the rumour we had heard from his brothers was true. He had met Beth. Mel and I couldn't wait to meet her but knew that Andrew would introduce us when the time was right.

We had no longer to wait than Andrew's birthday in early February. A bubbly, outgoing girl, Beth clearly made Andrew very happy and Mel and I found her very easy to get to know. Mel was particularly delighted not to be the only female in the house! The next few days were spent showing her some of our and Andrew's favourite places and restaurants, including lunch at the Lugger in Portloe. We were to see much more of them both in the weeks ahead.

We were, however, going to see much less of Justin. His burgeoning income was now able to support not only a car but his share of a flat as well. It was late February that saw Mel and I drive to Bath with a car load of his gear. There he was going to share a flat with James. Our emotions were pulled two ways. A small part of us relished the prospect of being relieved of the financial burden of our third and final dependant and of having the house to ourselves once more. But a huge part of us knew the last of three very bright lights was about to go out in our daily lives and we knew we would miss him as we still did Andrew and James.

As ever, Andrew joined us in Bath to help with the unloading and carrying and, later, after Mel and I had set off for Cornwall, by making his experience available to them in the matter of buying household equipment and furnishings! To our delight, though not surprise, Beth mucked in as if they were her own brothers.

Inevitably, despite having had more time than many parents to prepare for this important day in our lives, Mel and I felt unexpectedly empty as we headed for home. We found ourselves looking back over the years which had cheated us by flying by so fast. But, far from making us sad, this gave us a feeling of accomplishment.

In the days ahead we were to slowly emerge into a life we had not known for over twenty-eight years: a glorious life without the responsibilities of children!

～✶～

Soon afterwards we were to finally see the rumblings about Iraq turn into earnest action. How far away all that mess seemed from us. It was difficult to understand how the human race could be so diverse in the way its members ranged from the ultra good to the utter evil. If only the whole world could come round to the idea that, in the long run, good was the only thing to be to really lead a full and rewarding life. Evil had a habit of coming to grief throughout history.

On St Piran's Day Mel celebrated Cornwall's saint by buying cushions for Dandy and Cloey. She was very pleased with herself for finding at Trago Mills double-sided ones which were smooth tartan on one side and fur fabric on the other: a winter side and a summer side. Dandy loved hers and immediately settled down to a snooze on it, furry side up, on the top of the kitchen cupboards. Cloey, however, refused to go near hers. We left her to get used to it but later she had still not been on it. That was not to change until Mel experimented by turning one over. The response from Cloey was instant. She had her first sleep on hers, smooth side up, and could not be budged!

It was still early March when I walked the dogs early one evening as dusk was encroaching. There to the south was a smoked mackerel sky, the first I had seen. The mackerel was provided, of course, by the well-known high cloud formation while the smoke was courtesy of neighbour Malcolm's bonfire from which smoke streaked upwards towards the clouds!

Despite all our efforts, Max, meanwhile, was fast taking on the appearance of a third world cow with protruding ribs and hips.

We then knew urgent action was required. Ron Fraser, the practice horse vet, checked Max over thoroughly and reached the tentative conclusion that it might be a liver problem. He took a blood sample and, days later, the analysis confirmed his initial thoughts. The prognosis was poor, he said, though he explained that the liver is one organ capable of regenerating itself. Max's best hope, he thought, was the time of year. It was late January and within a few weeks fresh spring grass could just be enough to carry him through. Meanwhile he recommended a particularly easily absorbed type of horse feed and common sense energy-conservation. In practice this meant reducing or cutting out riding and keeping him as dry and warm as possible.

In short our task was to put weight on him as fast as possible. Mel found a special food supplement and, as it was flavoured with peppermint, Max needed no encouragement to wolf it down! Belatedly, as usual, my thoughts started to wander to aloe vera. I scoured David Urch's wonderful book which was encouraging. Relatively large quantities were called for with the objective of first helping to flush the toxins out of his system - the very ones that had shown up in his blood test - and secondly aiding the absorption of nutriments. Within days the quantity could be reduced and ultimately he would need to continue with a lower amount for some weeks.

Max had slowly but surely been losing his old zest. The well-known joke was never more true. 'Is life worth living? It depends on the liver!'

By mid-March he had not only stabilised but we thought he was beginning to put on weight. After careful thought I concluded that, on balance, he was fit enough to go out for a ride and his system might even benefit from it. But I promised Mel that if I thought he was labouring with the effort we would return home immediately. In fact we had a perfectly good ride with Max only showing signs of fatigue after a canter but from that point on his condition was to improve markedly.

I was sure that the prayer I offered up for him when he was at what was now evidently his lowest point had been answered. I had gone out on my own to assess him in his stable after he had eaten one evening. The sight of his protruding ribs and general poor appearance had upset me. There I stood with my arms wrapped round his huge though shrunken neck and my cheek resting against its warmth. How could such a magnificent animal be wasting away before my eyes? I wished him better with all the strength at my command.

The whole family, now including Beth, came to us for the Mothers' Day weekend. We enjoyed a boisterous Saturday afternoon on the beach at Polzeath, playing with a frisbee and a weird transparent plastic cylinder which could be thrown reproducing all the characteristics of a spinning American football, the difference being that a collision with it didn't hurt at all!

Lunch on the Sunday had to be somewhere special and the Nare it was! Mel and I had our chance to check up on the stability of the newly anchored cliff. The signs were indeed good, with even more huge granite boulders now protecting its foot. Once more, the weather in the afternoon was sunny and warm so we spent a couple of hours playing with a ball on the beach, Andrew revelling in the still cold sea. He was to end up semi-immersed while fully-clothed and was glad when his car warmed up on the way home.

We spent our third day running on the beach for the first time together since our last family holiday. After a light lunch at the Rashleigh Arms at Polkerris we went for a last stroll, and James a last rock-climb, before they were all gone again.

Mel was the one to spot the first swallow the next day but because of the colder-than-usual spring it was just the one that she saw shivering on the TV aerial cable to the cottage. She said she felt sorry for it! Three more weeks were to pass before we saw them descend on the barn en masse.

It was soon Easter and the boys were back, with Beth. James, having failed to sell his red VW Golf on taking delivery of his first company car, a BMW, had agreed that we should 'look after' it for him. We would use it and maintain it for a fee in case he wanted it back. And we always said we would never have another red car!

Our Easter was completed by a brilliant ride with Max looking better than he had for months. The aloe vera had apparently done the other job it was noted for and had freed up his stiff joints. In the days ahead it was clear the old Max was back with his sense of humour restored. We could only hope the recovery was permanent.

We had dinner at the Blisland Inn and seeing a poster advertising Morris Dancing there on Monday, Andrew, Beth, Mel and I returned, Justin and James having returned to Bath.

I was down to earth with a bump on Tuesday, having to go to London for a board meeting. News that Paddington, closed for engineering works over the weekend, was not to reopen until the Tuesday afternoon only added to the contrasting gloom of leaving Cornwall so abruptly. But I was in good company as the Governor of the Bank of England joined my train at Bodmin. But where I turned right at the exit from the platform at Ealing Broadway to catch the tube into the city, he turned left to be met, no doubt, by his car. I toyed with the idea of asking for a lift but decided against it!

At the end of April I was to take delivery of my birthday present from Andrew. On my birthday in January he had given me a voucher for the most unusual gift I had ever been given. Remembering my gift to him and Mel a few years earlier of a day's car racing at Thruxton, near Andover, he had returned the compliment of a day's racing in Devon but not of cars but of JCBs: digger racing!

To the likes of Steve Masters it would have been an easy task but driving a JCB flat out round a course and then performing a simple manoeuvre - picking up and setting down a traffic cone with the jaws of the digger at pre-determined spots - was not so easy for first-timers, or old-timers come to that. My first heat was my most exciting. After starting last following my unfamiliarity with the handbrake safety lock, I stormed round the course and crossed the line first. Apparently I broke a few safety rules, including the one about keeping all four wheels on the ground at all times. Despite not making it to the final, I received The Best Sport of the Day Award after 'an entertaining performance'! I was happy to settle for that.

In the last week of April, Mel and I took a momentous decision. Perhaps prompted by the scare we had experienced with Max, we considered our future with horses. It was not given to us to know how long we would have him with us. Even if he recovered, at nineteen his riding days could be limited to two or three years if not less. Perhaps I would at that stage consider buying another horse: even at sixty I would be far from too old to continue riding. People were known to ride into their eighties! 'It would have to be another Westphalian,' I concluded in my discussion with Mel.

To this day I have no idea how Mel introduced into the conversation the topic of Smartie having a foal. All I know is that I was eventually convinced, by her and others, that there was no reason why a 15.2 hand Morgan could not carry my weight, though it might be an idea if I lost some of it, and that it had been my decision!

The plans are in place for her to return to Monnington, where she was born, at the end of May where the most handsome stallion will be waiting for her. The excitement of this new development is offset by the fact that for the five or six weeks she will be away there will be an enormous gap in our lives and that of a very special convalescent.

My May Day celebration this year was very special. It started at around 7.30am when I opened the gates for the postman as usual. The clearest most complex and earnest birdsong was emanating from the very top of the tallest tree in the garden. I stood, watched and listened as the song thrush ran through its entire repertoire. But this was no rehearsal: it gave a virtuoso performance for all who wanted to listen, no ticket being required, in the most natural of concert halls.

And how did it make me feel? Lucky! Very lucky. Lucky to be alive. Lucky to have heard it. Lucky to have had the time to appreciate it. Lucky it chose my garden, of all the open countryside available, to give its rendition. And lucky to have Mel to share it with. Yes, I concluded, life was worth living.

24 New Dawns

The unusually cold May wind across the top of the field froze the expression on my face, reddened by the climb up from the house below. I turned to look at my view: I still found it inspiring, the pale orange of the early sunlight catching the tops of the green rounded hills on the far side of the valley. This time, as I slowly took it all in, I thought about the day that was coming when I would never see it again. Looking back over the tightly packed years since we came to Cornwall, I knew that in time to come I would look back again saying to myself how happy we'd been in they days!

While the eerily familiar feelings of a new life beckoning encouraged me, as ever, to look forward, a strange nostalgia begotten by no more than a few years in this place swept over me.

It really was no time at all since that first day at Upper Penwithiel in July 1998. How many more dawns would I see here? Where would I be seeing them in time to come? As I peered down through the early morning light I could just make out the movement of red shirts in front of the garage, carrying garden tools in from the removal van. Beside me were the quiet, slightly confused figures of two Great Danes, an ageing brindle dog and shy fawn bitch, followed by an eager, optimistic little black American Cocker propelling himself through the damp grass by his small wagging stump of a tail. He looked up at me and knew I was looking at him because he wagged even more furiously.

As I ambled slowly back down I could hear the drumbeat of hooves on the hard ground, getting closer, nostrils pumping out air as they investigated their alien new territory. After I returned once more to the drive through the five-bar gate from the field, I saw a bundle of black fur scurry across in front of me to hide in the safety of the skirts of a rhododendron. Two amber eyes peered out suspiciously at me.

Two lilac Burmese, one young and one old, looked out quizzically from the safety of the car parked there. A young man was sitting in it playing with them with a stem of hay. A young man and woman stood gazing at the house. 'It's so different from your last house,' the young woman said.

I saw a very tall man get out of his car with a bemused look. '...I went to Lostwithiel where I realised I was, well, lost!'

A harassed-looking woman shot out of the cottage and across to the house clutching a notepad. She turned briefly towards me and smiled a tired smile. 'I'm just looking for the kettle, darling.'

An old fawn Great Dane, her face almost completely white, hobbled over to me for a fuss. Sitting on the step was a lilac Burmese cat waiting patiently to be let in while a bewhiskered man in a deer-stalker busied himself with a TV mast on a pole. A pleasant-looking man was waiting for me, a box of eggs and a bottle of red wine in his hand.

The tanker driver stood by the septic tank, dextrously shifting a self-rolled cigarette from one side of his mouth to the other as he prepared to tell me something. He stood aside as the post van screeched to a halt and a bundle of letters and newspapers were left on the mat in the hall. Above them on the wall was a beautiful painting of the house and my mind filled up with the picture of another young man sitting under the oak tree by the gate, with an old Great Dane dozing on her side next to him in the late summer sun while a grey cat chased a dead leaf.

The same young, large, floppy, cuddly cat walked along the stone wall by the side lawn, gently pursued by a small black, tan and white dog and a large brindle puppy, in single file, a fawn one, wobbling uncertainly, bringing up the rear.

The tears welled up in my eyes as I mentally readied myself for the day we would be leaving and leaving so much behind.

'Are you alright?' asked Mel when I got indoors. I nodded and explained. 'I thought I was going to enjoy moving,' she said. 'I've been so excited about starting life in a new house. But this sad feeling has come over me. I don't really understand it.'

'It's a feeling of loss, I expect,' I replied. Mel looked puzzled.

'Loss?'

'Yes. When you think back to when we first arrived here, so much has changed. But somewhere in the back of your mind you're probably thinking of the animals who won't be coming with us. And the boys...' The warm, silent tears on my chest told me I was right.

Then she looked up into my face, smiled, and said brightly, 'but we'll have the patter of tiny hooves.'